The Classics in Black and White

The Classics in Black and White

BLACK COLLEGES, CLASSICS EDUCATION,
RESISTANCE, AND ASSIMILATION

Kenneth W. Goings and Eugene O'Connor

The University of Georgia Press

ATHENS

© 2024 by the University of Georgia Press
Athens, Georgia 30602
www.ugapress.org
All rights reserved
Designed by Mary McKeon
Set in 10.25/13.5 Minion Pro

Most University of Georgia Press titles are
available from popular e-book vendors.

Printed digitally

Library of Congress Cataloging-in-Publication Data
NAMES: Goings, Kenneth W., 1951–author. | O'Connor, Eugene Michael,
1948–author.
TITLE: The classics in black and white : Black colleges, classics education,
    resistance, and assimilation / Kenneth W. Goings and Eugene O'Connor.
DESCRIPTION: Athens : University of Georgia Press, [2024] | Includes
bibliographical references and index.
IDENTIFIERS: LCCN 2023050676 (print) | LCCN 2023050677
    (ebook) | ISBN 9780820366616 (hardback) | ISBN
    9780820366623 (paperback) | ISBN 9780820366630 (epub) |
    ISBN 9780820366647 (pdf)
SUBJECTS: LCSH: Historically black colleges and universities—
    Curricula. | United States—Intellectual life—1783–1865. | United
    States—Civilization—Classical influences. | United States—Civilization—
    Greek influences. | United States—Civilization—Roman influences. |
    Civilization, Classical—Study and teaching—United States—History—19th
    century. | Classical literature—Study and teaching—United States—
    History—19th century. | Classicists—United States—Biography. |
    Discrimination in higher
    education—United States. | Educational equalization.
CLASSIFICATION: LCC LC2781 .G65 2024 (print) | LCC LC2781 (ebook) |
    DDC 909/.09821071173—dc23/eng/20240201
LC record available at https://lccn.loc.gov/2023050676
LC ebook record available at https://lccn.loc.gov/2023050677

Homo sum: humani nil a me alienum puto
(I am human. I regard nothing human as alien to me).

—*Publius Terentius Afer*

This book is dedicated to all the founders, students,
teachers, and administrators of historically Black colleges,
who achieved so much against such great odds.

CONTENTS

Acknowledgments   xi

Introduction: Our Heritage Too   1

CHAPTER 1.   The Formative Influences of Classical Culture in
Colonial America and the Early Republic   18

CHAPTER 2.   The Founding of Black Colleges and Universities
and Their Classics Curriculums   41

CHAPTER 3.   A Survey of the Classical Texts Read at Black
Colleges and Universities   78

CHAPTER 4.   The Classics as Tools of Empowerment and Resistance   97

CHAPTER 5.   Practicality and the End of Classics   115

EPILOGUE   Bridging Two Worlds   124

Notes   129

Bibliography   149

Index   165

ACKNOWLEDGMENTS

This study is the culmination of more than thirty years of research, writing, and scholarly collaboration, beginning with our joint article on classical and African American models of the trickster in Ralph Ellison's novel *Invisible Man*, which appeared in the journal *LIT: Literature Interpretation Theory* in 1990. As our research has expanded, we have benefited greatly from the opportunities extended by the Society for Classical Studies at their 2004 and 2012 annual meetings; Tara Welch and the Department of Classics, University of Kansas; Judith Peller Hallett, University of Maryland, College Park; Daniel Orrells and Tessa Roynon, University of Warwick; Lorna Hardwick, Open University; Thomas Strunk and Shannon Byrne, Xavier University; John Ramsey and the late Allan Kershaw, University of Illinois, Chicago; Andrew Alwine and the Classics Department of the University of Charleston; and Jacob Mackey, Occidental College, to participate in classroom and panel discussions on African Americans and the classics. All along the way we have benefited from the expertise of numerous friends and colleagues, chief among them Patrice Rankine, Shelley Haley, Stephanie Shaw, Emily Greenwood, Margaret Malamud, Tom Hawkins, and Michele Valerie Ronnick. Our gratitude extends to Stephen Hall for his comments on our early efforts and suggestions for further research and to Polly Kummel for her substantive editing of our manuscript. Great thanks are owed to our acquiring editor at the University of Georgia Press, Nathaniel Holly; our copyeditor, Susan Silver; our indexer, Matthew White; and the press's anonymous readers. Last and by no means least, we express our profound debt to all the librarians, archivists, and staff at the Black colleges and universities for xeroxing and collating the surviving course catalogs, which provided the core of our research. We thank in particular Brian Page, who helped assemble all the college catalogs, and David Jackson at Florida A&M University, for supplying FAMU's catalogs. Without the aid of these dedicated individuals, this book would not have been possible. Portions of chapters 1, 2, 3, and 4 (on the colleges' histories, philosophies, and courses) and the epilogue are revised versions of earlier published material. We are grateful to the following publishers for permission to reprint the following:

"'Tell Them We Are Rising': African Americans and the Classics." *Amphora* 4, no. 2 (2005): 6–7, 12–13. Published by the American Philological Association. We thank the Society for Classical Studies, founded in 1869 as the American Philological Association, for permission to reuse material from the article.

"Lessons Learned: The Role of the Classics at Black Colleges and Universities." *Journal of Negro Education* 79, no. 4 (2010): 521–31. Reprinted by permission of Howard University, School of Education.

"Black Athena before *Black Athena:* The Teaching of Greek and Latin at Black Colleges and Universities during the Nineteenth Century." In *African Athena: New Agendas,* edited by Daniel Orrells, Gurminder K. Bhambra, and Tessa Roynon, 90–105. Oxford: Oxford University Press, 2011. Copyright © Oxford University Press 2011. All rights reserved. Reproduced with permission of the Licensor through PLSclear.

"Into the Republic of Letters: The Classics, Church/College Politics and the 'Firing' of Professor William S. Scarborough." In *Purgatory between Kentucky and Canada: African Americans in Ohio,* edited by Marsha R. Robinson, 61–68. Newcastle upon Tyne: Cambridge Scholars, 2013. Published with the permission of Cambridge Scholars Publishing.

"The Classical Curriculum at Black Colleges and Universities and the Roles of the Various Missionary Aid Societies." In *Classics in Practice: Studies in the History of Scholarship,* edited by Christopher Stray and Graham Whitaker, 75–96. London: Institute of Classical Studies, School of Advanced Study, University of London, 2015. Reproduced by permission of the Institute of Classical Studies and University of London Press.

The Classics in Black and White

INTRODUCTION

Our Heritage Too

You have seen how a man was made a slave; you shall see how a slave was made a man.
—Frederick Douglass, *Narrative of the Life of Frederick Douglass*

In U.S. educational institutions from the time of the American colonies until the midtwentieth century, a "classical education" was associated largely with elites—that is, White gentlemen. The Greek and Latin classics, as they traditionally were taught, reinforced codes of strict segregation—by race *and* class. The received wisdom of the time was that those outside this select group, especially African Americans, lacked the requisite mental capacity as well as the necessary leisure to study the classics.

Our study focuses on the teaching of Greek and Latin at Black colleges, mostly in the U.S. South, from the late 1860s through the 1940s, as tools not of exclusion but of self-formation and self-affirmation. This tradition began before the Civil War but gained ground after the war's cessation, as formerly enslaved African Americans, northern missionaries, the Union Army, and northern philanthropists all began the immense task of trying to educate a newly freed people, first with basic literacy for beginning students and, for the more advanced, college-preparatory or college courses in Greek and Latin, as well as the liberal arts more broadly. Given the dearth of primary and secondary education for African Americans, principally in the South following the Civil War, Black colleges had to be all things to their students, from primary schools to places of more advanced study with a traditional education that heavily emphasized Latin and Greek.

It is important, however, to understand that the adoption of Greek and Latin at Black colleges was not merely a mimicking of the northern, European-inspired curriculum then standard at American colleges. It was as well a deliberate choice that African Americans and others (including the White teachers who came from the North and from abroad) made for a variety of

1

reasons. The classics curriculum had long been the traditional pedagogy of the White elite, and, as such, it had been Europeanized, racialized, and weaponized. African American teachers and their students worked to break down these racial and classist barriers to appropriate the classics for their own purposes and, indeed, to decolonize the classics to make them a tool of resistance against White oppression. We refer throughout this book to the classics as tools, because, for African Americans, that is what they indeed were—instruments not only of resistance but of self-affirmation and self-formation—in short, good things to think with.

Much scholarship already exists on the education of African Americans during and after Reconstruction and the difficulties they encountered and overcame in setting up schools. Studies such as Heather Williams's 2005 *Self-Taught* examine the importance of Black agency and determination in directing their own education. Beyond chronicling the achievements of singular Black classical scholars, the literature is now beginning to examine how the classics have informed Black agency and provided tools to battle White supremacy.[1] A traditional focus of the historiography of African American education for the past century has been education's role in the so-called civilizing of Black Americans and their assimilation into the mainstream. This mission lay in African Americans' appropriation of Western culture for their own ends.[2] More needs to be written, however, about the formative role, for good or ill, that Greek and Latin have played in the education and lives of African Americans from the founding of the republic.

But why this focus on Latin and Greek? As early as the 1830s, people questioned the practicality and applicability of this focus to a modernizing, industrializing America, and, with the steady decline of enrollment in Greek and Latin courses, they still ask that question today. Recent literature on education has presented arguments for and against the liberal arts generally, particularly as marketable tools, in ways that recall the reasons given for the correct training of newly freed African Americans at the end of the U.S. Civil War. The March 4, 2012, issue of the *Chronicle of Higher Education* included several pseudonymous letters to the editor in response to "The Future of American Colleges May Lie, Literally, in Students' Hands," an essay by Scott Carlson it had published the previous month. The consensus of the spirited responses was that American college students, in our throwaway society, are too cosseted and lack practical knowledge. As one respondent put it, "They don't tinker, don't fix, don't have any idea how even the most basic items work, because if anything ever breaks, they just replace it." Said another, "Leaving the 'manual arts' programs out of schools over the last 20 years has been a disaster for our students and hence our country."[3]

2 INTRODUCTION

In 2009 the *New York Times Book Review* published an article by Drew Gilpin Faust, then president of Harvard University, in which she pondered the future of higher education in the United States in the wake of Barack Obama's election to the presidency. It contains a telling paragraph on practicality vis-à-vis transcendence in education: "American universities have long struggled to meet almost irreconcilable demands: to be practical as well as transcendent; to assist immediate national needs and to pursue knowledge for its own sake; to both add value and question values. And in the past decade and a half, such conflicting and unbounded expectations have yielded a wave of criticism on issues ranging from the cost of college to universities' intellectual quality to their supposed decline into unthinking political correctness."[4]

This ambivalence, Gilpin Faust tells us, has haunted American higher education since passage of the first Morrill Act of 1862, which established landgrant colleges meant for the "practical education of the industrial classes." While American higher education has indeed increased the nation's collective earning power, Gilpin Faust takes pains to remind the reader that the study of the liberal arts is about something more: acquiring "the kind of critical perspectives that look far beyond the present," even as the number of students majoring in the liberal arts has declined since the 1970s.[5]

Similar questions concerning the point of an elitist education for the newly manumitted Black citizens of the United States often were posed, not only by White power holders but also by many African Americans themselves at a time when Blacks in the United States faced limited options for employment. And while they might pursue careers in medicine or law, a degree in classics seemed a far-fetched option beyond the few prospects available for Latin (and, less often, Greek) teachers in high schools and colleges for Blacks.

To think of young men and women studying the languages and civilizations of ancient Greece and Rome is to envision pampered, rather otherworldly, individuals sitting in isolated splendor (or, more realistically, Spartan classrooms), poring over arcane texts, parsing irregular verb forms, and grappling with grammar and syntax. Such a picture may summon, for the more historically inclined, humanists of the Renaissance and later, who were drilled in Greek and Latin when knowledge of the classical languages, particularly Latin, meant patronage and privilege as a scholar, poet, or diplomat.

By the latter half of the nineteenth century, advanced study in Greek and Latin was becoming a specialized discipline and as such was considered increasingly arcane and elitist and therefore out of step with a rapidly industrializing United States. As a marker of intellectual privilege as well as social class, the classics were reserved for the select few with both the time and resources: such elite study imparted cultural enrichment, but it did not automatically translate into financial gain.[6]

What, then, would be the appeal of a classical education to a people just emerging from slavery, so recently brutalized and, with the passage of race laws in the South, still harassed and marginalized—an education that smacked more of the seventeenth-century Jesuit *Ratio studiorum*, which prioritized the Greek and Latin classics, than of training that would fit its students for life in a segregated America? Further, what constructive role could the study of classical civilizations play, given that these civilizations condoned slavery, regarded slaves as less than fully human, and looked on people of color as exotic? What had these civilizations to do with Blacks in America? In short, what good would a knowledge of the classical languages do a people long consigned to being (to invoke Joshua 9:21) "hewers of wood and drawers of water"?[7]

The founding of Black colleges and universities in America coincided with the rise of the modern university with its system of course electives and conferral of professional degrees. With modernity came a reduced emphasis on the classics, as the applied sciences gained primacy and foreign-language instruction shifted to the modern languages, principally German and French. The traditional classics course, while hallowed by centuries of primacy in higher education, was inexpensive in comparison with the hard sciences, for which students needed equipment and labs; the classics required nothing more than paper, pens, a few grammar and other textbooks, likely to be shared, and a blackboard for writing out lessons. Greek- and Latin-language classes consisted of rote learning and repeated class recitation of declensions and conjugations. Such a traditional pedagogy was a staple at the majority of small American liberal arts colleges founded in the mid-nineteenth century; many, at least at their beginnings, were church affiliated and financially insecure. Fiscally stressed Black colleges, especially, were under additional pressure from funding agencies to relinquish or at least reduce their own classics programs in favor of industrial education and domestic science, either as required courses or as electives, to fit their graduates for life in a racially divided America.[8]

For defenders of the classical curriculum, however, it was not merely a question of cost; it was a matter of racial pride and, indeed, equality. African Americans newly released from bondage after the Civil War and seeking their full manumission—their full humanity—knew that in the United States, knowledge of Greek and Latin was the irreproachable sign of an educated White elite. As early as the late eighteenth century, African American scholars and poets had been connecting northern Africa, the Mediterranean, and the classical civilizations of Greece and Rome. Therefore, in a very real sense, these scholars and their students believed that "the classical civilizations" belonged as much to them as they did to White Europeans. If African Americans were to be equal, they too would need to gain mastery of these languages and use them as tools of racial uplift. They could therefore, like their White counterparts, draw inspiration from classical Greece and Rome as models for the politics and culture of the early United States. Classical culture influenced in a profound fashion the rhetoric of educated African Americans and their ways of dealing with contemporary problems. This is evident when one takes a critical look at the Greek and Latin texts they read and how scholars and activists such as William Sanders Scarborough and Mary Church Terrell, as well as students themselves, used these texts as a way of speaking to, and thinking about, their own culture and their place in the world. African Americans thought of the classics, and the liberal arts more generally, as tools of racial uplift, tools they could employ as readily as the skills acquired in industrial education—that is, in courses in mechanical and domestic arts imposed on black colleges and universities in return for badly needed financial support from various philanthropic agencies.

In the college coursework across Black colleges and universities, African American teachers and students of the classics were building up, if not economic, then cultural capital—that is, "cultural knowledge, tastes, habits, social networks, and institutional affiliations."[9] They were privileging themselves with what they saw as the finest fruits of Western civilization—the *artes liberales*, the studies of free men and women. As the classics had been for scholars of the Renaissance, they were for African American teachers and their students nothing less than the *studia humanitatis*, whose purpose was to impart an intellectual dignity and a moral ethos.[10] This cultural capital would in turn form tools of self-empowerment. It would not, however, translate automatically into civic equality or economic improvement. Colleges for Blacks would remain chronically underfunded; to bring in desperately needed monies, they had to provide practical courses, such as woodworking for men and household science for women, to prepare their graduates for life outside as manual workers and domestics. The first Black teachers at historically Black colleges were themselves often the sons and daughters of slaves.

The tenacity with which later Black educators fought to retain the classical curriculum speaks also to the idea of African American agency. Traditional histories of Black education in the United States, particularly the history of Black colleges and universities, have depicted African Americans as objects in this history, not subjects. Things were always being done *to* them; they were never, or rarely, the agents of their own history. They were being kept

OUR HERITAGE TOO **5**

out of White schools, angry Whites were burning down Black schools, and teachers at Black schools were being run out of town and even lynched. Even the best-intentioned studies, based in part on accounts by early missionary teachers, too often dwelled on the newly freed people's lack of preparedness, as well as their so-called docility and childishness, which the teachers regarded as the doleful legacy of their students' African past.[11] However, African American history since the 1990s has seen a dramatic shift from this essentially race-relations model—which placed African Americans on the periphery, where things were always being "done to them"—to an agency model that finds that African Americans were seeking greater autonomy in their educational choices. Indeed, in the early republic, Blacks who had been educated in the North or abroad were already establishing a strong link between Africa and the classical world, thereby putting the lie to Whites' conviction that the classics were not for those whom they deemed their racial and intellectual inferiors. Such an inclusive philosophy of education, which was adopted by Black colleges and universities founded after the Civil War, would prove to be profoundly unsettling to the White establishment, for it undermined the entrenched notion of White racial superiority.

Much of the literature on Black pedagogy published in the past three decades has focused on Black teachers and students; the founding agencies, principally the American Missionary Association; and the placement of education within larger social and political contexts. In their discussion of the establishment of Black education in general, and especially the role of White philanthropy in the creation and maintenance of historically Black colleges, Marybeth Gasman and Nelson Bowman III, in their *Guide to Fundraising at Historically Black Colleges and Universities* (2012), cite especially James Anderson's *The Education of Blacks in the South, 1860–1935* (1988), as well as *Dangerous Donations* (1999), by Eric Anderson and Alfred A. Moss Jr. Scholars from the 1980s onward, for example, Henry N. Drewry and Humphrey Doermann, authors of *Stand and Prosper* (2001), have paid more attention to student activism, as well as to Black fraternities and sororities and the role of sports. Black and White faculty members have been the subjects of several works, notably, Gabrielle Simon Edgcomb's *From Swastika to Jim Crow* (1993), which recounts the lives and careers of émigré German Jewish scholars who brought high European standards to impoverished colleges for Blacks.

Recent studies have paid closer attention to curricular issues as well as educational leadership and administration, and they have contextualized philanthropists within the ideological and power structures from which they sprang. Michele Valerie Ronnick has done much to recover the lives and works of prominent African American classicists, in particular Wilberforce classics professor and race activist William Sanders Scarborough.[12] Scholars also have focused on the role of Black and White women in Black education, from the northern missionaries after the Civil War to well into the twentieth century. These studies include a reissue of classically trained Fanny Jackson Coppin's *Reminiscences of School Life, and Hints on Teaching* (1913) and Yolanda N. Watson and Sheila T. Gregory's *Daring to Educate* (2005), about the first four presidents of Spelman.

By the 1880s courses in Greek and Latin language and literature at Black colleges were enjoying what could be called a golden age. The listing of classical courses at the more elite schools, such as Fisk and Wilberforce, rivaled those of White institutions. A number of prominent classicists were Black, most notably Scarborough, the son of slaves, whose *First Lessons in Greek*, published in 1881, was adopted as a textbook by both Black and White institutions, including Yale University.[13] Scarborough and the small cadre of African American classicists extended themselves beyond the academy and became true public intellectuals, involving themselves in civil rights work, state politics, women's suffrage, and the fight against Jim Crow.

Historians of African America have rejected Rayford W. Logan's nadir model, which he described in *The Betrayal of the Negro* (1965). Logan called the period after the end of Reconstruction through the Progressive era (the same time period covered by this study) the worst for African Americans, except for slavery. According to Logan's analysis, the high rates of lynching and other forms of racial violence during this time served as an expression of White power and Black victimization. But as Kenneth W. Goings and other historians have suggested, that is a misreading of what was happening. The rising rate of lynching was not merely an expression of White power but also a reaction to Black insurgency and activism, such as Scarborough's.[14] In this book we apply these same shifts to the history of Black colleges and universities.

Within such a context of insurgency and self-empowerment, the classics may be read as dangerous: in the hands of the dispossessed, they are a tool of subversion; they foster disobedience of authority, destruction of property, and other lawlessness. However, the classics are also constructive: they provide the tools of self-empowerment and civic engagement—again, when in the hands of the dispossessed.[15]

What is more, many African Americans, among them some classically trained educators and others, saw the classics as African, beginning in the antebellum period. They argued for a link between North Africa, particularly Egypt, and the classical world. They viewed the classical authors whom they read in class and the distinct emergence of classics as a scholarly discipline in the eighteenth and nineteenth centuries, not as mere emblems of White European hegemony and exclusion but as a means of liberation and social uplift.[16] Clearly, placing the origins of the classical civilizations in North Africa complicated the relation between Eurocentric and Afrocentric studies. It was part and parcel of the wholehearted embrace by African Americans of classical culture, because, among other reasons, they felt it was theirs. This embrace, in effect, disrupted the racist and imperialist narrative of classics as exclusively European and White. The link between the classical world and Africa made by African Americans in the early republic would play a vital role in the Black insurgency that took place later in the nineteenth century.

That African American classicists—and, more broadly, teachers of the liberal arts and those college officials determined to retain the liberal arts program—were ultimately not successful at resisting the imposition of trades-oriented instruction at Black colleges and universities makes their efforts no less heroic. The literature, including primary documents, notably the extant college and university catalogs, attests to the continuance of the classical curriculum, even if in attenuated form, despite the inroads of the Hampton-Tuskegee model of trades-oriented instruction. Letters, campus publications, and other writings by African American students of the classics chronicle their efforts to resist being limited to industrial education, which they saw as part of the selling out of racial equality and accommodation to the wishes of White supremacists, who, especially after Reconstruction, wanted to retain an acquiescent Black workforce that would not resist and would not demand equal rights in education or in other areas of intellectual or social life. Despite the withdrawal of funds and even the risks of closure and interference by African Americans themselves, Black educational institutions fought against becoming mere engines for what they considered the perpetuation of Jim Crow. In this book we examine, and by doing so celebrate, the efforts of African American educators and their students to resist the watering down of liberal arts education, against the grain of the traditional historiography of Black education in the United States. Devotion to the classical curriculum at Black colleges and universities would continue as the primacy of the classics was being phased out, even at such elite institutions as Harvard University, in favor of the sciences and modern languages.

African Americans applied tools often learned under slavery to counteract Whites' engines of educational oppression—tools of outright resistance but, just as often, those of dissimulation and what we might term invisibility. Their tightly curled hair, broad noses, and especially their dark skin made African Americans supremely visible to White Americans. But at the same time, Blacks remained unseen by most Whites, beyond, say, a pair of gloved hands proffering a cup or carrying a tray. To remain invisible African Americans had to simulate deference and agreement. Black servants working in White homes would carry to their communities information about how Whites behaved and how to articulate strategies for countering and resisting White oppression—all done under the cover provided by condescending White attitudes toward those whom they regarded as "the lower race" and done with the obsequious smile that Whites associated with "those happy darkies," pleased to work for their masters. The first Black students of the classics applied these strategies when coping with often condescending White teachers and college officials who considered their charges to be still brutalized by the effects of slavery and the heathenism of their African past.

Our work is therefore informed by African American agency and resistance. The very idea of *resistance*, in the case of African American scholars—particularly, for our purposes, classical scholars—is, in a real sense, an unorthodox retelling of the history of what happened. The canonical account of Black higher education in the United States focuses on the triumph of the Hampton-Tuskegee model of industrial education trumpeted by Booker T. Washington and how it replaced the more traditional classics-oriented, liberal arts curriculum at historically Black colleges and universities. This account also states that all subsequent writing about African American education fell into line. The history that we propose is one of defiance, resistance, and dissemblance by those very scholars whom one would not expect to be social movers and shakers: the teachers and students of the Greek and Latin classics. It seems clear, based on our research, including a review of Black college catalogs from the late nineteenth century to the mid-twentieth century, that African Americans thoroughly assimilated their reading of the classics and truly used them for their own political, social, and intellectual advancement, even as the White majority continued to view Black students as powerless and inferior. To see them as otherwise would have been to regard them as a threat to White hegemony.

The topic of inclusiveness in the discipline of classics has been a concern of scholarly inquiry since the 1990s, with the crucial question being "Who are the classics for?" The program of the spring 2019 meeting of the Classical Association of the Middle West and South included a panel titled "Who Owns the Classics in the College Classroom?" Similarly, the January 2019 meeting of the Society for Classical Studies in San Diego featured a panel titled "The Future of Classics," which explored the degree to which racism and sexism still pervade the discipline and how the defense of "pure philology," which is the study of the structure and development of a language, crowds out classical reception as well as studies of women and minorities in antiquity.[17]

Indeed, the question of who owns the classics was being asked two centuries ago by European and American classical scholars who brought their own racist reading to classical texts, which went against the very "scientific philology" they were espousing. (This scientific philology was more broadly known by the German term *Altertumswissenschaft*—literally, the "science of antiquity.") But, as we show in chapter 1, this so-called pure science itself became infected with elements of romanticism and outright racism. As if to illustrate the racist component of *Altertumswissenschaft*, Thomas Jefferson, adducing examples from Roman history, described, in his *Notes on Virginia* (1784), what he regarded as the degraded, uneducable status of Blacks based on his classical reading and, in so doing, penned some of the most repugnant avowals of White supremacy.

We cannot, then, explore the subject of African Americans and the classics without a consideration of Whiteness as a marker of Eurocentrism and therefore of racial and cultural superiority. Cultural and racial imperialists argued that the Greeks and Romans had been White, after all, and that their gods were White. Africans and their African American descendants, by reason of their non-Whiteness, were feral, degraded, childlike, natural slaves. Indeed, hegemonic Whiteness, like hegemonic heterosexuality, had long gone unquestioned and had therefore become invisible. White people do not have to see themselves as White or as heterosexual—these are the unquestioned default modes. All others not conforming to these hegemonic models must by default be described as different, Other, and therefore deviant. Deviance in the case of African Americans begins with the color of their skin, from which emanate other bodily markers, such as modes of speech and movement and perceived intelligence. How, then, could a people so marked by their skin color enact Whiteness by a study of civilizations and languages so long dominated by Anglo-Europeans and thus so manifestly White? Indeed, how could they master a discipline so long regarded as the exclusive marker of White racial and class privilege? Classically educated African Americans responded by painting the classics Black and making a connection between northern Africa, the Mediterranean, and the classical civilizations of Greece and Rome. As John Levi Barnard argues in *Empire of Ruin*, African American artists and writers from the antebellum period "have appealed to biblical and classical sources both to challenge exclusive Euro-American claims to a Greco-Roman heritage and to advance the notion of African and Asian civilizational precedence." Thus they could call out Jefferson's vaunted "empire for liberty" as nothing more than an imperialist empire built on slavery and oppression.[18]

They did so, we argue, in part by applying those very skills learned under slavery: tools of dissemblance and subtle resistance while maintaining the appearance of submission and obsequiousness. Their learning the classics was in some ways a literal performance, a realization of the *hypokrisis*, or adoption of masks, such as was done by Greek and Roman dramatic actors who, while they wore these masks to impersonate mythical or historical characters, kept their own identities secret and intact. But the assignment of race, in addition to class, remained unavoidable. One could, in theory, be a sensitive, well-taught Negro. But one remained a Negro and ipso facto of an inferior race and a lower caste. In light of this, we need to consider the catalogs of Black colleges and universities themselves as performative pieces, in a way. Therefore, we asked, among other questions, Who is the perceived audience? What message do the catalogs convey and how well or badly? To what degree, if any, do they propagate racialized language? The catalogs' injunctions against gambling, drinking, smoking, dancing, and wearing any but the most conservative clothing, which would have been familiar to students at White religious institutions, were enforced to police Black students. Such language would have assuaged the concerns of White trustees and funding organizations who believed Black students needed not only to be supervised but also cured of unwelcome behaviors associated with their African past. For the Black audience, the catalogs' message would ensure, as well, that strict adherence to approved social norms would propagate habits of thrift, sobriety, and self-improvement and with that racial as well as social uplift.

Beginning just after the peak of the golden age, with the founding of the Tuskegee Institute in Alabama and the rise of racial violence in the South, the tide began to turn sharply against the classical model. But while traditional histories would have us believe that the ascendancy of the Hampton-Tuskegee model of industrial and utilitarian education was, with the exception of a few small bumps (most notably the resistance by W. E. B. Du Bois and a few other Black intellectuals), a smooth and inevitable one, our study demonstrates that the resistance to the diminution of the classics, by Black and White students and faculty alike, was widespread, from prep schools to universities, often at the risk of losing one's livelihood or the school's accreditation and funding. For example, at Florida State Normal and Industrial School (now Florida A&M), the all-White board of trustees fired the first two presidents for their refusal to drop the classics from the curriculum. In addition, the school suffered a reduction in funding because of this resistance. Some of the resistance was an outright refusal to change the classical curriculum to one of exclusively industrial and utilitarian training. As often as not, this resistance came in the form of deliberate dissemblance—that is, touting industrial training and domestic science to please White funding agencies and overseers even while pursuing a liberal arts education.

This dissemblance can be understood within the context of what Henry Louis Gates Jr., in *Figures in Black*, has shown to be the subversive capabilities of the appropriation of masks.[19] It may also be understood within the parameters of African American signifying, passing, and secrecy discourse. This tactic began under slavery, when slaves were forced to conceal what instruction they could obtain from sympathetic White householders or from the covert acquisition of spelling books, atlases, or other texts, in "pit schools"—literal pits dug in the ground and concealed with twigs to escape detection. They thus practiced an art of hiddenness, sometimes in plain sight of their masters, who were too blinded by their prejudice against African Americans' capacities for learning to see what was clearly before them. The desire to learn among slaves assumed a quasi-religious significance. At funerals slave children held their spelling books, which to them had the power of scripture. In what became the stuff of folklore, Nat Turner claimed to have been taught his alphabet by a hidden voice, with the letters themselves inscribed on the leaves of trees. Other slaves claimed similar miraculous instruction and thus gained the status of ministers or seers.[20]

In the end all this resistance could not turn back the forces arrayed against classical education. Increasingly, after the 1890s, funding by benefactors, foundations, and state and local governments were tied to the schools' willingness to adopt the utilitarian model (which was also becoming the dominant educational philosophy for most nonelite education in a rapidly industrializing United States).[21] In the rest of the country, White education was being segregated along class lines so that the industrial model was for working-class White students, while elite students still had access to a classical education. Within African America, racial segregation took the place of class segregation, so almost all African American students were shunted into some form of industrial and utilitarian training. Even colleges that stressed the liberal arts began to introduce, as part of students' overall instruction, courses for men such as woodworking and carpentry and domestic science for women. This was necessary to secure badly needed monies from funding agencies and was a pragmatic move by the colleges to better prepare their graduates for the lives they would soon lead in the segregated world outside.

As evidenced by the extant catalogs, such as those of Tougaloo, Spelman, and Wilberforce, the colleges encouraged (or reluctantly required) students in liberal arts courses to spend a few hours each week mastering practical instruction. Such accommodation, if one wants to call it that, was actually a way of melding the training of the hand and mind to produce citizens with both intellectual capital and ready tools for employment beyond college. Black educators were not idle dreamers. They realized that there could not

12 INTRODUCTION

be an either-or approach to education—that is, either liberal arts or industrial training. Rather, they saw it as a both-and approach. As the catalogs show, the two were combined in a single curriculum, even if, it must be acknowledged, not always comfortably. Sometimes weird juxtapositions included courses in needlework for women and blacksmithing and woodworking for men offered alongside instruction in classical languages and civilizations.[22]

In 1930 there were 121 Black colleges and universities. Currently, there are 101. Reasons for a decline in number include increasing enrollments for students of color in predominantly White institutions, including the Ivy League, which are able to offer full scholarship aid. In an effort to maintain enrollment and thus to remain viable, many Black colleges have moved to diversify their own student populations. By 2015 White, Hispanic, Asian, and Native Americans composed 22 percent of students at Black colleges.[23]

Black colleges and universities have learned to survive in the face of demographic changes and challenges from White institutions. The fate of the classics course, however, has not fared as well, having been phased out over time at various schools, most recently, at Howard University, which closed its classics department in 2021, though not without an outcry from faculty, students, and others. Our emphasis in this book, however, is not on classics' decline but on its seminal role in the pedagogy and lives of African American teachers and students. It seems clear, based on our research, including a review of Black college catalogs from the late 1860s to the 1940s, that those African American students enrolled in classics courses thoroughly assimilated their reading of the Greek and Latin classics and truly used them for their own political, social, and intellectual advancement. This process of assimilation has persisted in African American rhetoric long after the classics ceased to be the core of the curriculum at Black colleges and universities, a most glorious witness to which would be the rhetoric of Dr. Martin Luther King Jr. We may add here President Barack Obama, who, while he did not attend a Black college, picked up Black rhetorical style from his work as a community organizer in Chicago and also from listening to other Black orators.

It is to be lauded, but also lamented, that the classical liberal arts curriculums at many—though by no means all—Black colleges and universities have been the victim of African Americans' increasing inclusion in American society, including access to educational institutions formerly closed to them. But it is also the result of an essential misreading of the purpose of the classics by some twentieth-century African Americans who decried them as irrelevant to racial and social uplift. Nonetheless, beginning in the 1950s, more far-seeing Black classicists were turning, once again, to Africa and emphasizing the need to promote the role of Africans in classical culture. We may mention here as examples Howard educator Frank Snowden Jr.'s groundbreaking works, *Blacks in Antiquity* (1970) and *Before Color Prejudice* (1983). These were followed by Martin Bernal's three-volume work, *Black Athena* (1987–2006), and Daniel Orrells, Gurminder K. Bhambra, and Tessa Roynon's edited volume, *African Athena: New Agendas* (2011), which includes responses to Bernal's controversial *Black Athena* and the effect of the Western classical tradition on Black humanism. Eric Ashley Hairston's *The Ebony Column* (2013) shows how African Americans since Phillis Wheatley have used the classics as a means of African American liberation and self-affirmation. Barnard's *Empire of Ruin* describes how African Americans have used the classics to critique American racial imperialism.

The literature on classical education for African Americans during the later nineteenth and early twentieth centuries attests to the continuance of the classical curriculum despite the inroads of the Hampton-Tuskegee model of industrial and trade-oriented education. Part of our work, therefore, has been to consider the efforts by select African American educators to contest the watering down of liberal arts education against the traditional historiography of Black education in the United States. This includes outright resistance as well as the more covert (and, some would argue, accommodationist) tactic of dissemblance. Much of this book is the result of retrieving and reading primary documents meant to be ephemeral and subject to disposal, including Black college and university catalogs, some nearly in tatters and falling apart. Other ephemera, including surviving school bulletins, newspaper articles, and letters, also played an important part in revealing to us how African American students and educators felt about the role and value of a classical education against the broader background of classical studies at the time. However, the paucity of surviving material, including information on the identities and careers of classics teachers at individual Black colleges, is the direct result of colleges' lack of resources to keep extensive archives, beyond the factor of the passage of time.[24]

We begin in chapter 1 with the prehistory—that is, the move by educated northern African Americans in the colonial period and early republic (the late eighteenth century through the 1850s) to promote a link between Africa and the classical world, even as the classics were being encoded as exclusively European and White. During this time the small number of educated Blacks established reading rooms and other venues for African Americans of both sexes, again in the North, for the purpose of engaging in soul-enriching intellectual activities. But this was also a time when the Greek and Latin classics became areas of contestation between White and Black America. In his *Appeal to the Colored Citizens of the World* (1829), David Walker used his understanding of Roman history to oppose the racial imperialism of Thomas Jefferson, as expressed in Jefferson's *Notes on Virginia*. Racial categories were calcifying during a period of colonization and the so-called rescue of Greek antiquities from what the White elite called the dissolute East.

Our second chapter discusses the founding of Black colleges and universities that sprang up, mostly in the South, for the express purpose of educating newly freed African Americans during the period of Reconstruction following the Civil War. The question of how best to teach the freedmen and women in the South after slavery became a question of paramount importance. As Susan C. Jarratt puts it, "At stake in the debates over curriculum were issues of great magnitude: What place should formerly enslaved African Americans have in the new social, intellectual, and economic arrangements of their regions and states, and in the nation at large? What kinds of educational institutions and curriculums would best prepare them for newly imagined futures? How did the enterprise of southern Black higher education, and the situation of Black intellectual life more generally in the decades following the Civil War, look from the perspective of southern Black students?"[25] This chapter assesses the important influence of Oberlin College's racial and gender inclusiveness, as well as the vitality of its classical curriculum, on the formation of Black colleges and universities.

In this chapter we also examine the extant catalogs of Black colleges and universities dating from the 1860s to the 1940s. The catalogs provide the clearest evidence of the extent and role of the classical curriculum. But the number of courses offered and their duration were not the same among the colleges. Institutions founded by the American Missionary Association, a White antislavery society whose mission was to proselytize free Blacks, limited their classics offerings (Fisk being among the exceptions) in favor of domestic and industrial training. Other colleges, those founded by the African Methodist Episcopal Church, held on to the classics longer as tools of empowerment, even as funding for the liberal arts was being reappropriated to industrial education.

In the third chapter, we discuss several of the classical authors taught at Black colleges and universities, as evidenced by the catalogs, to determine what lessons they may have imparted and how course offerings changed over time. Notable is the role played by classical rhetoric in the formation of the "whole man"—that is, a man or woman Whites could understand and even respect for their correct speech and deportment, whose rules could be found in Greek and Roman authors, notably Demosthenes, Cicero, and Quintilian, all of whom were taught in the Black colleges. While the curriculums in general conformed to those of White colleges of the period, which classical authors were favored and how they were read is a question worth examining. Adopting the language of "toolsism" again, as Hairston so elegantly articulates, in the period extending from the late eighteenth to the early twentieth century, African Americans deployed the classics as "essential cultural tools . . . to build civic and spiritual virtue, encourage heroism, value and pursue civic equality, and cultivate cultural and artistic life."[26] During this era of increasing racial stratification and segregation under Jim Crow, the alien Other of classical culture offered new ways of thinking and writing about history, through a radical encounter with antiquity.

The fourth chapter describes how various modes of resistance, from dissimulation to outright rebellion in the early twentieth century, were practiced at select institutions, including Avery Institute, Fisk University, Georgia State Industrial College, Florida A&M College, Jackson College, Palmer Memorial Institute, and Howe Institute. Students themselves played an operative role in their own self-empowerment and resorted to strikes and even physical resistance when they saw their liberal arts education being undermined, whether by racist Whites or by accommodationist faculty, trustees, and other college officials. Student voices often provide the clearest indication of the tenor and direction of Black education in the South.[27] But we also look more broadly at how Black educators and activists resorted to more subtle forms of resistance and "the power of the pen" to promote the interests of the race and to resist the imposition of second-class citizenship.

Chapter 5 describes the attrition in the teaching of classics at Black colleges and universities during the twentieth century, a trend that sadly continues as the colleges themselves pass out of existence or have their classics program eliminated. Another reason is African Americans' increased access to White institutions following the *Brown v. Board of Education* decisions of 1954 and 1955 and the civil rights movement of the 1960s. In this chapter we discuss as well the increasing stress on and coding of the notion of usefulness in education as the twentieth century progressed.

In the brief epilogue we describe how, to claim their full right to the civilizations of Greece and Rome as their African birthright, educated African Americans have had to bridge two worlds, using the tools of double consciousness and dissemblance to negotiate with entrenched racism. The role played by the classics and the liberal arts generally in promoting Black autonomy and racial pride is the pivotal concern of our study. It was not our intention to write an exhaustive history of Black education in America nor to compose a detailed catalog of Black colleges and universities from the midnineteenth to the midtwentieth century. Our purpose throughout this book, we emphasize, is to provide for the general reader a broader understanding of

16 INTRODUCTION

the ennobling and empowering roles of Greek and Latin in the lives of educated African Americans during that period.

The surviving college catalogs document the extent of the course lists as well as the schools' ethos. The catalogs list not only classics but the other courses available, dependent on the needs, requirements, and resources of the particular institution. Emphasized for the comfort of their readers, particularly by those schools founded by the missionary societies and financially assisted by various funding agencies, was the centrality of morality and character: their commitment to mold their students into upright, God-fearing citizens.

The inherent recognition that these colleges must be all things to their students, including guardians of students' morals, mandated strict rules of dress and deportment, especially for women. However, Black educators could turn these very strictures to their advantage by using them to put their best face forward to White power holders to enhance the institutions' stature, their solvency, and ultimately their autonomy, as well as to fight racial prejudice. That self-empowerment, by Black classicists and their supporters, is what we recount and champion in this book.

CHAPTER 1

The Formative Influences of Classical Culture in Colonial America and the Early Republic

WHILE *an intrinsic ardor prompts to write,*
The muses promise to assist my pen;
'Twas not long since I left my native shore
The land of errors, and Egyptian *gloom:*
—Phillis Wheatley, "To the University of CAMBRIDGE, in New-England"

The Negro, however sincere, is the slave of the past. None the less I am a man, and in this sense the Peloponnesian War is as much mine as the invention of the compass.
—Frantz Fanon, *Black Skin, White Masks*

Although classical culture was traditionally encoded as European and White, free educated African Americans in the antebellum period argued for full Black humanity, based on their reading of biblical and classical sources. This was occurring during a period of Western European colonialism and racist imperialism in Africa and parts of Asia. By arguing that classical culture had itself originated in northern Africa, Black activists offered a radical rereading of antiquity, one that placed people of color at the center of that culture.

By their campaign of racial equality and arguments for full human dignity, educated Blacks were building on the efforts of enslaved African Americans to educate themselves and their children, even in the face of virulent White opposition.[1] As Vincent P. Franklin notes, "Education and literacy were greatly valued among Afro-Americans enslaved in the United States because they saw in their day-to-day experiences—from one generation to the next—that knowledge and information helped one to survive in a hostile environment."[2] Literacy also reinforced self-worth. Numerous accounts from slaves mention that learning to read made them feel "like a man" or made them feel equal to Whites. The ability to read and to acquire knowledge was also important as a communal act. Slaves could and did pass along information that they garnered from newspapers and books, including the Bible, often circumventing the master's desire to keep the slaves uninformed. Additionally, learning to read was often a blatant political act of resistance done in defiance of state laws, local ordinances, and the master's orders. While we do not have definitive figures for the number of literate slaves, Janet Duitsman Cornelius notes, in *When I Can Read My Title Clear*, that approximately 10 percent of slaves had some level of literacy.[3] Slaves achieved literacy, often in collusion with a sympathetic member of the slave owner's family, at great personal peril: amputation of fingers or thumb to prevent slaves from holding a pen, whippings, or even death.[4] Educated African Americans in the North used this drive to learn as a point of departure, based on their own reading of biblical sources and later evidence from classical culture, to argue for Blacks' full humanity, self-empowerment, and liberation from White racial hegemony.

Traditional Racist Arguments for "Natural Slavery" Based on Notions of Black Inferiority

As members of a so-called inferior race, but at the same time the primary mode of production and source of income for landowners in the South until the outbreak of the Civil War, enslaved African Americans had been subjected to a totalizing institution with a strict hegemonic structure at all levels. Southern Whites used legal controls, residence patterns, and work schedules to highly regulate the lives of slaves. Such control even extended to eye contact, clothing, comportment, association, marriage, and diet.[5] Slavery's objective, then, was to turn human beings into automatons with no will, no voice of their own—at least no articulate voice—and to reduce them to the status of children or animals. Therefore, slavery reinforced and ratified already held Anglo-European notions of Black inferiority and powerlessness. Indeed, Whiteness itself was regarded as a property right that excluded people of color.[6] Ruminating on the state of Black humanity in "Query XIV" of his *Notes on Virginia* (1784), Thomas Jefferson stated, "I advance it, . . . as a suspicion only, that blacks, whether originally a distinct race, or made distinct by time or circumstances, are inferior to the Whites in the endowments both of body and mind. . . . This unfortunate difference of color, and perhaps of faculty, is a powerful obstacle to the emancipation of these people."[7]

Expressing a similar biologically racist sentiment, the eighteenth-century English philosopher David Hume stated in his essay "Of National Characters" (1753): "I am apt to suspect the negroes and in general all other species of men (for there are four or five different kinds) to be naturally inferior to the whites. There never was a civilized nation of any other complexion than white, nor even any individual eminent either in action or speculation. . . . Such a uniform and constant difference could not happen, in so many countries and ages, if nature had not made an original distinction between these breeds of men."[8]

Such racial attitudes would be officially codified in the United States a century later by the *Dred Scott v. Sandford* decision of 1857.[9] This decision was historically important, according to Samuel DuBois Cook, "because the case marks the first time in the seventy-year history of the [U.S. Supreme] Court that it squarely addressed the rights of the African people in the United States":

> Speaking for a unanimous court, Mr. Chief Justice Roger B. Taney declared that a person of African descent, whether a slave or not, belonged to "a subordinate and inferior class of beings," and was not, under a Constitution, included "in the people," and was not and could not be a citizen of a state or of the United States. The Court went on to maintain that persons of African descent had no rights that whites were bound to respect. Black rights depended on the arbitrary and capricious whims, desires, and decisions of whites. Whatever rights whites gave blacks, they could take away at will. Persons of African heritage "had for more than a century before," concluded the august and majestic Supreme Court of the United States, "been regarded as beings of an inferior order, and altogether unfit to associate with the white race, either in social or political relations; and so far inferior, that they had no rights which the white man was bound to respect; and that the Negro might justly and lawfully be reduced to slavery *for his benefit.*"[10]

This stress on inherent Black inferiority, fallacious as it is in light of African Americans' efforts to teach themselves, would impact all efforts to teach African Americans both during and after slavery. The overriding questions were what to teach them and for what purpose. In the antebellum South, several missionary efforts targeted the religious instruction of the Negro. White slaveholders themselves worked to counter what they saw as their charges' dullness and immorality through regular biblical instruction and church attendance. Slaveholders promoted enough literacy to enable African Americans to read the Bible for themselves and in turn spread scripture to those others who could not read. But literacy for slaves served a practical purpose as well for their White overlords. Grey Gundaker provides examples of the tolerance for education, for example, in the low country of South Carolina: for large numbers of absentee owners and overseers clearly overwhelmed by their workload, "a certain degree of literacy [among slaves] was regarded as advantageous for key enslaved personnel to keep accounts, order supplies, and communicate by letter with the property owner."[11] Owners established Sabbath schools to teach the slaves basic literacy as well as to school them in Christianity.

20 CHAPTER ONE

But plantation owners were wary of too much education for their Black charges, since it could bring with it greater autonomy and, with that, the danger of upsetting the status quo. In his *Narrative of the Life of Frederick Douglass* (1845), Douglass recounts efforts by his former mistress, Sophia Auld, to teach him to read and how her husband thwarted those lessons: "'Now,' said he, 'if you teach that nigger (speaking of myself) how to read, there would be no keeping him. It would forever unfit him to be a slave. He would at once become unmanageable, and of no value to his master. As to himself, it would [do] him no good, but a great deal of harm. It would make him discontented and unhappy.'"[12] Similar arguments by powerful Whites, citing discontentedness and unfitness for duties assigned to slaves, would later be used against the teaching of the liberal arts to African Americans, lest it delegitimize the racist trope of natural slavery and, with that, Blacks' exclusion from White culture.

Colonialism, Imperialism, and the Essential Westerness (and Whiteness) of Classical Culture

Racialist arguments such as these were taking place against the background of the imperialism and colonialism practiced by Britain and Western Europe in the late eighteenth and nineteenth centuries. Its field of colonization included the Near East and North Africa, which by then had become subject to European hegemony. Including Egypt in "the Orient," the British explorer and writer Sir Richard Burton (1821–90) called Egypt a "treasure to be won" and "the most tempting prize which the East holds out to the ambition of Europe not excepted even the Golden Horn."[13] As a prize, Egypt, like the Orient, was therefore to be plundered. Edward Said's statement about Orientalism as a way of thinking about a subject, and therefore an abject, people is worth quoting at length here:

> For any European during the nineteenth century—and I think one can say this almost without qualification—Orientalism was such a system of truths, truths in Nietzsche's sense of the word. It is therefore correct that every European, in what he could say about the Orient, was consequently a racist, an imperialist, and almost totally ethnocentric. Some of the immediate sting will be taken out of these labels if we recall additionally that human societies, at least the more advanced cultures, have rarely offered the individual anything but imperialism, racism, and ethnocentrism for dealing with "other" cultures. So, Orientalism aided and was aided by general cultural pressures that tended to make more rigid the sense of difference between the European and Asiatic parts of the world. My contention is that Orientalism is fundamentally a political doctrine willed over the

Orient because the Orient was weaker than the West, *which elided the Orient's difference with its weakness.*[14]

Essential to the concepts of imperialism and colonialism is that the colonized are naturally supine and ready recipients of the superior fruits of so-called Western civilization.[15] Said states in his later work, *Culture and Imperialism,*

> Neither imperialism nor colonialism is a simple act of accumulation and acquisition. Both are supported and perhaps even impelled by impressive ideological formations that include notions that certain territories and people *require* and beseech domination, as well as forms of knowledge affiliated with domination: the vocabulary of classic nineteenth-century imperial culture is plentiful with words and concepts like "inferior" or "subject races," "subordinate peoples," "dependency," "expansion," and "authority." . . . Without significant exception the universalizing discourses of modern Europe and the United States assume the silence, willing or otherwise, of the non-European world. There is incorporation; there is inclusion; there is direct rule; there is coercion. But there is only infrequently an acknowledgement that the colonized people should be heard from, their ideas known.[16]

Indeed, what we now consider the lawless plundering of Greek artifacts by the Western European powers in the early nineteenth century was then seen as the rescue of priceless works of art, most famously the Elgin marbles and the Aphrodite of Melos, more popularly known as the Venus de Milo, from the dissolute, exotic, and effeminate non-White world. Greece itself, in the throes of a war of independence from the Ottoman Empire, was regarded as having degenerated from its glorious classical past. As such, it was no longer a safe haven for what was regarded as quintessentially Western art. So says Gonda Van Steen in her book *Liberating Hellenism from the Ottoman Empire*: "The classical age, in particular, was given the 'honor' of not belonging to the Orient; that is, it alone firmly belonged to the West. . . . The West that leaned on ancient Greece for its own self-worth could not possibly admit that its roots were partly Oriental and therefore 'inferior,' according to the classifications of its own making." Such were the thoughts, for example, of Marie-Louis-Jean-André-Charles Demartin du Tirac, comte de Marcellus, a French diplomat stationed in Constantinople, who purchased the newly discovered Venus in 1820 for relocation to the Louvre. A thorough romantic, Marcellus "assumed the role of the courageous male protagonist who 'saved' the desirable Venus . . . from sexual violation in the Turkish or Arab harem."[17]

The plundering of the Parthenon's pedimental sculptures by Lord Elgin and their relocation to the British Museum also occurred at this time, for similar reasons. By the time of their recovery, these magnificent sculptures had long since lost their overlay of paint. This reinforced the already encoded model of beauty as overwhelmingly European and White, even though nineteenth-century neoclassical sculptors were certainly aware that their ancient predecessors had suffused their marble figures with colorful, indeed sometimes garish, pigments. The German art historian and archaeologist Johann Joachim Winckelmann (1717–68) had already worked to suppress such knowledge in the eighteenth century, and other scholars similarly dismissed the mounting evidence for polychrome statuary.[18] Even in the visual and plastic arts, White racial privilege could be upheld, says Charmaine A. Nelson in *The Color of Stone*, only "by the racial marginalization that produced blacks, Arabs, and Natives as Others and the economic control of land that ensured the eventual geographical displacement of Natives and barred blacks from legitimate and legal landownership, which can activate social independence and full citizenship."[19]

From Indentured Servant to Classically Inspired Poet

Faced with the remarkable talent of the Black-slave-turned-classical-poet Phillis Wheatley (ca. 1753–84), Jefferson tried to explain her away inasmuch as she failed to conform to the entrenched dogma of Blacks' racial and intellectual inferiority. Wheatley challenged Jefferson's colonialist and racialist concepts and indeed broader Anglo-European doubts about the humanity and intellectual ability of people of color. As Jefferson dismissively stated, "Misery is often the parent of the most affecting touches in poetry. Among the blacks is misery enough, God knows, but no poetry. . . . Religion, indeed, has produced a Phillis Whately [sic]; but it could not produce a poet. The compositions published under her name are below the dignity of criticism."[20]

Wheatley, born on the West Coast of Africa, was the first published Black woman and the first Black female poet of distinction in America.[21] She was purchased as a slave by the Wheatley family of Boston, who taught her to read and write, granted her access to her master's extensive library, and encouraged her poetry. In 1773 Wheatley's *Poems on Various Subjects, Religious and Moral*, was published in England, since no Boston publisher would accept it. It was a slender collection, composed mostly in heroic couplets, of pastoral, epic, religious, and elegiac poetry inspired by the classical authors, including Homer, Vergil, Ovid, and Horace, all standard texts read in colonial America. But coming from a young slave woman barely out of her teens, it was an extraordinary achievement. On the strength of her considerable literary reputation, Wheatley gained her freedom. However, the very quality of her poetry raised the specter of authorial fraud. Subsequently, Wheatley had to undergo an examination by eighteen of Boston's most illustrious citizens to determine whether she possessed the requisite ability and educational background to produce such a book—as indeed she did, having been instructed by the Wheatleys' children and later receiving more formal instruction in the classical languages.[22]

Wheatley mined the classics to describe her American experience. She exalted her Blackness by claiming special kinship with the Roman playwright Terence, in that he had been born in Carthage and thus was African and, according to Suetonius, in his *Life of Terence*, *colore fusco*, or "of a dusky hue" (*Vita Terentii* 5). Moreover, Terence, like Wheatley, had been a slave. Drawing from Suetonius's portrait of Terence, Wheatley describes herself as "one . . . of *Afric's* sable race."[23] Upon her book's publication, Wheatley became something of a sensation in both America and England. An astute reader of her classical sources, Wheatley, in her poems to various high-ranking addressees, including Gen. George Washington, calls attention to her ambiguous social status.[24] Born a slave, she appropriates the classical *captatio benevolentiae*, or appeal, in this case, to her free-born and even aristocratic addressees' kindness.[25] Nonetheless, she self-consciously plays the role of a teacher with both the moral and spiritual authority to instruct her readers, who themselves assume the role of students. She also, by her frequent references to Egypt, calls attention to the prominent role of Africa in the classical world.

The very fact of a Phillis Wheatley, as Vincent Carretta states in the introduction to his edition of Wheatley's classically inspired poems, "was frequently cited by opponents of slavery and the slave trade, especially in Britain, as evidence of the humanity and inherent equality of Africans."[26] Indeed, says John Levi Barnard, Wheatley's "use of classical tradition—as evident in 'Niobe' as it is in 'Ocean'—to emphasize the violence of slavery and empire only thinly veiled by the veneer of 'civilization'—would anticipate the critical mode of black classicism . . . emerging as an integral part of African American literary and political writing of the nineteenth century and beyond."[27] Recent work by classicists and literary scholars acknowledging the centrality of classical sources to Wheatley's poems, says Barnard, "has tended to evaluate Wheatley's classical appropriation for its subversive potential, discovering the ways her revisions of Greco-Roman mythology challenge both the slavery and the White supremacy for which the classical tradition had typically provided authorization."[28] Indeed, by appropriating the classics as material for her own original body of work, Wheatley and later generations of African Americans undermined the notion of classical study as a tool exclusively of White cultural and imperialist domination.[29]

Jefferson's dismissal of Wheatley's poetry and his speculations generally on Black inferiority in the *Notes* signaled the beginnings of a significant shift in the racial sentiments of the new nation. The ideological fervor of the American Revolution, which had led to widespread condemnation of the institution of slavery, was giving way to the calcification of racial categories, extending even to the so-called scientific classicism being formulated at this time. These categories helped define which race would dominate and which would submit.

The Racism Inherent in So-called Scientific Classicism

Western Europe and then North America thought they had the right to the classical world in that it contained the seeds of Western culture. This picture of antiquity was idealized but also racialized, imperialistic, and romanticized: philhellenism, as opposed to the Otherness (read non-Whiteness) of Oriental culture. Arguments for the essential Europeanness of classical antiquity found a home in the *Altertumswissenschaft* (literally, "science of antiquity") model first promulgated in Germany and then in France, Britain, and North America during the nineteenth century. This was a time when classical study was moving away from being merely part of the trappings of an elite social class and evolving into a specialized academic discipline that required rigorous training and, for those pursuing advanced degrees, a record of research and scholarly publication. Essentially, *Altertumswissenschaft*, as it was developed in Germany in the late eighteenth century by Friedrich August Wolf (1759–1824) and others, was, as defined by Christian Kaesser, "the redefinition of classics as a historic and objective mission, the notion that this discipline affords its practitioners direct and unmediated access to the spirit of the classical Greeks (but not so much to the Romans), the idea that classics' various subfields must collaborate in an interdisciplinary way to achieve this purpose, and the invention of the Seminar as its institutional venue."[30] But for all its avowed "objectivity" and "purity" in truly recovering the ancient world and applying a rigorous analytical approach to the reading of classical texts, *Altertumswissenschaft* was an outgrowth of Prussian racial and cultural imperialism.

Indeed, *Altertumswissenschaft* had grown out of an earlier Romantic Hellenomania of the godlike Greeks of classical antiquity as the pure, unsullied exponents of Western culture.[31] Prominent among the early, more Romantic, Wissenshaftlers was Karl Otfried Müller (1797–1840). In the first volume of his *History of Greek Tribes and Cities: Orchomenos and the Minyans* (1820), Müller argued, on so-called scientific, albeit highly racialized, grounds, that the early and thus pure Greeks were descendants of the Minyans, a northern tribe related to the Dorians. Müller attributed to a corrupting "Egyptomania" or "barbarophilia" the later writings of the ancient Greek historian Herodotus about borrowings from Egypt and other cultures.[32] During the later nineteenth and early twentieth centuries, the German cult of identification with the Dorians and Lakonians (i.e., Spartans) continued to gain adherents, says Martin Bernal, author of *Black Athena*, "until it reached its climax in the Third Reich."[33] Briefly put, there never was a purely scientific classicism. With the White racial bias inherent in classics at this time, how much more alien would an African American classicist have seemed to those who fully embraced and endorsed the racialist and imperialist classical model. And they would have been the White majority both in the United States and abroad.

For most nineteenth-century Whites, the bodies of African Americans, if considered as a text, were read as dirty, ugly, and offensive. They were likewise inferior in mind, by some lights hardly better than animals. The very idea of an educated African American who could demonstrably translate Latin or Greek was unthinkable. Having been assigned the lowest place in the American social hierarchy, an African American even attempting to imitate educated Whites by, for example, reciting Greek or Latin was seen as an anomaly or even a danger, because they would be attempting to move beyond their place and therefore to violate the larger social body. Indeed, such so-called soiled people could quite literally leak into White society, as sewage might into a public well, thus contaminating all who drank from it.[34]

The classical world, then, to maintain dominance in the eyes of White European and American cultural and racial imperialists, had to be dissociated from these areas of subjection and hence enslavement. Extending Said's arguments, we may infer that this is why early African Americans' advocacy of and association with the classical world and Africa were so heretical. As a subject, abject, and weaker people, African Americans had no rights to the fruits of Western civilization, nor had they the intelligence, in Whites' eyes, to appreciate it. At best, in the opinion of White racists, who regarded classical culture as their exclusive domain, African Americans could parrot Greek declensions or quote a few lines from a classical author without truly understanding them—all in a failed effort to appear White.

Such elitist and racist attitudes may be expressed in the following (perhaps apocryphal yet telling) anecdote from the Reconstruction era. Walter Hines Page, a publisher and diplomat who had studied Greek at Johns Hopkins under the famed American classicist Basil Lanneau Gildersleeve, once visited a school for young Blacks in the South, where, Page says,

> I heard a very black boy translate a passage from Xenophon. His teacher was also a full-blooded Negro. It happened that I went straight from the school to

26 CHAPTER ONE

a club where I encountered a group of gentlemen discussing the limitations of the African mind. "Teach 'em Greek!" said old Judge So-and-So. "Now a nigger could learn the Greek alphabet by rote, but he could never intelligently construe a passage from any Greek writer—impossible." I told him what I had just heard. "Read it? Understood it? Was black? A Black man teaching him? I beg your pardon, but do you read Greek yourself?" "Sir," he said at last, "I do not for a moment doubt your word. I know you think the nigger read Greek; but you were deceived. I shouldn't believe it if I saw it with my own eyes and heard it with my own ears."[35]

The incredulousness of an old White southerner at the idea of African Americans, newly freed from slavery, learning the classics is indicative of racist White attitudes toward African Americans' intelligence and, with that, their capacity to determine their destiny through their education, their freedom of movement, and their involvement in the public life of the nation. For the judge a classically trained African American reading Xenophon (whose *Anabasis* was a staple text assigned in Greek courses at Black colleges and universities) in the original Greek was impossible: it was a text the Black student, by reason of his blackness, could not read. By the same token, the old southerner could not contemplate the idea of a classically educated Black man or woman, even when presented with the facts. It was simply incomprehensible to him.

Approaching this philologically, it was as if the White southerner were reading through a screen of prejudices, misapprehensions, and reductive notions (in short, misreadings) about African Americans; therefore, the judge could not come to a clear and unbiased understanding of the evidence that lay visibly before him. To do so would indeed be, for him, an act of ultimate estrangement from the privileged racist world that he inhabited.[36]

Similarly, in 1834 John C. Calhoun (1782–1850), a South Carolina senator and slaveholder, could adduce Aristotle's concept of the "natural slave" to argue for the inferiority of Blacks.[37] J. Drew Harrington, in his essay "Classical Antiquity and the Proslavery Argument," states that "as early as 1820, Calhoun admitted to John Quincy Adams that he thought slavery 'the best guarantee to equality among the whites.'" By 1837 Calhoun, in his *Speech on the Reception of Abolition Petitions*, stated, "But let me not be understood as admitting, even by implication, that the existing relations between the two races in the slaveholding States is an evil: —far otherwise; I hold it to be a good, as it has thus far proved itself to be both, and will continue to prove so if not disturbed by the fell spirit of abolition."[38] In fact, Calhoun, like other nineteenth-century southerners, thought that advanced civilizations, such as that of ancient Rome, were possible only because of the institution of slavery, which provided for the elite class the leisure necessary to devote themselves to intellectual and cultural pursuits. Calhoun's view of Rome therefore was reinforced by the racial and class stratification of his own place and time.[39]

Calhoun is said to have acknowledged that he would accept the Negro as human but only when it could be demonstrated that the Negro could master Greek syntax.[40] This occurred, according to Alexander Crummell, who recounted the episode, during "a period of great ferment upon the question of Slavery, States' rights, and Nullification."[41] Crummell (1819–98), a pioneering African American minister, academic, and African nationalist, argued that the "asininity" of Calhoun's remark implied that the Black mind would need to have an inborn knowledge of Greek syntax, whereas Calhoun himself had to go to Yale to learn it. But this remark points also to the centrality of the classical languages, and indeed the classical world itself, to the question of who is and is not fully human. Vital to this measure of who is fully human is the maintenance of the classics as White and European.

Basil Lanneau Gildersleeve and a Racist Reading of the Classics in the American South

In late nineteenth- and early twentieth-century America, one of the principal embodiments of the scientific yet romanticized and racialized *Altertumswissenschaft* was Basil Lanneau Gildersleeve (1831–1924), a native of Charleston, South Carolina. Gildersleeve's classical study began at home; he continued his studies at the College of Charleston (from which he graduated at eighteen), followed by two years at Princeton. Because a passion for German language and scholarship had become all the rage among American intellectuals, Gildersleeve traveled to Germany to study classics at the University of Göttingen, receiving his doctorate at twenty-two in 1853.[42] After returning to the United States, Gildersleeve worked as a journalist until his appointment as professor of Greek at the University of Virginia in 1856. In 1876 Gildersleeve moved with his family to Baltimore to take up his position as chair of Greek at the new Johns Hopkins University with its German-style doctoral program, the first such program in the country. There Gildersleeve's reputation as a scholar flourished. During his long career at Johns Hopkins, he would supervise sixty-seven dissertations.[43] He founded the esteemed *American Journal of Philology* and published a Latin grammar, as well as commentaries on the Roman satirist Persius, on the *Apologies* of Justin Martyr, and on Pindar's *Olympian* and *Pythian Odes*.

Gildersleeve nonetheless remained a passionate son of the South, convinced of the righteousness of the secessionist cause and the strict separa-

28 CHAPTER ONE

tion of the races. He never gave up his devotion to journalism, publishing articles and editorials in the *Richmond Examiner*, the *New Eclectic Magazine*, the *Southern Review*, and the *Atlantic Monthly* with titles ranging from "The Hazards of Reviewing" to "The Creed of the Old South." Summoning both classical and biblical examples to bolster his racist arguments, Gildersleeve inveighed against miscegenation with almost hysterical fervor in an editorial published in the *Richmond Examiner* in April 1864, when events were turning against the South. Sharing his fellow Whites' opposition to "the damn Yankee's import of evil," he called this a plot by Abraham Lincoln, the Republicans, and Northern "she-men" to dilute the White race. Such an insidious practice, he argued, would lead inevitably to the pollution of the English "pure blood" and the "intrusion of mongrels."[44]

Gildersleeve was by no means alone in his views. During this period the classical curriculum throughout the South had been preparing the White elite to take their place in a segregated society and to strengthen their sense of their own racial and cultural superiority. For example, professors at South Carolina College, before the outbreak of the Civil War, chose classical readings to furnish lessons for the training of the Southern landed gentry, for the resistance to Northern tyranny, and for the continued maintenance of White dominance. Texts read included the Greek New Testament, Xenophon's *Cyropaedia* (*The Education of Cyrus*), Vergil's *Aeneid*, Cicero's political speeches and his *De oratore* (on the training of the orator), and Longinus's *On the Sublime*. In "The Power of Ancient Words: Classical Teaching and Social Change at South Carolina College, 1804–1860," Wayne Durrill argues that the teaching of the classics at South Carolina College in the first half of the nineteenth century not only prepared South Carolina's White male elite to take their proper place in society but, perhaps even more important, prepared to them to defend their culture and society, which was coming under increasing attack by the North as the nation moved inexorably toward the Civil War.

Durrill points out that, between 1800 and 1835, the classics read by students at South Carolina College focused on oratory and persuasion, the state, and aesthetics and taste. The texts were concerned largely with character and the persuasive argumentation needed for membership in the debating societies; thus, Cicero, particularly his *De oratore*, was seen as important. They ignored texts that did not fall into this category or that were critical of authority, such as Juvenal's *Satires* or Tacitus's *Histories*. The chief lessons to be learned from classical sources were the proper comportment of the public self, the harmony of the outside and inside person, courage in adversity, a sense of purpose, the nurturing of virtue and friendship, and calm acceptance of death. The curriculum could be adapted to changing times. On the eve of the Civil War, Demosthenes's speeches against Philip of Macedon were read as historical analogues of Northern aggression against the South.[45] Gildersleeve himself, in his *Atlantic* articles "The Creed of the Old South" (January 1892) and "A Southerner in the Peloponnesian War" (September 1897), reflecting on the events of thirty years before, compared the war between the States to the contest between Athens and Sparta.[46]

In light of this view and the bias of classical study, especially in the South (that is, as training for a White Protestant ruling class), how could African Americans not have felt alienated from something so racist and elitist? Classically trained Black educators argued that the civilizations of Greece and Rome belonged as much to them as they did to White Europeans and Americans. It was precisely *because* classical study was such a culturally empowering enterprise that African Americans from the time of the early republic would use the classics as a scholarly tool available to them to resist and even to subvert the very idea of White racial domination and cultural supremacy.

Classics to the Defense of Black Humanity and Equality in the Antebellum Period

From the earliest days of the U.S. republic, educated African Americans in the North had been making a distinct link between northern Africa and the cultures of Greece and Rome to declare their full humanity and their right to complete civic participation in the political and social life of the nation.[47] Says Albert J. Raboteau, "Nineteenth-century blacks needed to reclaim for themselves a civilized African past in order to refute the charge that they were inherently inferior." Indeed, Barnard states, "Looking back to Egypt and Ethiopia allowed [antebellum] African American writers to claim a history not only prior to enslavement, but prior even to the Greek and Roman civilizations White Americans claimed as their own legitimating antecedents."[48]

Black intellectuals disseminated their work in publications such as the *African Repository and Colonial Journal* and especially *Freedom's Journal,* founded in 1827 by Samuel Eli Cornish (1795–1858), a Presbyterian minister in New York, and John Brown Russwurm (1799–1851), the first African American to graduate from Bowdoin College. From its inception *Freedom's Journal* addressed such pressing issues as slavery, colonialism, and the achievements of the civilizations of sub-Saharan Africa. Other Black writing of this period decried the evils of slavery and called down vengeance on the United States for hypocritically espousing republicanism while brutally enslaving a large portion of its population based on the notion that Blacks were inherently inferior to Whites, that they were indeed subhuman and therefore meant, whether by divine providence or by the laws of nature, for a degraded position within American society.

In 1817 Jacob Oson (d. 1828), a self-described "descendant of Africa," addressed the free Black populations of New York and New Haven to clarify the relationship between Africa and American society and the evolution of Western civilization. He adduced Herodotus and Josephus to demonstrate that Egypt and Nubia were the earliest seats of the arts and sciences. Indeed, he argued, the ancient Egyptians, to whom the Greeks were indebted for their art, learning, and even religion, were Black.[49] Oson's argument followed an assertion made by writers of the French Enlightenment of a racial connection between ancient Egypt and African America.[50] In the introduction to her edition of David F. Dorr's nineteenth-century travelog, A Colored Man Round the World, Malini Johar Schueller addresses the concern roused by this connection:

> Egyptology had created considerable consternation for both phrenologists and theorists of racial classification because of the non-Caucasian features of Egyptian monuments like the Sphinx and the existence of people with Negroid-African features in many of the carvings, paintings, and parchments of Egyptian antiquity. While proslavery anthropologists strove to demonstrate the lowly status of black peoples in Egypt, prominent African-Americans like Frederick Douglass, Henry Highland Garnet, and later Pauline Hopkins, used Egyptology to validate the idea of Africans being the originators of civilization.[51]

Oson's own somewhat quixotic list of "African" notables with links to the classical world included the second-century CE Christian apologist Tertullian, the emperor Augustus, and Scipio Africanus, who defeated Hannibal in the Battle of Zama. Invoking biblical time, the Haitian-born scholar Pompée Valentin Vastey, Baron de Vastey (1781–1820), stated in his article "Africa," published posthumously in Freedom's Journal on February 7, 1829, "The enemies of Africa wish to persuade the world that for five of the six thousand years that the world has existed, Africa has been sunk in barbarism. Have they forgotten that Africa was the cradle of the arts and sciences? If they pretend to forget this, it becomes our duty to remind them of it." De Vastey went on to say that "everyone knows that the Greeks, so celebrated for the polish of their manners and the refinement of their taste, were in a state of the grossest ignorance and barbarity, living like beasts upon herbs and acorns until civilized by Egypt." Another early African American historian and author, Robert Benjamin Lewis (1802–58), wrote in Light and Truth (1843), "I have therefore searched for light and truth, in sacred and ancient history, in those works translated by English historians—truths which have long been concealed from the sons of Ethiopia—and will now present the results of my investigations to the public."[52] These truths, Lewis asserted, were the greatness of African civilizations such as Ethiopia and Egypt, thus refuting the commonly held perception of Africa as a vast jungle inhabited by creatures who, if they were above the animals, were only slightly above them.

Still another example is provided by Hosea Easton (1798–1837) in his *Treatise on the Intellectual Character and Civil and Political Condition of the Colored People* (1837). In this work Easton presented Africa as a place with a wide range of racial and ethnic groups and as a font of wisdom for the Western world. Easton asserted, "It is evident from the best sources extant that the arts and sciences flourished among this great branch of the human family, long before its benefits were known to any other."[53] The American abolitionist and feminist Lydia Maria Child (1802–80) wrote in 1833, "It is well known that Egypt was the great school of knowledge in the ancient world. It was the birth-place of Astronomy. . . . Herodotus, the earliest of the Greek historians, informs us that the Egyptians were Negroes [*Histories* 2.104]. This fact has been much debated and often contradicted. But Herodotus certainly had the best means of knowing the truth on this subject, for he traveled in Egypt and obtained his knowledge of the country by personal observation."[54] Turning to the ancient world, then, meant more than fanciful versions of a mythical past. Rather, it allowed both Black writers and some sympathetic Whites to use the lenses of history to bolster the belief that all humankind shared one common origin, thus undercutting the then-current notions of a vast racial divide in the human family.

The classically trained scholar Edward Wilmot Blyden (1832–1912) mined the classics to support the primacy of Africa in the progress of civilization. Born the son of free Blacks on the island of Saint Thomas in the Danish West Indies, Blyden was brought to the United States at the age of seventeen to complete his studies for the ministry. Despite his promise, however, he was denied entrance to the theological college at Rutgers because of his race. Disillusioned, Blyden emigrated to Liberia, courtesy of the New York Colonization Society.[55] There he served as professor of classics at Liberia College, secretary of state, and minister to England. In Sierra Leone he held government positions relating to education.[56]

Relevant for our purposes is that Blyden espoused a pan-Africanism and was a supporter of the immigration of American Blacks to Liberia. As a student at mission schools in Liberia, Blyden had a strongly classical education. Contrasting African accomplishments in antiquity with the degraded state of

Blacks in the United States, Blyden argued, as had Black American abolition-ists before him, that this was the result of enforced racial inequality and not an innate lack of ability. This was in opposition to nineteenth-century anthro-pologists who argued that differences in physical appearance reflected racial inferiority or superiority. Blyden advocated the study of Arabic and African languages as well as the culture and mythology of African tribes alongside study of the classics. Robert W. July calls this a "curious *non sequitur*" and "all the more astonishing since [Blyden] was one of the first African intellectuals to insist that Africa had an authentic history and a valid culture of her own, and to proclaim repeatedly and at length the accomplishments and contribu-tions of Africans to the civilization of the world."[57] This, however, jibes with our argument about the powerful link that had already been made between Africa and the classical world. Blyden is being perfectly consistent with other Black and African American scholars who made this link. African Americans should study the classics because the classics were indeed African and there-fore part of the history of Africa.

Adducing evidence from classical antiquity and scripture, de Vastey and other early Black intellectuals argued that the current degraded status of Blacks in the United States was the result not of innate inferiority but of Whites' transgression against God. As such, the problem called for divine intervention. Invoking Psalms 68:31, they argued that Ethiopia would again stretch forth her hands unto God, and America, like the biblical Babylon, would suffer for its sins.[58] Thus the status quo would be turned upside down, and African Americans would assume their rightful place in the social, polit-ical, and economic life of the nation.

Reading Rooms and Other Learned Societies for African Americans

This same fervor that linked Africa to the classical world was responsible for the rise of the literary, mutual aid, artistic, and historical societies that be-gan to be formed in the large northern cities, such as the Minerva Society of Philadelphia, during the antebellum period. These societies were racially egalitarian; their ostensible purpose was to uplift the race by demonstrating mastery of the intellectual currents of the day and to promote literacy. But they did more than that. Separate literary associations for women, which in-cluded weekly readings and recitations of classical literature, "strove to pro-mote piety, truth and justice."[59] As Elizabeth McHenry convincingly argues in *Forgotten Readers*, these societies were also conscious sites of resistance, refuges from the racial attitudes that denied African Americans citizenship and often even personhood. "Literary societies planned reading lists; they provided regular opportunities for authors to 'publish' original literary creations and for audiences to encourage, discuss, and criticize their ideas and presentation," McHenry writes. "The societies helped train future orators and leaders by sponsoring debates on issues of importance to the black community. In supporting the development of a literate public they furthered the evolution of a black public sphere and politically conscious society."[60] Susan C. Jarratt quotes William Lloyd Garrison's *Liberator*, in which he states that "the endorsement of traditional rhetorical education can have radical implications" in the service of an oppressed people.[61] This tradition would continue at Black colleges and universities and their various literary and debating societies.

Freedom's Journal and other publications addressed to African Americans encouraged reading as an activity that promoted both opportunities and moral conduct, in that reading expanded the soul: "By reading you may ascend to those remote regions where other spheres encircle other suns, where other stars illuminate a new expanse of skies, and enkindle the most sublime emotions that can animate the human soul."[62] Literary societies long remained a vital center for African Americans. A 1902 recommended reading list compiled for the Boston Literary Society in response to the African American community's "needs of the hour" to encourage "more reading and thinking" included the following classical authors: Homer, Aeschylus, Pindar, and Sappho. History and oratory were also favored. Educated Blacks in the early republic advocated the reading of classical authors who demonstrated a clear link between Africa and the classical world.

African Americans appropriated the millennial and teleological concerns of American Protestantism to show that African Americans would be vindicated and that their White transgressors would be humbled. Samuel Cornish, speaking on the infrastructure of Black churches and benevolent societies, stated, "Our general agent whose duty it shall be to continue travelling from one extremity of our country to the other, forming associations communicating with our people and the public generally, on all subjects of interest, collecting monies, and delivering stated lectures on industry, frugality, enterprise, etc. thereby [might link] together, by one solid claim, the whole free population, so as to make them think and feel and act, as one solid body, devoted to education and improvement."[63]

Nathaniel Paul (1793–1839), pastor of the African Baptist Church in Albany, New York, in his July 5, 1827, address to a freedom celebration, spoke of the religious need for education:

34 CHAPTER ONE

The God of Nature has endowed our children with intellectual powers surpassed by none; nor is there anything wanting but their careful cultivation in order to fit them for stations the most honorable, sacred, or useful. And may we not, without becoming vain in our imaginations, indulge the pleasing anticipation that within the little circle of those connected with our families there may hereafter be found the scholar, the statesman, or the herald of the cross of Christ. Is it too much to say that among that little number there shall yet be one found like the wise legislator to Israel, who shall take his brethren by the hand and lead them forth from worse than Egyptian bondage to the happy Canaan of civil and religious liberty?[64]

Against this background of Black activism and advocacy, David Walker's pamphlet, *Appeal to the Colored Citizens of the World,* may be seen as a call to arms to refute what he saw as the brutality, sinfulness, and criminality of racism as manifested in Black American slavery.

David Walker's *Appeal* as a Rebuttal of Thomas Jefferson's Racialist Classicism

David Walker (1785–1830), born in the Cape Fear region of North Carolina to a free mother and an enslaved father, settled in Boston in the 1820s. There are no extant records of his having had any formal education, but Walker was clearly literate from an early age. In Boston Walker ran a used clothing store and became involved in the activism of the vibrant Black community, which included the Massachusetts General Colored Association and the Reverend Samuel Snowden's Methodist church. He also served as a Boston agent and writer for *Freedom's Journal.*

Out of his familiarity with a broader Black intellectual class and their involvement in local politics, Walker published in 1829 his *Appeal to the Colored Citizens of the World,* but in particular, and very expressly, to those of the United States of America, his jeremiad against what he saw as not only slavery but brutality against people of color generally. The *Appeal,* which was privately printed in Boston, combined African American interests in social and secular history with a plea against the injustice of slavery. More than an abolitionist, Walker was an outspoken representative of the Black intelligentsia of his time. However, Walker could do this only because previous African American intellectuals, by using not only biblical but classical sources to claim Black personhood, had claimed a kinship with classical antiquity and had thus appropriated the classical heritage as their own. Walker's *Appeal,* published in three editions between 1829 and 1830, served as a direct rebuttal of Jefferson's views of slaves and Black people in general. For any Black person

FORMATIVE INFLUENCES OF CLASSICAL CULTURE **35**

to refute a president of the United States, indeed one who had died only three years before, was audacious and dangerous enough. Walker, however, went one step further. He attacked the scholarly Jefferson not only for his pseudo-scientific argument for White supremacy but also on his understanding of the classical past.[65]

Walker circulated his book as widely as possible, disseminating it among free Blacks and slaves in the South. It enflamed Whites, who began confiscating copies wherever they found them. The governor of Virginia tried and sentenced to hard labor anyone, White or Black, he found distributing copies. Not surprisingly, Walker's pamphlet resulted in a hardening of White racial attitudes and increased strictures against slave literacy. Nonetheless, the *Appeal*'s message reverberated throughout the antebellum South and, according to Peter Hinks in the introduction to his edition, may have led to the slave rebellion directed by Nat Turner in 1831.[66]

Walker's *Appeal* offered an alternate reading of classical sources and an argument for Black intellectual achievement in the persons of Augustine, Hannibal, and Cleopatra. Ancient slavery, Walker argued, was not racially specific and was mild in comparison with the condition of enslaved Blacks in early nineteenth-century America. Ignorance among African Americans, Walker contended, resulted not from a biological inferiority but from a lack of education. Walker predicted that one day the world would be turned upside down and that African Americans, as descendants of the initiators of civilization, would assume their rightful place in the social, political, and economic life of the nation.

The preamble of the *Appeal* adduces examples from both the Middle East and the classical world to contrast ancient and contemporary slavery:

> They tell us of the Israelites in Egypt, the Helots in Sparta, and of the Roman slaves, which last were made up from almost every nation under heaven, whose sufferings under those ancient and heathen nations, were, in comparison with ours, under this enlightened and Christian nation, no more than a cypher—or, in other words, those heathen nations of antiquity, had but little more among them than the name and form of slavery; while wretchedness and endless miseries were reserved, apparently in a phial, to be poured out upon our fathers, ourselves and our children, by *Christian* Americans![67]

Walker takes care to separate heathens from Christians or, in America's case, "professed Christians" who will bring down on themselves the wrath of the Almighty. Walker's book being nothing less than a spirited lamentation against American racism, he invokes the deity in detailing his grievances. The separation of heathens from Christians lies at the core of Walker's argument.

Here he rebuts Jefferson's famous passage, in *Notes on Virginia*, about slave torture in antiquity: "With the Roman, the regular method of taking the evidence of their slaves was under torture. Here it has been thought better never to resort to their evidence. When a master was murdered, all his slaves, in the same house, or within hearing, were condemned to death. Here punishment falls on the guilty only, and as precise proof is required against him as against a freeman."[68]

Walker adduces a classical example to challenge this assertion, once again the helots under the Spartans:

> The sufferings of the Helots among the Spartans, were somewhat severe, it is true, but to say that theirs were as severe as ours among the Americans, I do most strenuously deny—for instance, can any man show me an article on a page of ancient history which specifies, that, the Spartans chained, and handcuffed the Helots, and dragged them away from their wives and children, children from their parents, mothers from their suckling babes, wives from their husbands, driving them from one end of the country to the other? Notice the Spartans were heathens, who lived long before our Divine Master made his appearance in the flesh. Can Christian Americans deny these barbarous cruelties?

Once again Walker pointedly juxtaposes pagan antiquity and Christian America. He especially calls Jefferson to account to answer "at the bar of God." Once more adducing history (but not naming his source), Walker states, "Every body who has read history, knows, that as soon as a slave among the Romans obtained his freedom, he could rise to the greatest eminence in the State, and there was no law instituted to hinder a slave from buying his freedom. Have not the Americans instituted laws to hinder us from obtaining our freedom?"[69]

In his rebuttal to Jefferson, Walker returns to Africa and cites the example of Hannibal in an effort to pit the African against the White race, with the African the victor: "When I view the mighty son of Africa, Hannibal, one of the greatest generals of antiquity, who defeated and cut off so many thousands of the White Romans or murderers, and who carried his victorious arms, to the very gate of Rome, and I give it as my candid opinion, that had Carthage been well united and had given him good support, he would have carried that cruel and barbarous city by storm."[70]

Regarding Jefferson's assertion that Epictetus, Terence, and Phaedrus, though slaves, were White, Walker becomes especially animated: "See this, my brethren!! Do you believe that this assertion is swallowed by millions of the whites? Do you know that Mr. Jefferson was one of as great characters as ever lived among the whites? See his writings for the world, and public labours for the United States of America. Do you believe that the assertions of such a man, will pass away into oblivion unobserved by this people and the world? If you do you are much mistaken. . . . I say that unless we try to refute Mr. Jefferson's arguments respecting us we will only establish them."[71] Walker appears to be arguing about what constituted a slave in ancient Rome and in contemporary America. In Jefferson's version of Roman history, former slaves could rise to the greatest eminence in the state. Walker's animus is raised against Jefferson in this particular instance because Jefferson emphasized that White slaves specifically could become eminent, whereas Black slaves in America cannot precisely because they are Black. Walker uses this in support of his claim that Whites are truly murderous. Walker's scholarship may become shaky, his arguments ad hoc. However, Walker was writing not as a scholar but as an evangelist and a reformer. As Hinks states in his introduction to the *Appeal,* "Walker believed that one of the most urgent assignments for African Americans now was to attack and refute [Jefferson's] nefarious doctrine, because it was the ideological centerpiece of American racism."[72] Walker preached his message to the Black population, many of whom were illiterate. Thus his work would be read aloud and, in the recitation, invoke the same sorts of passionate feelings as the scriptures.

Walker reverts again and again to examples from Greek and Roman history whose names, at least, would be familiar to many of his readers and listeners, since classical names were regularly used for slaves.[73] Walker does this to point up the difference between the pagans and Christians. In the case of the United States, Walker shows how superior in morals the heathens were to the White population of Walker's own time, people who stand condemned before history and before God.

Clearly, the civilizations of Greece and Rome, for both Jefferson and Walker, were a ripe area for plunder to advance their respective ideas of racial superiority or inferiority. In the spirit of the time, Jefferson's writing is deemed scientific, though he shared with his peers an elitism regarding the purpose of a classical education, which was, in his day, to inform and enlighten a privileged class. Hovering in the background is the colonialism that in this period pitted the White man against the unmanned and inferior East, including northern Africa. Since White Anglo-Americans were believed to embody the best of Western, classically inspired civilization, being subjected to White hegemony through colonization was to the benefit of the colonized. Drawing on the writings and advocacy of earlier generations of Black abolitionists, Walker

38 CHAPTER ONE

exploited classical examples to argue that the professedly Christian America of his time was far worse in its treatment of Black slaves than antiquity had been at its worst moments. Combining biblical with classical sources, Walker and other Black evangelical reformers argued that White America was on a road to perdition and that the Black underclass should rise up against its oppressor.

The classics themselves, then, could serve as tools of liberation and self-empowerment, as they would later in the nineteenth century, when, following Emancipation, Black colleges and universities were founded on a classical curriculum to educate the newly freed slaves. But the classics also became sites of contestation between Black leaders and White racists. Black educators would learn to hone more effectively the tools of resistance against White authority and the entrenchment of the classics as the sole property of a White elite.

The sources for Walker, Blyden, de Vastey, Easton, Oson, and others were the Bible first and then, just as important, classical sources, including Pliny's *Letters*, Eusebius's *Ecclesiastical History*, Plutarch's *Notable Lives*, Dionysius of Halicarnassus's *History of Rome*, Tacitus's *Histories* and *Germania*, Polybius's *General History of the Greeks and Romans*, and Isocrates's *Orations* and *Epistles*.[74] For those who did not know the classical languages, English translations, such as those published by Harper's in its Classical Library series, were available.[75] Thus they grounded their Afrocentric view of history in the works of Greece and Rome and combined with that the eschatology of scripture to argue for the inevitable rise of African Americans to equality and even dominance.

Throughout the early U.S. republic, American intellectuals argued about the Europeanness versus Africanness of the cultures and literatures of Greece and Rome. The arguments for either position were racially specific at their core. One side stressed the superiority and racial hegemony of Whites; the other, the worthiness of people of color to participate as free citizens of the republic. As worthy participants, African Americans therefore had the right to form educational societies to promote intellectual and social uplift and to receive the same education as their White brethren.

This call for Black education and uplift was one African Americans themselves had been making even under slavery. The Black colleges and universities founded after the Civil War would, however, not answer the call evenly. The extent to which they did so would depend on the educational and evangelizing philosophy of the founding institution as well as on the availability of funds, access to which often determined the courses that would and would not be taught. In chapters 2 and 3 we look at the founding and course lists of select institutions. The surviving catalogs are our primary evidence, from the late 1860s to the 1940s, and show that not all these institutions would be able to fully realize or even address the early Black abolitionists' dream of a promised land of equal opportunity for African Americans as well as the full realization of a classical education as an African birthright.

CHAPTER 2

The Founding of Black Colleges and Universities and Their Classics Curriculums

*Whether the work is easy or difficult, it must be done, or woe to this nation. . . .
It is no time to sit down and cry. The voice we hear today, is Go! Work—This people
must be educated and may we rejoice that God permits us to aid in such a work.*
—*American Missionary*

Following emancipation, African Americans, particularly in the South, quickly moved to gain what had been denied them under slavery—namely, a formal education. As Harriet Beecher Stowe observed in 1879, "They rushed not to the grog-shop but to the schoolroom—they cried for the spelling-book as bread, and pleaded for teachers as a necessity of life."[1] Almost every account of this period notes the cry for universal education from the freed men and women for themselves and their children.

While cut off from most educational venues, African America still had managed to train a ministerial and intellectual class by relying on private northern liberal arts colleges and seminaries, educational opportunities abroad, self-help, and communal initiatives. The achievements of these men and women countered the then accepted White American narrative of racial supremacy. This counternarrative, based on Blacks' own reading of classical and biblical sources, discussed Africa's formative role in antiquity and thus the right of African Americans to participate in the intellectual life of the American nation. The "Report of the Course of Instruction in Yale College," better known as the "Yale Report of 1828," had argued for the primacy of the classical course in American higher education, in that "the study of the classics was superior to all other subjects for acquiring mental discipline and cultural refinement for later life."[2] Therefore, it should come as no surprise that when African Americans could have a say in the direction of their own higher educational endeavors, the classics, long the bastion of a free man's intellectual formation, would form a central core.

The first report on schools issued by the Freedmen's Bureau in 1866 commented on the "self-teaching" that had already been taking place and the "native schools" that were in operation. With the assistance of the Freedmen's Bureau, missionaries from New England and Black and White church groups began to standardize primary education. In accordance with their newfound status, the freedmen and freedwomen wanted to create and control these schools themselves. As William Channing Gannett (1840–1923), a White teacher from New England affiliated with the American Missionary Association, noted, "What they desire is assistance without control." A variety of funding agencies founded Black colleges and universities, mostly in the South, after the Civil War, a period that saw explosive growth in the founding of both White and Black colleges in the United States.[3] We examine the extent of the classics curriculum at Black colleges and universities during a roughly eighty-year period, from Reconstruction to the mid-twentieth century.

While the records are incomplete, several studies have shown that the first teachers and leaders in the South were literate former slaves.[4] Clearly, literacy and leadership were connected. In the introduction to her study *Self-Taught* (2005), Heather Williams states, "Literate men who escaped slavery to enlist in the Union Army, for example, became teachers in regiments of Black men, and once the war ended, these same men taught in local communities. They also advocated for political and economic equality, underscoring with each letter or petition precisely why literacy was such an urgent priority to an oppressed group living within a literate society."[5]

In his history of Fisk University in Nashville, Tennessee, Joe M. Richardson describes the hunger for learning among the newly admitted students. When Fisk opened for classes in the fall of 1866, it had to serve as both a primary and secondary school as well as a college (a consistent pattern across Black colleges): "One teacher had a class of pupils ranging in age from seven to seventy, all reading at the same level. Parents and children, husbands and wives—all were trying to learn."[6] This cry for education is most eloquently and poignantly expressed in the opening pages of Fisk's first academic catalog (1867):

> Ignorance is the bane of republics. Can there be safety, either to the people or to the government, when nearly two-fifths of the whole voting population are unable to read and write; and when not more than one in seven can be said to be educated up to the proper standard of citizenship?
>
> *The true policy of reconstruction is to educate the people.* But how can we educate without teachers? Ten thousand colored teachers are needed in the South, to-day, to give the bread of knowledge to those who, with out-stretched hands and pleading hearts, are famishing for the want of it. Shall they ask in vain, when *our* safety and *theirs* depend on their receiving it?[7]

We must emphasize that throughout their history Black colleges and universities across the board struggled with tight budgets and inadequate teaching staff; additionally, they had to offer basic remedial instruction, including reading, writing, and spelling, for incoming students who had only rudimentary instruction. Therefore, before these students could be admitted to the college level, they had to go through the equivalent of at least the upper grades of primary school and then high school before entering either the normal school, for the express training of teachers, or the college courses.[8] In our discussion of individual Black colleges and universities, we indicate the levels of instruction, from primary grades to college level, that they were offering.

Once they had achieved literacy, numerous African Americans viewed studying the classics as the next step for creating leaders. Typical was the assessment by Kelly Miller (1863–1939), dean of arts and sciences at Howard University and known as "the Bard of the Potomac," who in 1895 observed that the Greek and Latin classics and ancient history were important because, "if any race needs leaders we do."[9] This speaks to the determination of Black educators and students to become classically educated and, with that, to lift themselves out of oppression. Thus what the students read would help determine who they would become. The 1912–13 Fisk catalog sums it up nicely: "The Classical Course is intended to give those who pursue it a *liberal* education. Its purpose is not so much to give specific or professional knowledge as it is to give power in thought, correctness of judgment, breadth of view, standards of refinement and established character. The experience of history justifies this course."[10]

Compare with this the statement in the 1881–82 catalog of Simmons University, founded in 1879 as the Kentucky Normal and Theological Institute, in Louisville, Kentucky: "To build, fashion and develop young men and women intellectually and morally for the higher vocations and duties of life—and particularly to secure an educated ministry and competent teachers."[11] There was great stress laid on good moral character and industry. The statement of purpose of Morris Brown University in Atlanta emphasized application and industry, as well as good moral character, which contravened the commonly held caricature of African Americans as shiftless and lazy. Indeed, the Ten Commandments were and remained the foundation of the school's ethos. But practicality had to be joined with ideals. Morris Brown, like other Black colleges and universities, inaugurated an industrial department early in its history, with dressmaking, crocheting, knitting, embroidery, chair caning, and cooking and canning, with other departments to be added "as soon as possible."[12]

Beyond these general assumptions about what the study of classics did for African Americans, we must ask, in light of Black intellectuals' stress on the

Africanness of classical literature, whether African Americans would bring a specifically subversive reading to the classical texts. The most well-documented cases we have of classical readers among African Americans emphasize the qualities of leadership, authority, and autonomy, which, in the nineteenth and early twentieth centuries, were commonly regarded as the virtues of White males, with few exceptions. Moreover, the pride of place long held by the classics within the broader curriculum of American education, coupled with a conservative Christian mentality, reinforced Whites' notions of elitism and exclusivity. These included the tacit acceptance of a graded society, with males in positions of leadership and women subservient, and thus the performance of conformity, heteronormativity, and the strict separation of the races. The achievements of Black classicists would undermine this racial and gender hierarchy.

Oberlin's Role in the Formation of African American Higher Education

African American educators were not the only early promoters of the classics as an essential element of Black education. A vital site not only in the abolitionist and evangelical movements but also in the importance of the classics for the uplift of African Americans was Oberlin College in Ohio. Nineteenth-century evangelicalism stressed social reform: two of the chief causes evangelicals in the North took up were abolitionism and women's rights, causes advocated also by transcendentalists and the Quakers. In his history of the Second Great Awakening and the transcendentalist movement in the United States, Barry Hankins emphasizes the strong link made by both the evangelicals and the transcendentalists between social reform and salvation: "The Transcendentalist goal was that individuals be free. Evangelicals also believed that God intended for individuals to be free, but they possessed as well the vision of a just society built on the principles of the kingdom of God. For them, the sin of slavery was not just that it denied African Americans their freedom, but also that it violated the biblical norms of a just society. They believed that God would judge America for this national sin."[13] In addition, the transcendentalists advocated egalitarianism and communal living, with the same rights and responsibilities accorded to both male and female members. These societies fostered lofty social ideals to be inculcated through education, from primary grades on to advanced study in Latin, French, and other subjects.[14]

Within these egalitarian, redemptive, and teleological concerns, it is important to discuss the formative role Oberlin played in setting the classical curriculum and the educational philosophy of Black colleges and universi-

44 CHAPTER TWO

ties. While not a Black college as such, Oberlin, founded by the clergyman John Jay Shipherd (1802–44) and the missionary Philo Penfield Stewart (1798–1868) in the newly formed state of Ohio in 1833 as the Oberlin Collegiate Institute and rechartered in 1851 as Oberlin College, was dedicated to the idea that a liberal arts education should be within the reach of all, regardless of sex, race, or color.[15] Indeed, as part of its Christian character, Oberlin advocated freedom for the slaves and was an important stop on the Underground Railroad. Oberlin's chief aim was to produce qualified teachers "for the pulpit and for schools." It advocated education for men and for women (though women would be routed into the separate Ladies Course until 1875). In a letter to parents on August 6, 1832, Shipherd outlined the purpose of the college, which was that "all the children of the [Oberlin] colony are to be well educated, whether destined to professional or to manual labor."[16]

In accordance with the college's staunch Congregationalist beliefs and inculcation in its students of a Christian lifestyle, Oberlin officials prohibited alcohol and even tea and coffee as improper stimulants. Student housing was strictly segregated by sex and student life closely regulated. Chapel attendance and four hours of daily labor were mandatory. This Puritan stress on Christian conformity would have been commonplace at the time and was indeed practiced at both Black and White sectarian colleges.[17] Oberlin stressed the scriptures; according to the official history of Oberlin's first fifty years by James H. Fairchild, *Oberlin: The Colony and the College, 1833–1883*, the classical curriculum eliminated some of the more objectionable pagan authors.

An examination of the available course catalogs, beginning with the academic year 1864–65, bears this out to a large degree. Students read the Greek New Testament, and the college emphasized Greek and Roman history, oratory, and philosophy, including Demosthenes's *On the Crown*, Plato's *Gorgias*, Cicero's *De officiis* (*On Duties*), the Greek tragedians, Hesiod, and Theocritus. Latin became a required study in 1849. The first commencement, in 1834, featured a Greek and a Latin oration as well as a colloquy whose aim was to maintain an orthodox opinion on the subject of classical education—that is, students may gain life lessons by reading the best classical authors, whereas they were to avoid the more scurrilous writers. However, some of the authors deemed more questionable do appear in the syllabus, despite the college's claimed castigations.[18] Judging by the course listings in classics at Oberlin, the definition of "scurrilous" depended on the reader. We may also deduce that teachers at these schools taught what they themselves had learned and that they stressed their favorite authors. Clearly, they did favor the canonical writers. The curriculum followed at Oberlin, largely replicated at Black colleges and universities, would provide a model of classical education in America for the next century.

Oberlin's importance for African Americans and the classics is, first, that it provided a site of training for young African American men and women seeking a liberal arts education. In his letter to the trustees on December 15, 1834, Shipherd said he wrote "to secure the passage of the following resolution, to wit: 'Resolved. That students shall be received into this Institution *irrespective of color.'"*[19] Teachers at Oberlin, and at Black colleges and universities, had arrived with training in the classics and liberal arts from normal schools, female academies, and colleges in the North, in cities like Baltimore, Boston, Cincinnati, Pittsburgh, and Washington, D.C.

Second, Oberlin became in turn a feeder for teachers who went to the Black colleges and universities that opened in the South after the Civil War. As *Oberlin: The Colony and the College* states, as part of the school's missionary activity, "Oberlin students have been connected with this work in large numbers . . . in the institutions for higher education, such as Berea College, Ky.; Fisk University, Nashville, Tenn.; Talladega College, Ala.; Atlanta University, Ga.; Straight College, New Orleans, La.; Emerson Institute, Mobile, Ala.; Howard University, Washington, D.C.; and other similar schools for the colored people."[20] Oberlin could boast many distinguished African American graduates. Among them was the activist and educator Mary Church Terrell (1863–1954), who took the "Gentleman's," or classical course, earning her bachelor's degree in 1884. While at Oberlin, Terrell was imbued with the college's abolitionist credo. Throughout her career she devoted herself to education and to the cause of liberation for African Americans. Other prominent Oberlin graduates were Thomas De Saille Tucker (1844–1903), first president of Florida A&M College, and William Sanders Scarborough (1852–1926), who with Terrell became a professor of classics at Wilberforce and author of *First Lessons in Greek*. Scarborough, who earned his degree in 1875, states in his autobiography that his coming to Oberlin after two years at Atlanta University had been providential.[21] Indeed, in Wilberforce's first thirty years, one-third of its teachers were graduates of Oberlin.[22]

The providential nature of Oberlin for its African American graduates cannot be overstated. Oberlin encouraged social activism, service, and moral and spiritual rectitude as well as scholarship in its students. Since the classics curriculum was dominant, the faculty believed that study of the best Greek and Roman authors would impart valuable life lessons to their students. Oberlin students demonstrated at least token resistance to the classical authors. During the presidency of Rev. Asa Mahan, some students burned classical texts; however, Fairchild reports, "the young men who burnt the books prepared their lessons in Virgil for the next day, as usual. The boyish freak was widely published through the country as 'The burning of the Classics at Oberlin,' and was accepted very generally, not unnaturally, as a declaration that such studies were to be repudiated. No such impression prevailed at Oberlin, and no such result followed."[23] While this was construed as mostly a student prank, it does speak to the sometimes ambivalent attitude toward these pagan authors that would be evident not only at Oberlin but at other educational institutions, including Black colleges and universities, that were founded on religious principles and whose main purpose was to train ministers and spread the Gospel.

The Founders of Black Colleges and Universities

Black colleges and universities were founded largely by White and Black denominations, from the 1850s to the early twentieth century.[24] These included the American Missionary Association (AMA) and the African Methodist Episcopal (AME) Church. Other Black colleges and universities were founded by philanthropical industrialists. Still others were founded by ex-slaves. Initially, Black land-grant universities, such as Alcorn and Florida Agricultural and Mechanical College, were few. These institutions did not impose any color barriers; therefore, they were open to both White and Black students— that is, when the law permitted. They had Whites among their faculty as well. "Indeed," says Gabrielle Simon Edgcomb in *From Swastika to Jim Crow*, "the historically black colleges were about the only places in Jim Crow America where white Americans and African Americans could communicate on the basis of equality and mutual respect."[25]

Those colleges established by missionary societies were based on the New England academic model. Their founders often demonstrated a condescending attitude toward African Americans, whom they considered to have been depraved by slavery, but devoted themselves to providing Black students with a training necessary for advancement in civil and political life. This emphasis shifted gradually during the latter part of the nineteenth century, as the course catalogs themselves attest, from antiquity to Europe, as stress was placed on mastery of not only Latin and Greek but also philosophy and the modern European languages, chiefly French and German.

Given the evidence of the catalogs at least (although this likely gives us a somewhat idealized picture), a percentage of students, small in relation to the number of those enrolled in the lower grades, managed to progress from primary subjects to elite, college-level courses in Latin (and in fewer cases Greek) and later, with the broadening of the curriculum, modern foreign languages and English courses.[26] However, at colleges affiliated with the American Missionary Association, these elite courses had to be balanced by industrial education for men and domestic science for women, even at schools that stressed the liberal arts. This combination of industrial and liberal arts training was a popular model in midnineteenth-century America.[27]

Each group had its own philosophy regarding a classical curriculum. This philosophy had to do with the way in which the group viewed the relationship between higher education and the African American's place in the New South. Taking as evidence their educational and social philosophies as revealed in the extant college catalogs, we demonstrate how these White and Black organizations felt about the role of higher education—specifically, a classical, liberal arts education—for African Americans and how that belief, coupled with financial and other exigencies, contributed to the demise or survival of the classics at Black colleges and universities.

The American Missionary Association

The largest single founder of Black high schools and normal schools, colleges, and universities in the South was the American Missionary Association, which had been founded in 1846 as an antislavery society.[28] This new organization clearly rejected the earlier mission societies' unwillingness to denounce slavery and acceptance of donations from slave owners. The AMA became an umbrella organization for the home mission societies of the Congregationalists, Methodists, and Episcopalians. Immediately after the Civil War, the AMA started its educational project for the newly freed Black people in the South, although faculty at its schools faced constant harassment by Whites who inveighed against those "nigger teachers." The AMA began by establishing primary and secondary schools, primarily for freed people, but which were "open to illiterates regardless of color."[29] But when the South started instituting its own public primary and secondary education for Blacks, the AMA largely restricted its efforts to founding normal schools, for the training of teachers, and colleges. The professed goals of the AMA were "the incorporation of blacks into a casteless American society" and the preparation of the freed people for a "full, rich, and productive life" and for citizenship.[30] AMA teachers required stamina, energy, sobriety, good character, and, ideally, teaching experience, including experience as strict disciplinarians. The AMA was therefore interested in hiring good teachers, both Black and White, who could do the work required.

However, the schools' expressed goals would often bring their teachers into conflict with the very people they were called on to assist. For example, while the AMA schools had largely adopted the New England classical curriculum, these organizations, for all their concern about the welfare of African American students in their charge, did not see them as yet equal to Whites.[31] Typical of their view is the following paternalistic, indeed colonialist, comment by the secretary of the Methodist Freedmen's Aid Society: "The colored people are yet children, and need to be taught everything."[32]

James McPherson offers a more nuanced assessment of the White missionaries' educational purpose in the South. According to McPherson, the missionary teachers went south with the best of intentions—namely, to lift up newly freed African Americans by giving them an education equal to that available in the North.[33] The teachers brought with them northern pedagogical models based on the classics-oriented liberal arts education, whose professed goal was to end racism and to transform the South. This indeed was the ideal, though study of the liberal arts could not initially be implemented at many of the AMA-founded schools, for the majority of students they set out to teach were illiterate or possessed only basic literacy. Even so, the AMA colleges offered classics courses for qualifying students in response to the demands of the Black community, particularly in the larger cities such as Nashville, Atlanta, and New Orleans, where the more affluent Black middle classes insisted on the traditional course for their sons and daughters. The evidence of the surviving catalogs indicates that students, at least in the more elite AMA institutions, were more successful in the aims of a liberal arts education.

In their concern with thrift and industry, AMA colleges required that students perform manual labor in addition to paying their tuition, to defray expenses and to inculcate morality through good work habits.[34] Cynthia Griggs Flemming illustrates the paternalistic attitude of northern missionaries toward the former bondsmen they were trying to mold into dutiful Christians: for example, they forbade the ex-slaves to express themselves by singing and dancing.[35] The extant college catalogs often detail stringent codes of behavior and dress, all in an effort to encourage "right living." This stress on dress and manners was meant to further inculcate Christian morality. It is also important to remember that any traces of so-called licentious behavior by these Black students not only would damage the students' reputation but also could threaten the very existence of the college. For example, the 1917–18 catalog of Benedict College, an AMA institution founded in 1870 in Columbia, South Carolina, contains rigorous requirements for women's clothing:

1. No white dresses, white waists or white petticoats for school wear. No silk, satin, velvet or ribbon girdles. No elaborate girdles at any time. Very thin waists and dresses are not allowed. Waists are to be fastened with buttons or hooks, not pinned. . . .
4. Only plain black or white stockings. No thin stockings, no silk dresses, or

silk poplins, no net or crepe de chine waists. For special occasions a plain (not plaid or stripe) black or navy blue silk waist may be worn. No other silk waists allowed. No fancy dresses at any time.[36]

This injunction would be repeated in subsequent Benedict catalogs until 1920. Other religiously affiliated schools also followed a strict dress code. An example is provided by Simmons University, focusing once again on female attire: "The dress of students must be simple and inexpensive. Whatever their circumstances, elegant attire and jewelry are out of place. Low-necked dresses, short sleeves and French heels must not be worn by the young women. . . . Dresses for Sabbath must be plain and neat, subject to the above restrictions. Plain white dresses may be worn for entertainments and socials." The 1910–11 Simmons catalog went beyond policing merely the matter of dress: "Not only silence is enjoined, but things like keeping one's feet off the furniture." Talladega College, an AMA school founded in 1867 in Alabama, similarly mandated simple clothing, censored mail, and even required permission to play the piano.[37] Atlanta University's dress code expressly demanded "conservatism and simplicity." Women students especially were discouraged from "the use of expensive and showy dresses."[38]

Strict separation of the sexes, codes of dress and behavior, the prohibition of alcohol and tobacco, and compulsory chapel attendance and Bible reading inculcated a "culture of civilization"; the rules also worked to insulate the college against a racist White community that needed only the flimsiest of excuses, including so-called loose behavior or lewd and suggestive dress, to prosecute, harass, or lynch African Americans.[39] The stringent regulation of student behavior was partly geared to the children in the primary grades, for whom the college was acting in loco parentis. Nonetheless, those students in the normal and college courses, who were already young adults, must have sometimes chafed at being treated like children themselves.[40] This strict code of student conduct recalls that statement by the Methodist Freedmen's Aid Society: "The colored people are yet children, and need to be taught everything"—with "everything" extended to how not to abuse the institution's furniture.

With the notable exceptions of Fisk University in Nashville, Tennessee; Avery Institute in Charleston, South Carolina; Atlanta University (now Clark Atlantic); and some others, AMA-founded educational institutions had in fact fairly limited offerings in the classics. The "classical course" typically included, in addition to Greek and Latin (and later Latin only), modern languages (typically French and German), the sciences, mathematics, and economics.[41] There were two main reasons for this, beyond the disparagement of African Americans' ability to handle the rigors of higher education: the

50 CHAPTER TWO

devotion of AMA schools to training missionaries to Africa and the Hampton-Tuskegee model of industrial education for African Americans, which was gaining ground and, despite increasing Black objections, would soon become the predominant impulse for African American higher education.[42]

The missionaries had come south, after all, to save souls and therefore to redeem African Americans. While they may have believed that their charges would one day be equal in mental ability to Whites, the missionaries still thought that slavery had made the freed people somehow feral; moreover, the missionaries believed that the heathenism of the African continent from which they came had left its mark. The catalog of Atlanta University for the 1882–83 academic year addressed these twin challenges to Black education in the South (note the address's not-so-subtle contrasting of African backwardness and Anglo-American enlightenment):

> It is no ordinary school-teaching that we have undertaken to carry on in the South. Our pupils bring to the class-room absolutely no inheritance of scholarly mind. Only two or three generations separate them from the heathenism of the most uncivilized continent in the world. Some of them come with the most meagre vocabulary—a few hundred tattered and torn remnants of English words. Many of them have no equipment of general information, such as other children absorb from their parents. But worse than all is the evil inheritance which many of our pupils bring from centuries of heathenism and slavery. Let us be frank and add that even the great boon of freedom, so righteously conferred, has, by the very suddenness of its bestowal, unavoidably brought peculiar peril and damage to many of the freedmen.[43]

An important part of the mission of reforming African Americans' heathen legacy was, in addition to academic achievement, the development of a reliable work ethic.[44] Typical was the mission of Spelman College in Atlanta, which had been founded as a women's college in 1881 by the American Baptist Home Mission Society explicitly to make African American women better homemakers and mothers, thus reinforcing both racial and gender roles. In this capacity, then, courses in domestic science would not have been unwelcome. Not only would such practical courses assuage the desires of benefactors and White boards of trustees to instill the work ethic in their students, but they would also prepare the students themselves for gainful employment beyond what slim prospects there were for their graduates to become teachers or scholars. In the more religiously oriented colleges, such as Tougaloo and Spelman, the work ethic was instilled to promote fully rounded Christian character.

Tougaloo College

Tougaloo College, founded in 1869 by the AMA in Tougaloo, near Jackson, Mississippi, provides an example of the extent and duration of the classical liberal arts course at an AMA college, as seen in the extant course catalogs from 1901 to 1945. Because of the dearth of primary and secondary education available to African Americans in Mississippi at the turn of the twentieth century, Tougaloo incorporated both primary grades one through eight and a secondary academy level, including Academy Classical, which taught Latin and elementary Greek in addition to algebra, rhetoric, physics, bookkeeping, and English literature. (At this time it had no college department.) Striving to maintain a curriculum that harmonized education of the hand and mind, Tougaloo offered a manual-training department, including woodworking, blacksmithing, mechanical drawing, agriculture, "household science," and needlework (which constituted its own department). Nor was religious training neglected. As the 1918–19 catalog states, "The institution is Christian in its work and aim. The Bible is studied daily in each grade. Church services, Sabbath school, the religious societies and the general religious tendency, help to make Tougaloo an advantageous place for the growth of Christian character."[45]

By the 1905–6 academic year, the scientific course included Latin and Greek, "to be given as desired." By the 1912–13 academic year, Latin was still offered in the freshman and sophomore years, but Greek had disappeared from the college course, replaced by German in junior and senior years. The 1916–17 course catalog listed Latin, along with French, as an optional subject, with mechanical courses increasing in number. Thus the classical course included English, mathematics, science, history, civics, and economics, along with Latin, which was offered in the first three years. Sociology was offered in fourth year. Relevant to the times, the concentration in the 1918–19 catalog was "Problems of Race Relationships. Based on Commons' 'Races and Immigrants in America' and Mecklin's 'Democracy and Race Friction.'"[46] By the 1923–24 academic year, in a further progressive move, the college department had been broken down as follows: education, English, social sciences, Spanish, science, mathematics, and philosophy. A separate music department would be added later in the decade.

Latin, meanwhile, had been relegated to the academic, or high school, level, and varied from year to year, as a requirement or as an elective. The sciences, biology and chemistry, gained primacy in the late twenties and early thirties. The 1931–32 catalog listed, under history, "Ancient Civilizations.—An outline study of Hellenistic and Roman civilization during the pre-Christian eras."[47] After a lengthy absence, Latin was restored to the college curriculum as an elective at the elementary and intermediate levels. It remained so until the 1936–37 catalog, when it disappeared altogether, replaced by Spanish and French.

The wobbly stature of Latin and the short life of Greek at Tougaloo, which was replicated at other Black colleges and universities, had at least something to do with increasing or decreasing student demands and enrollments and the availability of competent teachers, as well as with a decreasing emphasis on classics generally as the hard sciences became more prominent in response to a changing academic climate. But, especially in Tougaloo's early years, the relatively low place of Latin and the quick disappearance of Greek in favor of the "mechanical arts" and "needle work" do speak to the AMA's emphasis on training African Americans to be efficient workers rather than scholars. Other AMA schools were more able to fight this backslide, however. We focus on three: Avery Normal Institute in Charleston, Atlanta University in Atlanta, and Fisk University in Nashville.

Avery Normal Institute

Founded in Charleston in 1865 with the assistance of the AMA, Avery was initially organized around primary, intermediate, and advanced divisions.[48] In 1882 the institute reorganized its curriculum into a three-year primary department, which stressed basic natural science, reading and writing, and drawing and singing; a grammar school, which focused on natural science (including geography and botany), reading and composition, arithmetic and bookkeeping, and history; and a classical course, which included Latin, chemistry, philosophy, theology, rhetoric, and, in spring term, the choice of Greek, French, or German. Avery later streamlined its course list to focus on the normal course, to prepare students to teach in the lower grades, and on the college-preparatory track. By 1910 Avery's normal and college-preparatory tracks had developed into four-year programs. Although Latin was still required, electives were allowed, reflecting changes in college-entrance requirements.[49]

In 1883, under pressure from the AMA, Avery, which had seen itself progressing to become another Fisk or Howard, added stenography and bookkeeping to its curriculum. Avery's 1882–83 "Circular of Information" made clear its willingness to introduce industrial education, but not for the purpose of creating mere workers:

> Hitherto there has been but little attention to industrial education in our school. It is not now our plan to teach trades or crafts; not that we depreciate really practical education, for such instruction is the need of the hour; but it is not within

our province to make carpenters or shoe makers. We believe, however, that it is within our province to train the hand and eye as well as the brain. And for this training we shall introduce tools, a knowledge of the use of which will better qualify those who go out from us to meet the exigencies of life.

We are confident that mental culture will be furthered in its connection with hand culture, and that industrial training will develop possibilities in the pupils, which might otherwise have never been discovered.[50]

In 1890 the AMA's governing board asked Avery and all the other AMA schools to cut back on classics and to incorporate more practical courses like those at Tuskegee and the Hampton Institute. The Black community (including teachers, alumni, and students) was outraged. Although Avery had always had a few practical courses, Charleston was home to a large artisan class, and the Black elite in the city saw the change of curriculum as retrograde and insulting. Working with some sympathetic Whites (New England missionary educators), the Black community petitioned the AMA, objecting to the new direction. When the AMA refused to back down, Avery constructed a building for industrial training separate from the rest of the school. While all students were required to take some training in the industrial arts, such as woodworking and domestic science, the rest of the curriculum was not changed.[51] One reason for this was that the Black community in Charleston was fairly prosperous—parents of Avery students had helped to fund the school initially, then paid half the costs of the school through their children's tuition, one of the highest rates of any AMA school, thus partially relieving the national office of money-raising worries.[52]

But unfortunately for Averyites, funding again became an issue in the 1940s as a result of Avery's retention of its liberal arts program. In 1946 Joe M. Brownlee, the AMA secretary, issued this statement to justify the organization's decision to withdraw all financial support: "The curriculum was set along New England classical lines, and has so remained to the present day. French, Latin, English, the sciences and mathematics still hold first place in the list of offerings." Avery paid the ultimate price for its intransigence: it was merged with the public school system in 1947 and closed in 1954.[53]

Atlanta University

Atlanta University, an AMA school founded in 1865, used as its motto "I will find a way or make one."[54] The AMA began by establishing primary and secondary schools, primarily for freed people but which were "open to illiterates regardless of color." It was one of the few AMA institutions that persisted with its classics program, though in gradually diminishing form, until at least 1940

54 CHAPTER TWO

(the most recent of the Atlanta catalogs in our possession). Among the illustrious students in classics were William Henry Crogman (1841–1931), class of 1876, who had a long career at Clark University, and William Sanders Scarborough, member of the first class of 1869, who transferred to Oberlin, where he graduated in 1875.

The city of Atlanta provides a remarkable illustration of the role of classics at Black colleges and universities, since four colleges for African Americans were located there: besides Atlanta University, Atlanta Baptist College (renamed Morehouse in 1913), founded in 1881; Morris Brown College (founded in 1881), later Morris Brown University; and Spelman College (founded as the Atlanta Baptist Female Seminary in 1881). All four were church affiliated: Atlanta with the AMA, Atlanta Baptist and Spelman with the American Baptist Home Mission Society, and Morris Brown with the AME Church.

Given Atlanta's troubled and sometimes violent racial history, it seems all the more remarkable that four such distinguished institutions should be located in one urban space following the failure of Reconstruction and the segregation of African Americans. While Atlanta, as indeed other cities in the South, was a site of White supremacy, Black disenfranchisement, and Jim Crow, it was also a place of Black resistance as well as accommodation within the context of respectability. In his Cotton States and International Exposition Address, more commonly known as the Atlanta Compromise speech, of 1895, Booker T. Washington spoke of how African Americans and Whites, in all social settings, "can be as separate as the fingers, yet one as the hand in all things essential to mutual progress," which (appropriate to the analogy) played into the hands of White separatists and set the boundaries for racial segregation.[55] Nonetheless, educated Blacks worked within these strictures to promote a degree of autonomy and racial pride. The colleges speak to both motivations, for self-improvement and for accommodation to the limitations set by Jim Crow in all public facilities. Indeed, as the college catalogs themselves attest, Atlanta University and its sibling institutions tried to be all things to African Americans, in that they provided both an elite liberal arts education in the college course but also primary schooling to help make up for the lack of public school education for Blacks in Atlanta.[56]

Echoing Washington's advocacy of separate status for Blacks and Whites, the *Atlanta University Bulletin* for 1910 opens with a statement that might seem to play into the "Black victim" narrative: African Americans "ought to be taught by the best of the upper [i.e., White] race, and then to give themselves for their own race."[57] Surely this speaks to the need for respectability and hence accommodation, which is also why Atlanta University and other Black colleges and universities inaugurated, for both male and female students, at least some industrial courses: household science for women, wood- and metalworking for men, to teach the principles of these disciplines but also to provide practical training for gainful employment after college. However, the 1894–95 Atlanta catalog, in its appeal for contributions to its permanent endowment, addresses the evils of slavery and thus the need to create a great educational institution that will lift African Americans up, and "which will enable it to do for a race, which has been the victim of man's avarice and brutality till its degradation is a national and personal disgrace to every inheritor of the American name and American privileges, a work that is unexampled in its promise and reach." In the catalogs is a palpable sense of pride in the statements of the colleges' purpose and their expectations for their successful graduates. For example, Morris Brown University, whose Latin motto was DEO AC VERITATI (for God and truth) was dedicated to training teachers and preachers for the "Christianization of Africa." The Morris Brown 1913–14 catalog stated the aim of its classical course: "To equip students for the mastery of the great problems of life, offering special training in Latin and Greek, as well as Higher Mathematics."[58]

In this spirit of "mastery of the great problems of life," even Atlanta University's scientific course was heavy with Latin and English literature, including Horace's *Odes* and Tacitus in the junior year. In the college-preparatory department, first-year students took Latin grammar along with "Reading Writing and Spelling." In the scientific-preparatory department Latin grammar and composition were taught, which remained the case at least through the 1870s. However, women in the higher normal course were taught "household science," embracing "Plain Sewing, Cookery, Nursing the Sick, etc." This would remain pervasive in the higher normal and college-preparatory departments: household science for women, woodworking and metalworking for men. (The expectation, at least implied, was that young African Americans, even those classically trained, would have something practical to fall back on. But it also instilled the idea that Blacks were primarily workers.) The 1884 catalog described the inauguration of the "Mechanical Course" required of all male students, in addition to regular studies in other courses: two years of woodworking, one of metalworking, whose aim was to teach the use of tools and the principles of wood- and metalcraft.[59]

By the 1885–86 catalog, as part of the normal course, there was "metal-working for boys; dress-making and cooking for girls." Illustrating the great socioeconomic rift between White and Black students, the 1882–83 catalog states that even normal- and college-level students should learn "the wood-working or the iron-working tools" and apply the same industry to those as "the Harvard and Yale boys . . . to wield the oar and the bat."

56 CHAPTER TWO

This stress on usefulness would remain the pattern in the collegiate and college-preparatory departments for years. The 1888–89 catalog states that any student without "an earnest desire to fit himself for usefulness" will be sent home.[60]

Atlanta University's early years showed success in its pursuit of a thorough liberal arts education. The 1872–73 Atlanta catalog lists the examinations to be taken before admission to the collegiate department. Those for classics were "Ancient History and Geography, Latin Grammar and Prose Composition, the first Book of Caesar, four Orations of Cicero, four Books of Virgil's Aeneid, Greek Grammar and Prose Composition, and three Books of [Xenophon,] the Anabasis."[61]

The "Report of the Board of Examiners" dated June 12, 1884, describes the overall satisfaction of the examiners, although perhaps mixed with incredulity. Note the telling line at the end that bespeaks the examiners' idea of the tentative nature of Black higher education:

> Your committee [members] desire to express their gratification at the uniformly creditable character of these examinations. Such scholarship as we have witnessed in so large a representative body of the colored people has impressed us with their capacity for education, as well as for application to study. In the highest as well as the lowest branches of the curriculum, we found correct information, mastery of detail and ability to communicate clearly. Alike well posted, they seemed to be, both male and female, in such difficult branches as advanced Latin and Greek, geometry, physics, algebra and political science. The examinations were honestly made, and the committee were allowed full latitude in testing the pupils' knowledge. Nor did it seem to be a technical knowledge merely. It appeared to go to the substance of things. It was evident that the teachers had instructed faithfully and the scholars had studied zealously and learned correctly. The result was very interesting and full of good augury. *It has seemed to be a favorable issue to the experiment of colored education.*

No creditable argument, therefore, could be made for the incapacity of African Americans to learn college subjects. The examiners add for good measure that the written examinations "showed, in addition to knowledge of the subjects, neat penmanship, correct grammar and accurate spelling as well as the valuable quality of tidiness."[62]

The October 1910 *Bulletin* lays out a good history of the question of educating African Americans after Reconstruction, but at the same time is deeply racist in its narrative: Negroes have to be led from the darkness of slavery to self-control in place of the external control of masters. Through education Negroes can get the help that will enable them to help themselves, which was part of the missionary work of the AMA. Once again African Americans "ought to be taught by the best of the upper race, and then to give themselves for their own race." Therefore, the clear implication is the existence of a racial hierarchy, with Whites at the top. However, the *Bulletin* recognizes that industrial education, while indeed part of the university curriculum, is not all, and that race leaders are needed. The *Atlanta University Bulletins* of 1911 and 1912 speak to the poor state of many Black schools and neighborhoods and link them to disease, both physical and moral. The 1912 *Bulletin*, beneath the heading "The Common School and the Negro American," addresses inadequate funding for Black schools. Atlanta University itself lost its annual AMA appropriation, in accordance with the AMA's policy that its institutions be self-sufficient. As a consequence, the catalogs made yearly appeals for contributions from alumni as well as appeals to other organizations. With the loss of AMA funding, Atlanta University moved to an independent life, with its own board of trustees, "like the great colleges and universities of the country."[63]

The constant search for funds would lead to changes in the curriculum to suit the requirements of subsequent donors and to assuage the state legislature, which remained hostile to higher education for African Americans, particularly in the liberal arts. During the 1920s Atlanta University suffered the same attrition in classics as that of other AMA-founded institutions. In the 1925 catalog, Latin was still taught during all four years of high school. The high school English course was inaugurated in 1900–1901, at junior, middle, and senior levels, with industrial training each year, to make up for deficiencies in public education available for African Americans in Atlanta. The 1922 catalog states that Greek would be taught, "if called for by a sufficient number."[64] Later classical courses included mythology and courses in translation, requiring no previous training in the languages. Latin language and literature courses were no longer offered every year. In 1931 Atlanta became a graduate school only, with undergraduates attending Morehouse and Spelman. In 1988 Atlanta University merged with Clark College to become Clark Atlantic University.

Fisk University

In his history of Fisk University, Richardson recounts an anecdote about the head of the J. K. Brick Industrial School at Enfield, North Carolina. A Fisk alumnus, he was successful in setting up rural engineering projects on the school's eleven hundred acres and had engines in his shops that impressed even the local White engineers. When asked where he had learned to do all this, he replied, "Oh, studying Greek at Fisk." He had probably been a student of Adam Knight Spence (1831–1900), professor of Greek at Fisk, who had been recruited from the University of Michigan.[65]

John Ogden (1824–1910), Rev. Erastus Milo Cravath (1833–1900), and Rev. Edward Parmalee Smith (1822–76) had founded the Fisk School in Nashville in 1866 under the auspices of the AMA and the Western Freedmen's Aid Commission of Cincinnati. The school was named for Gen. Clinton B. Fisk, who was head of the Freedmen's Bureau in Tennessee. Like most institutions founded in the immediate aftermath of the Civil War, Fisk at its beginnings could not be called a college, since so many of its students had no formal education. In its first year of operation, most of the students attending Fisk were taking basic courses, learning to read and do math, but there were two sections of Latin. Fisk was dedicated to the highest academic aspirations, which meant providing not what was termed a "Negro education" but an American education—that is, training in the classical liberal arts. By 1867, with the opening of other educational institutions in Nashville, the Fisk School became Fisk University, with a preparatory school, a higher school, a normal school, and a college department.

Richardson describes the Fisk college curriculum during the college's formative years: "The number of students was small, but their program of studies was rigid. A skeptical visitor witnessed an examination of the college students in 1875. The freshmen were tested on Vergil's *Aeneid*, geometry, and botany. Sophomores stood [for] an examination in Latin, Greek, and botany. The visitor concluded that Blacks were capable of mastering the most difficult studies and of highest attainment in the best colleges."[66]

Students in the college-level classics course would have already had classics in secondary school, the best of them anyway.[67] College freshmen studied Latin, Greek, and mathematics; sophomores, Greek, Latin, French, math, and the natural sciences; juniors, German, natural philosophy, history, English, and astronomy. College prep pupils studied Latin, Greek, English, arithmetic, world history, and algebra. In keeping with Fisk's Christian ethos, all students received a Bible lesson once a week.[68]

The college curriculum as presented in Fisk's catalog was daunting and comparable to that in White educational institutions, but, like most Black colleges, Fisk was constantly in financial trouble. By 1871, just five short years after its opening, it was faced with closure. The first academic dean of Fisk, Dr. Adam Spence, who was a classicist by training, came up with an innovative idea. Having heard spirituals sung at chapel and in other venues, Spence put together a choir and sent them out as fundraisers for the university. On their first trip, they also took along the university's remaining money. The Fisk Jubilee Singers, as they came to be called, were an immediate success. The group toured Europe twice and sang before Queen Victoria and the kaiser of Germany. With the continued support of the AMA, the monies raised by the Fisk Jubilee Singers, friends of the university in the North, and student tuition, the university was able to survive, graduating some of the most illustrious members of the African American elite, including, most notably, W. E. B. Du Bois (1868–1963) but also graduates like John Houston Burrus (1849–1917), class of 1875, who had been born a slave but who earned a degree in classics. After a career in teaching, Burrus studied law and was admitted to the bar in 1881; in 1883 he accepted the presidency of Alcorn Agricultural and Mechanical College. This tale of success conceals a further challenge for funding and the pressure exerted by northern philanthropists, such as the John F. Slater Fund for the Education of Freedmen, to provide industrial courses in exchange for funds. While it did accede to some degree, Fisk did manage to maintain its liberal arts program.

Philanthropic Industrialist Founders

Hampton Institute and Tuskegee Institute

Schools founded by the industrial philanthropists provide perhaps the clearest example of the link between a founding group's view of higher education and the Negro's place in the New South. No other group of schools was as hostile to the classics and to the aspirations of African Americans themselves as these. Industrial training had been a part of Black education as early as the 1830s, and by the 1880s most Black colleges and universities had some form of industrial education, usually in the form of student work programs. Beginning in 1872, however, when the AMA-founded Hampton Institute, under the leadership of the former Union general Samuel Chapman Armstrong (1839–93), broke away from the AMA and later with the founding of Tuskegee Institute in 1881, the role of industrial education took on a quite different meaning. Initial support for Hampton Institute, founded as a normal school for teacher training, came from former New England (largely Boston-based) abolitionists. These financial backers wanted Hampton to develop along the lines of more traditional liberal arts colleges with their classical curriculums.

Armstrong and later his protégé, Booker T. Washington (1856–1915), were concerned, however, about the liberal arts focus. First, they were skeptical that African Americans had the intellectual capacity and background necessary to master the classics—indeed, they believed classical instruction posed a danger to African Americans' moral improvement.[69] Second, both Armstrong and Washington felt that a liberal arts education would place Black students in direct economic competition with their White brethren. Third, they believed that a liberal arts education might make African Americans feel equal to Whites and therefore present another arena of conflict.[70] Better

60 CHAPTER TWO

for African Americans, they thought, to be trained in occupations that they were intellectually suited for and that would not put them in direct competition with Whites. In short, they should be given an education that would not cause them to challenge the White establishment socially or politically. Both Hampton and Tuskegee were successful in developing curriculums that fulfilled those aims.

Indeed, by the turn of the twentieth century, the "Hampton-Tuskegee Idea" was clearly ascendant among the northern philanthropists who had become the principal funders of Black higher education, as the former New England abolitionists were either dying off or turning to other projects. The initial northern philanthropic foundations (based in New York) that funded the Hampton-Tuskegee Idea were the Peabody Educational Fund and the John F. Slater Fund, established in 1867 and 1882, respectively. John Fox Slater (1815–84) believed that manual labor provided not only useful skills but also moral training. Both foundations were particularly attracted to the maintenance of racial inequality in the South, with a trained workforce that knew its place and desired no other. Additional foundations included the General Education Board, the Anna T. Jeanes Foundation, the Phelps-Stokes Fund, the Carnegie Foundation, the Laura Spelman Rockefeller Memorial Fund, and the Julius Rosenthal Fund. The philosophy of these foundations is perhaps best summed up by William Baldwin (1863–1905), a philanthropist and Tuskegee trustee:

> The days of reconstruction were dark for all. Their sting has not yet gone. Then appeared from the North a new army—an army of white teachers, armed with the spelling book and the Bible; and from their attack there were many casualties on both sides, the southern whites as well as the blacks. For, although the spelling book and the Bible were necessary for the proper education of the negro race, yet, with a false point of view, the northern white teacher educated the negro to hope that through the books he might, like white men, learn to live from the fruits of literary education. How false that theory was, thirty long years of experience has proved. That was not their opportunity. Their opportunity was to be taught the dignity of manual labor and how to perform it. We began at the wrong end. Instead of educating the negro in the lines which were open to him, he was educated out of his natural environment and the opportunities which lay immediately about him.

Baldwin adds that "except in the rarest of instances I am bitterly opposed to the so-called higher education of Negroes."[71] As Anderson notes, "Of the one hundred black colleges and normal schools in 1914–1915, two-thirds had no endowment funds; and the remaining third had a combined total of only

8.4 million [dollars]." This would lead to what August Meier called the "vogue of industrial education," where schools desperate for funds to stay afloat would seemingly buy into these ideas while stealthily trying to maintain some semblance of a liberal arts education.[72] One of the methods used by African American educators to counteract this trend was to claim a devotion to industrial education while secretly pursuing a classical, liberal arts curriculum.

Hampton Institute, founded as Hampton Normal and Agricultural Institute in 1868 for African Americans and, from 1875 to 1923, for Native Americans, and Tuskegee Institute provide the clearest example of the opposition to the liberal arts and the belief that the classical curriculum was inappropriate for the newly freed Blacks. The curriculums listed in Hampton's catalogs from 1875 through the end of the 1920s are heavily geared toward industrial training, animal husbandry, agriculture, and domestic arts, the object of which was to turn out workers and teachers of these subjects. Armstrong's condescension toward African Americans may be summarized by the following comment prefacing the history offerings in the 1909 Hampton catalog, which at least gives a nod to "ancient civilization." It begins with biblical history, study of which "may destroy many of the superstitious notions of religion held by Negro and Indian students. . . . This course is intended to give the pupil a knowledge of the Bible, an acquaintance with ancient civilization, the numerous lessons which that civilization teaches undeveloped races, and a more accurate conception of religion and its relation to morals." Another equally condescending, indeed near fatalistic, attitude is expressed toward African Americans and Native Americans in Hampton's 1911 catalog, under "Training in Community Work": "This course is designed to give the knowledge and training needed in dealing with the perplexing and almost unsolvable problems confronting the young men and women of the colored and Indian races."[73] Appropriately, there are strictures against indolence, profanity, card playing, alcohol, and tobacco.

An examination of Hampton's catalogs does, however, reveal that some classics courses were taught, at least for a time. The 1894–95 catalog listed a senior class history course on Greece, Rome, and the ancient Orient, as well as three-year courses on harness making, cobbling, painting, and printing. For a brief period in the 1920s, Latin did make an appearance, first as an elective in the secondary school in the 1922–23 catalog. The 1925–26 catalog included Latin as an elective for a major, beginning with elementary Latin. Among the courses taught were Cicero's selected speeches and philosophical works; selections from Vergil's *Aeneid*; Catullus's poems and Horace's *Odes*; the work of the historians Livy and Tacitus; selections from Pliny (whether the Elder or the Younger Pliny is not specified); Plautus's and Terence's come-

62 CHAPTER TWO

dies; and prose composition. But by the 1926–27 catalog (perhaps as the result of a lack of trained teachers, administrative hostility, or student disinterest), the Latin courses had been reduced to elementary Latin, Cicero, and Vergil, although elective courses could be arranged for classes of five or more students. By the time of the 1929–30 catalog, Latin had disappeared from the curriculum. Nonetheless, the greater variety of courses, including modern languages and sociology, was a sign of not only the college's increased stability but also a recognition of broader opportunities for African Americans as the twentieth century progressed.

Similarly, Tuskegee Institute's stated objective was "to furnish to young colored men and women an opportunity to acquire thorough moral, literary and industrial education so that when they go out from Tuskegee, by putting into execution the practical ideas learned here, they may become real leaders of their community, and thus bring about healthier moral and material conditions."[74] Extrapolating from the few catalogs in our possession, Tuskegee's literary education extended as far as English grammar and composition and readings of classic American and British authors, such as Hawthorne and Shakespeare.

Land-Grant Institutions

Land-grant colleges were established following the passage of the first Morrill Act of 1862, which granted monies from the sale of federal lands to each of the states to establish institutions to teach citizens agriculture, home economics, the mechanical arts, and other useful professions. According to Eric Adler, however, "these new institutions did not abandon classical studies (in fact, the Morrill Act mandated them) but added an array of technical subjects to the curriculum. At the land grant universities, Latin and ancient Greek competed with a panoply of vocational disciplines, many of them new to American academia." As expressly stated by the 1862 act, "The leading object shall be, without excluding other scientific and classical studies, and including military tactics, to teach such branches of learning as are related to agriculture and the mechanical arts . . . in order to promote the liberal and practical education of the industrial classes in the several pursuits and professions in life."[75] This statement may help explain (or explain away) the bifurcated character of the curriculum at Black colleges and universities. But it does not account for the entrenched racism behind the curriculums and the policies applied to students across colleges, whether land-grant institutions or not.

This racism is reflected also in the very creation of land-grant colleges and universities. Many of these institutions were built on land forcibly extracted from Native American populations as the American nation moved west. As Margaret A. Nash argues in "Entangled Pasts: Land-Grant Colleges and American Indian Dispossession," "The Morrill Act was part and parcel of the federal government's quest to settle the continent with (mostly) white people. With that as a goal, establishing colleges and universities was the aside, not the Indian dispossession. Certainly, proponents of the Morrill Act had other goals in addition to conquering the West, such as using education as a means to catapult the nation into global prominence as an industrial leader."[76] This forcible appropriation of native land may speak also to the condescension shown to Native American students at Hampton Institute.

In the South African Americans were not permitted to attend those institutions established under the first Morrill Act, although the law did contain provisions for the establishment of "separate but equal" facilities for Blacks. In an attempt to rectify this situation, Congress passed a second Morrill Act in 1890, specifically to support Negro land-grant institutions. In this section we discuss three land-grant institutions: Alcorn A&M (Agricultural and Mechanical College) in Mississippi, Florida A&M, and Alabama A&M. Alcorn and Florida A&M were initially founded with funds from the first Morrill Act; Alabama A&M was founded by ex-slaves who also applied for monies from the first Morrill Act.

Alcorn Agricultural and Mechanical College

Alcorn Agricultural and Mechanical College (now Alcorn State University) was founded in 1871 in Lorman, Mississippi, as a college exclusively for men; it began admitting women in 1895. "Agricultural and Mechanical" is part of the name of several land-grant colleges, both White and Black, to reflect their devotion to industrial training. Writing in 1939, Lewis K. McMillan, who taught history at several of the Black colleges, discussed this nomenclature as racially demeaning in his article "Negro Higher Education as I Have Known It":

> The Southern Negro state college is indeed a southern institution. Just the name it bears reflects the Southerner's attitude toward the race—"Agricultural," "Mechanical," "Industrial," "Normal," "Institute." The southern White man will call the Negro by any name excepting "Miss," "Mrs.," or "Mr." Likewise he refused for a long time to allow state schools for Negroes to bear the name "college." Only in recent years did a state as northward as Virginia allow the use of the name "State College." And of course Florida, Mississippi, Alabama and South Carolina still forbid the use of "College" unless it is preceded by several qualifying words sufficient to carry the message that colored people are made to plow, cut wood, and shoe horses.[77]

Nonetheless, Alcorn did offer Latin and Greek instruction early in its history.[78] The 1873 catalog listed introductory Latin in the first year of the college-preparatory course and Cicero's orations and Vergil in second year, as well as beginning Greek. The catalog promised "Declamations and Compositions weekly, throughout the course."[79] The college department would admit students only after they had passed an examination in Greek and Latin grammar, Caesar, Cicero's orations, and Vergil.

Following this ambitious beginning, classics at Alcorn had suffered a marked decline by the time of the 1887–88 catalog. No classics courses were expressly listed; rather, a "scientific course" included "mensuration and surveying with field work, Armsby's 'Cattle Feeding,' and 'Evidences of Christianity.'"[80] The 1912–13 catalog listed Latin, using William Coe Collar and Moses Grant Daniell's *The First Latin Book*, for the first-year college course, as well as ancient history. A separate industrial department listed a "Blacksmithing, Carriage Making, and Horseshoeing Department," which seems more geared to the previous century. Other "departments" included printing, shoemaking, and leatherworking. The 1914–15 catalog, true to Alcorn's status as a land-grant college, listed husbandry and farm management and, with the admission of women, sewing and dressmaking, laundering, and nurse training. (Alcorn's nursing school opened in 1904.)[81]

In the 1920s Latin made a desultory appearance in the catalogs: the 1923–24 catalog listed the Roman historian Cornelius Nepos and Caesar's *Commentaries*, books 1 to 4, in the college course; the high school course offered three years of Latin, alongside such electives as blacksmithing, shoemaking, painting, and general manual training. By the time of the 1928–29 catalog, Latin was an elective for bachelor's degrees. Latin courses included Cicero's orations, selections from Vergil's *Aeneid*, Horace's *Odes* and *Epodes*, and prose composition. Instead of Latin, students in the bachelor of arts program could elect a modern language, such as French.

While the putative purpose of the classical liberal arts program at Alcorn was to "educate the whole man," by the third decade of the twentieth century, industrial courses had gained increasing primacy. The 1921–22 catalog promoted laundering for women, which they would need as homemakers but also "as breadwinners for themselves and of greater domestic value to the State."[82] That "domestic value," it was understood, would be as laundresses to White families.

Florida Agricultural and Mechanical College

Florida Agricultural and Mechanical College (now Florida A&M), founded in Tallahassee in 1887, had a classics curriculum comparable to Alcorn's in its early history. The 1894–95 catalog listed, under its preparatory department, for the junior year, beginning Latin and Greek. Seniors in that department would study Caesar's *Gallic Wars* in their Latin course and Greek. Students in the normal department would read Cicero's orations in junior year and Xenophon's *Anabasis*.

By the turn of the twentieth century, Florida Agricultural and Mechanical had undergone a reorganization into literary, industrial, and musical departments. Latin was retained as an elective in the preparatory and normal departments. Students could take Latin instead of general history or English literature. The 1909–10 catalog listed Latin 3–4 in the college scientific course; lower grades of Latin were offered in the high school scientific course. No Greek courses were offered. With the increasing encroachment of industrial and domestic courses, we find quixotic combinations, as in the 1915–16 catalog, of two years of Latin, alongside art needlework and millinery for the bachelor's degree in home economics. The same catalog, under "Courses for Teachers," touted the growing emphasis on industrial and domestic arts and therefore the increased importance of providing trained teachers for these subjects: "The number of schools in which domestic arts and sciences are being taught is rapidly increasing, and the demand for well trained teachers in these subjects is greater than ever before."[83] Students at the college level could take ancient history in the first year; in the second year either Latin or English history; in the third year Latin or agriculture; and in the fourth year, Latin 3.

By the 1920s Latin was disappearing, or listed as an elective, in the college course, while the high school retained Latin and ancient history. By the late twenties, students could take Latin at the college level to satisfy the language requirement, although that requirement was often left unspecified. By the 1929–30 catalog, the liberal arts and science concentrations included English and romance languages. The vaunted purpose of the department of industrial arts was made clear—that is, to "prepare young men for life's work in the trades as mechanics, contractors, teachers of trades and directors of departments."[84] By the end of the 1930s, Florida A&M's industrial department had become well developed. The curriculum for the bachelor's degree, however, still mandated two years of a foreign language. Physical education was required for this and other courses as well. The surviving catalogs do not address the often troubled history of student and faculty unrest at Florida A&M because of the increasing imposition of industrial education at the expense of the liberal arts.

66 CHAPTER TWO

Alabama A&M University

An examination of the surviving early catalogs of Alabama A&M, founded in 1875 as the State Colored Normal and Industrial School in Normal, near Huntsville, shows that this institution was trying to be all things to its students. The earliest catalog we found was for the academic year 1895–96, which shows a range of courses being taught. Alabama A&M's Model School (that is, grammar school) taught basic grammar and science. Caesar's *Commentaries*, book 1, was taught at the senior high school level. Cicero's orations (unspecified) and his dialogue *De senectute* (*On Old Age*), along with Vergil and Tacitus (works unspecified), were listed at the postgraduate level. By the 1896–97 catalog, the college had undergone a change of name to the Agricultural and Mechanical College of Alabama for Negroes. The normal course included, in second and third years, Latin (without being specific). Latin was also included in the first and second years of the college department's scientific course. The 1897–98 catalog showed that students were studying medieval history along with Latin in the first and second years.

The 1898–99 catalog listed specific authors in normal courses, beginning with the third year: the historians Cornelius Nepos and Eutropius (misspelled as Eutopius), Caesar (unspecified), Cicero (unspecified), and the grammarian Aulus Gellius. The scientific-literary course included, again, Cicero's *De senectute* and *De amicitia* (*On Friendship*); Vergil's *Aeneid*, books 1–4; Horace's *Odes*; Livy's selected books; and Tacitus's *Germania* and *Agricola*, all listed for the second year, with no Latin listed after that.

The 1905–6 catalog contains prefaces describing the range and purpose of the various courses of study. That for Latin, begun in the second year of the normal course and continued through the second year of the college course, lists the range of courses by academic year, including simple Latin prose and verse composition; selected poetry and prose; Caesar's *Gallic Wars*, "with special attention being given also to syntax and to the review of the declensions and conjugations"; Cicero's orations against Catiline; Vergil's *Aeneid* "and a study of meter and Roman Mythology"; Cicero's *De senectute* again; Horace's *Odes*; and the work of historians Livy and Tacitus. This preface concludes, "Aside from the fact that students may desire to pursue higher work in the study of the Latin language, there may be others who desire a broadening of the intellect by a continued study of Latin, and yet others of whom a rigid course in the Department of Science demands such a knowledge. It is the plan of the course described above to accommodate all these."[85] But sharing space with this are the descriptions of coursework in ironworking, brick making, carpentry, shoemaking, printing, tailoring, cooking, broom mak-

FOUNDING OF BLACK COLLEGES AND UNIVERSITIES **67**

ing, chair bottoming, sewing, millinery, nursing, laundering, bookkeeping, and secretarial duties. It seems at first a bizarre juxtaposition, but, again, this was a land-grant college for African Americans and thus was clear-sighted in its aim to provide a well-rounded training for its students for the roles they would be expected to fill in a graded, racist society that abhorred even the idea of the liberal arts for African Americans.[86] Latin continued to be offered at least until 1915, but by the 1920s, as evidenced by the 1923–24 catalog, Latin had been relegated to the senior high school level, and then it disappeared altogether, along with the bulk of the liberal arts beyond English composition.

Public and Nondenominational Colleges
North Carolina State Normal School

North Carolina State Normal and Industrial School (now Fayetteville State University) opened in 1867; in 1877 the North Carolina General Assembly allocated funds for a normal school for the education of African Americans. Its aim, as stated in the 1919–20 catalog, was "to give the students such a well rounded culture of head, hand and heart as should ever enable the industrious and conscientious teacher to do his best in assuming and discharging the weighty responsibilities of his great calling."[87] The first catalog we possess, for 1907–8, lists, as part of the normal course, Latin or economics for the third year, and for fourth year Collar and Daniell's *First Latin* textbook. Latin is listed for the third year of the academic course (though readings were not specified). By the 1916–17 academic year, Latin offerings had broadened, with beginning Latin in the first year of the normal course, followed by readings of Caesar's *Commentaries* (in Charles Bennett's Latin series) and Vergil's *Aeneid*, as well as prose composition in later years.[88]

Latin offerings continued until 1920, after which Latin does not appear in the remaining catalogs we located. The last we have, for 1937–38 (with announcements for 1938–39), includes in the four-year program courses geared more toward teaching in the twentieth-century classroom— that is, the priorities are the hard sciences, math, educational psychology, and economics. More traditional liberal arts courses are offered as electives. These include French, Negro literature, music appreciation, and American arts.

Howard University

Howard University, located in Washington, D.C., and today the premier institution of higher education for African Americans, with an enrollment of ten thousand, was chartered by Congress in 1867 as a nondenominational normal school and college, although resolutely Christian in its aims and character.

(Indeed, the AMA had been influential in the university's founding.)[89] The school was named after Gen. Oliver O. Howard (1830–1909), a Civil War hero prominent in national affairs and in promoting educational opportunities for newly freed African Americans.[90] Open to both Whites and Blacks, Howard had stringent requirements for incoming students to its law and college departments. The 1890–91 catalog stated that candidates for the classical course were examined as follows: "LATIN—four books of Caesar, five orations of Cicero, six books of Virgil's Aeneid, and twelve lessons on Jones' Latin Prose Composition; GREEK—Crosby's Lessons, four books of Xenophon's Anabasis, and one book of Homer's Illiad [sic]."[91] Later the entrance requirements would include sight translation of both prose and verse.

Nonetheless, in its pledge to harmonize both hand and mind, Howard offered a range of courses in manual and domestic science. These included "basketry weaving and cord work," model and simple needlework, and "Venetian iron and sheet metal work" but also more advanced courses like chemistry, psychology, and bacteriology and sanitation. Such courses provided practical instruction for life after graduation. We shall have more to say about Howard University in chapter 5, where we discuss in more detail the role of practicality in education.

The Role of Classics at AME-Controlled Institutions

Until roughly 1905 AMA schools had maintained largely White administrators and White faculties. This stance was bringing these schools increasingly into conflict with the larger African American community; all-Black congregations in the South had been led by Black ministers from the 1890s onward. As time went on, this would become an increasingly contentious dispute between the Black community and the schools' sponsors.[92]

The situation was different at institutions founded by the African Methodist Episcopal (AME), the African Methodist Episcopal Zion (AMEZ), and the Colored Methodist Episcopal Churches.[93] As Bishop Benjamin T. Tanner (1835–1923) wrote in *An Apology for African Methodism* (1867):

> The great crime committed by the Founders of the African Methodist Episcopal church, against the prejudiced white American, and the timid black—the crime which seems unpardonable, was that they dared to organize a Church of men; men to think for themselves; men to talk for themselves; men to act for themselves; a Church of men who support from their own substance, however scanty, the ministrations of the Word they receive; men who spurn to have their churches built for them, and their pastors supported from the coffers of some

charitable organization; men who prefer to live by the sweat of their own brow and be free.[94]

Clearly, Bishop Tanner was referring to that independence of spirit and desire for self-control that had led some African Americans to walk out of the White Methodist Episcopal Church in 1816 and to form their own denomination. These demands for autonomy were most closely reflected in the curriculums of the colleges controlled by the AME AND AMEZ denominations, all classical liberal arts colleges. James Anderson, in *The Education of Blacks in the South, 1860–1935*, goes even further in articulating the philosophy of these Black-owned and Black-controlled schools: "Nearly all the major colleges controlled by black organizations and their combined voice largely articulated the educational policy of the black community." Unlike numerous AMA schools, Anderson writes, "these [AME and AMEZ] institutions never adopted the Hampton-Tuskegee pattern of black industrial education, and they gave low priority to all forms of industrial training."[95] An examination of the course catalogs for some of these schools verifies this assertion. But while it is strictly true that AME institutions did not yield to the philosophy of industrial education, they did have to introduce some industrial training courses to obtain desperately needed monies.

Despite these financial exigencies, AME-founded colleges had a different motivation for classics, and it flowed out of educated African Americans' observations about the contributions made by northern Africa to the classical world. Indeed, they too had a mission but one that was less to save souls or to redeem an enslaved, unenlightened people and more to lift up those men and women to their rightful place as coequals in American society. Furthermore, unlike the AMA colleges, the administrators and most of the teachers at the Black denominational schools were Black. There remained a large minority of White teachers, however. Several White teachers had come from Oberlin College, which had a profound influence on African American education because many of its graduates took positions at AME colleges, such as Wilberforce University in Ohio.

Wilberforce exemplifies and may serve as a model of the ideals Blacks themselves set for African American education. Named for Britain's premier abolitionist, William Wilberforce (1759–1833), it was founded in 1856 in Xenia, Ohio, by the Cincinnati Conference of the White Methodist Episcopal Church to promote Black education in the North.[96] The school struggled financially for its first decade. In fact, it suspended operations and was on the verge of being sold to the state of Ohio as an asylum, when, in 1863, Daniel A. Payne (1811–93), bishop and leader of the African Methodist Episcopal denomination, who had been educated at the Lutheran Theological Seminary at Gettysburg, bought the school for $10,000, the amount of its debt. In doing so, Bishop Payne made Wilberforce the flagship institution of the AME Church.[97] Eager to make Wilberforce a normal school and liberal arts college, Payne hired the best teachers he could. By the second term of the academic year 1866–67, Payne had engaged Dr. William Kent, of England, to teach science; Professor Theodore Suliot, of Edinburgh, to teach Latin, French, and mathematics; and Sarah J. Woodson, of Oberlin, to teach English and Latin.[98] In accordance with its strict adherence to a philosophy of "Christianity and culture" meant to combat ignorance and superstition, under Payne's auspices Wilberforce University set out to become the premier institution of higher learning for African Americans.

The Wilberforce catalog of 1872–73 lists subacademic, academic, classical, scientific, normal, theological, law, and music departments. The classical department offered these courses: Cicero's *De senectute, De amicitia,* and *Tusculan Disputations*; Horace's *Odes, Satires,* and *Epistles*; Livy; Tacitus, *Germania* and *Agricola*; and Plautus and Terence. On the Greek side was listed Xenophon, *Anabasis* and *Memorabilia; Homer's Odyssey*; Herodotus; Aeschylus, *Prometheus Bound*; Plato, *Apology* and *Gorgias;* and the Attic orators.[99] Even after Payne's retirement as president of Wilberforce in 1876, his vision continued under the next two presidents, both of whom were Wilberforce alumni, Benjamin F. Lee (1841–1926) and Samuel T. Mitchell (1851–1901).

As was the case at other historical Black colleges being founded both in the North and in the newly emancipated South at this time, all this was accomplished by dedicated teachers who were overworked and underpaid and teaching all levels, from elementary to college. Mary Church Terrell, trained in the classics at Oberlin and later founder and first president of the National Association of Colored Women, recalled the many duties she performed as a young teacher at Wilberforce during her tenure there in the 1880s: "I taught everything from French to mineralogy in the college department to reading and writing in the preparatory department. . . . In addition to teaching five courses in subjects totally dissimilar, I was secretary to the faculty . . . and played the organ for the church services every Sunday morning and evening and gave a night every week to choir rehearsal."[100]

Following Payne's death, Benjamin William Arnett (1838–1906) was elected the seventeenth bishop of the AME Church. As David Levering Lewis describes it in his biography of W. E. B. Du Bois, in the absence of the restraining influence of Payne, Arnett quickly moved to rule the university "like a satrapy, monitoring and even controlling its curriculum, and periodically increasing its faculty with several of his five ambitious sons."[101] As part of his move for control, Arnett promptly fired the university's most distinguished faculty member, William Sanders Scarborough.

Born a slave in Macon, Georgia, in 1852, Scarborough had been at Wilberforce since 1877 and became one of the most prominent African American classicists of the nineteenth and early twentieth centuries. His wife, Sarah Cordelia Scarborough (1851–1933) (who was White), was an equally distinguished member of the faculty, first as professor of natural sciences from 1877 to 1884, then as professor of French from 1884 to 1887, and finally as principal of the normal department from 1887 to 1914.[102] William Sanders Scarborough authored several articles on classical philology, the textbook *First Lessons in Greek*, and the paper "Birds of Aristophanes." Given these accomplishments, Scarborough may best depict how, by mastering the classics, African Americans, even in the highly segregated America of his time, could nonetheless gain entry to the republic of letters, where they could be judged not merely by the color of their skin but by their intelligence and industry. Scarborough's *First Lessons* and other publications on classical philology were not only works of scholarship but testaments to the endurance and perseverance of all educated African Americans in the pursuit of racial equality.

In his autobiography Scarborough elides the particular circumstances of his firing, although we can glean the essential information from other sources. According to Lewis, "The courtly classicist had run afoul of Bishop Arnett's nepotistic practices." But Francis P. Weisenburger comes closer to the mark, we think, in his article on Scarborough's scholarship and politics. Scarborough clashed in faculty meetings with the university's vice president, Joseph P. Shorter, and its president, Samuel T. Mitchell, over educational ideals. Says Weisenburger, Scarborough "had gone too far and too fast to suit some people."[103] This clash went beyond the brilliance of, and resentment aroused by, Scarborough's classical scholarship. He had risen to the peak of his profession as a classicist; he was a member of the American Philological Association (now the Society for Classical Studies), only the third African American to join, after Richard T. Greener and Edward Wilmot Blyden, as well as the first African American member of the Modern Language Association.[104]

Beyond the classroom and the lecture hall, Scarborough became a tireless advocate of social equality for African Americans, including in the area of education, for he himself embodied the highest scholarly attainment. According to Weisenburger, speaking of Scarborough's early career at Wilberforce, "Scarborough was interested in scholarly progress, especially in the classics" and tirelessly advocated for educational and social equality in the popular press. In his 1898 article "The Educated Negro and Menial Pursuits," Scarborough asked why the Black man, given the position of African Americans in the America of the time, should not be given "a pick instead of Latin and Greek." "The answer," said Scarborough, "is that life should be intellectually ennobled for the Negro as well as for the White man, even for those serving in menial positions, hence all avenues of life's higher activities should be open to him."[105]

Scarborough held this conviction throughout his life, even as he himself was subjected to the most virulent racism. When invited to scholarly conferences to read a paper, he would be refused admittance to the convention hotel and have to find accommodations elsewhere, if not with a sympathetic family, then wherever he could. Scarborough writes of the difficulties he encountered when attending the 1896 annual convention of the Modern Language Association at Case Western Reserve University in Cleveland: "I was refused accommodation at every leading hotel though I had brought my credentials as a member of the Association. I had letters from some of these same hotels asking [for] my patronage. I was told the letters were simply sent to all members of the Association, not knowing my color, and they did not take colored guests. I had to undergo the humiliation and find an obscure room with scarcely a bowl and pitcher available."[106] At the 1909 meeting of the American Philological Association in Baltimore, Scarborough was barred from attending the subscription banquet at the Belvedere Hotel, since they refused to serve people of color.

Because Wilberforce was a denominational institution, other factors also lay behind Scarborough's dismissal. Despite the reputation of Scarborough and others of its faculty, Wilberforce was hampered from its beginning by the hostility of the White establishment, which, as in the case of AMA colleges, wanted a "Negro education" that further reinforced the racial segregation known as Jim Crow. The classical liberal arts program fostered by Scarborough and others did not do this. Therefore, what monies Wilberforce did receive from the state of Ohio and other funding agencies were directed toward building the college's normal and industrial departments, whereas the liberal arts program languished financially.

The history of Wilberforce University is one of high ideals and determination to pursue those ideals in the face of racial prejudice; it is also a history shaped by a chronic lack of funds. As W. E. B. Du Bois recounts about Wilberforce in his *Autobiography*, the university's overriding problem was lack of money: "There was no visible source of Negro income large enough to support a college. The members of the church were fighting desperately for food and clothes. Their labor was being exploited to the last dime by every white American who had a chance or could steal it."[107] The African American presidents and trustees of the university were therefore compelled to trade their own autonomy for desperately needed financial support to shore up the university's normal department by introducing industrial training along the lines of the Hampton-Tuskegee model. The firing of Professor Scarborough from Wilberforce and his so-called transfer in 1892 to Payne Theological Seminary, an independent theological school on campus, may be seen as part of this larger process that, while rescuing Wilberforce financially, also worked against the university's best interests.

All these forces worked to put an end to what some Whites saw as an education ill-suited for their racial and social inferiors. Thus, from the 1890s through the 1940s, there was a continual effort to eliminate classical education for African Americans at Wilberforce and at institutions in the South, an effort that Bishop Henry McNeal Turner, a strident Black nationalist, felt was teaching "Negro inferiority."[108] Funding agencies both withheld funds from programs they deemed inappropriate for African Americans and worked to take away from the Black colleges the ability to govern themselves—since, clearly, the liberal arts programs demonstrated how misguided the faculty and governing boards were about what was "right" for Negro education.

Wilberforce in particular was singled out as badly managed. Thus both the Phelps-Stokes Fund (a nonprofit fund established in 1911 by the will of the New York philanthropist Caroline Phelps-Stokes) and the U.S. Bureau of Education rated Wilberforce's "Combined Normal and Industrial Department" for the training of teachers and manual workers and its liberal arts department as separate institutions, with the former lauded and the latter denigrated. The Combined Normal and Industrial Department's courses included agriculture, carpentry, and woodworking; commercial courses such as bookkeeping, mechanical drawing, forging, and blacksmithing; "household arts"; and machine shop.[109] Wilberforce struggled to secure accreditation for its college department, which did come in 1938, at a time when the stress in Black education began to shift from industrial training back to the liberal arts and sciences. But this did not put an end to Wilberforce's problems. In 1947 the state of Ohio severed its ties to Wilberforce, and Central State University became the state-supported teachers' college. As a result, Wilberforce lost its hard-won accreditation.[110]

We might conclude from this that Wilberforce had its funding cut because it was failing; rather, Wilberforce had its funding cut precisely because, under Scarborough's leadership, it had been *succeeding* in its pursuit of a classical liberal arts curriculum, which funding agencies denigrated as unsuitable training for African Americans. Like other institutions of higher learning for African Americans, therefore, Wilberforce faced a Hobson's choice—that is, to either buckle under and receive badly needed monies or go its own way and do without.

The reaction against liberal arts education at Wilberforce was by no means an isolated phenomenon. White elitists and racists decried the teaching of the classics as irrelevant and wasteful, especially for those whose station—or race—prevented them from entering the higher echelons of society. Thus it spoiled them for the type of work they were meant to do. White supremacists especially preferred the Booker T. Washington–Tuskegee model of manual and industrial training, such as farming or domestic service, to tamp down African Americans' self-realization and uplift and to once again keep them "in their place."

African Americans, too, played a role in this. According to Booker T. Washington, who was educated at Hampton and had little contact with the classics, during Reconstruction Negroes engaged in both a craze for Greek and Latin and political ambition. Washington saw no need for the classics and discouraged his faculty from teaching them. Other conservative African Americans opposed classical education for more complicated reasons. First, because of the intensity of the racial climate, college-educated African Americans were often the targets of racial attack simply for being educated. Second, it was almost impossible for African Americans in the South to get jobs commensurate with their training. Third, Black education at all levels, but particularly at the college level, was dependent on White financial support, whether governmental, private, or philanthropic.

This was all the more reason, then, for Scarborough to combat what he saw as a watering down of Wilberforce's educational mission, particularly when, in pursuit of desperately needed state funds in the late 1880s, Wilberforce promised to provide buildings and teacher-training resources for a combined normal and industrial department that would be legally separate from the university and controlled not by its board of trustees but by the state of Ohio. This move eased the financial pressure on the university's normal department but did nothing to help the college department. The AME Church's decision to establish Payne Theological Seminary further eroded Wilberforce's liberal arts curriculum. We may cite two reasons for this. First, the infusion of public funds into Wilberforce University, which was an organ of the AME Church, raised the issue of the separation of church and state. Therefore, the church would fund the theological school with monies formerly channeled to the normal department. Second, the founding of a separate theological unit provided a way for the church hierarchy to disengage themselves from too close a devotion to the liberal arts, including the pagan classics, which they thought detrimental to religious training.

Meanwhile, prominent Black leaders argued that Wilberforce was playing into the hands of White bigots by promoting a form of manual and industrial training that they saw as too emblematic of segregated Black schools meant to keep Blacks in a subordinate social and economic position. Indeed, John P. Green (1845–1940), a Cleveland attorney and a prominent Black Republican, called on young African Americans to take advantage of the opportunities opening up for Blacks by enrolling in Ohio's other colleges and universities "and asking their parents to petition the [state] legislature against the Wilberforce claim [to federal funds] in order to preserve their right to do so."[111]

Scarborough himself addressed this situation as early as 1910, but with a determination to fight back:

> The competition is great and Wilberforce is the sufferer because other institutions are better equipped and better maintained as they have more money. In this State where the schools are mixed many students we ought to have do not come to us but go to the mixed schools because of the advantages. The first thing we ought to do is build up a distinctively College Department and secure as many students as possible. This means an outlay for better equipment, for if they find that we are not as thoroughly equipped as other institutions and that they can get just as good or better for the money elsewhere, they will not stay with us. And further, Wilberforce has won its way in the world, has made its mark, and is known, and it is for us to take hold of this work with determination and zeal and make it the literary center, not only of the AME Church, but as the oldest school, the Literary center of the Negro people, at least the United States.[112]

What happened to Scarborough at Wilberforce and the forces working against other Black colleges and universities may be set against the larger history of race relations in America. Scarborough was reinstated at Wilberforce University in 1896 as vice president and became president in 1908, a position he would hold until his retirement in 1920. However, his dream of establishing "the Literary center of the Negro people" at Wilberforce was dead, another casualty of the withholding of funds and the emphasis on normal and industrial training over the liberal arts.[113]

Despite the odds against it, the classical curriculum at many Black colleges and universities thrived, or at least persevered, even in an atmosphere of repression, discrimination, and lack of resources. Some institutions fared better than others, but all provided, to varying degrees, education that informed the hand and mind. The primacy of the Hampton-Tuskegee model of education for Blacks influenced the programs of even the most progressive Black colleges. But even at Hampton and Tuskegee could be found teachers and courses that valued at least something of the classical curriculum, no matter how small. Espousal of the virtues that the reading of Greek and Roman authors instilled in their students could be found across schools under the auspices of various funding organizations, whether religious or not. Chapter 3 offers a more detailed survey of the canonical texts read in the classical curriculum taught at Black colleges and universities. There we discuss how those texts informed Black agency and uplift.

CHAPTER 3

A Survey of the Classical Texts Read at Black Colleges and Universities

Negro education is no longer an experiment. The ability of the race to take rank in higher education is no longer questioned by reasonable minds. The facts speak for themselves.
—William Sanders Scarborough

Susan C. Jarratt points to the life-forming purpose of a classical education for African Americans when she states, "The traditional curriculum provided not only a content and a practice; the very educational controversy itself provided a common place for articulating competing visions of group identity, and for deliberating about social organization and political action." Of paramount importance was what to teach the students to further the mission of racial uplift and self-empowerment. Says Jarratt, "At stake in the debates over curriculum were issues of great magnitude: What place should formerly enslaved African Americans have in the new social, intellectual, and economic arrangements of their regions and states, and in the nation at large? What kinds of educational institutions and curricula would best prepare them for newly imagined futures? How did the enterprise of southern black higher education, and the situation of black intellectual life more generally in the decades following the Civil War, look from the perspective of southern black students?"[1]

As Meyer Reinhold, in *Classica Americana*, and Caroline Winterer, in *The Culture of Classicism*, argue, the classics were the gateway to knowledge and the moniker of the educated. Therefore, African American teachers and students' mastery of this discipline would vindicate their full personhood and discredit, once and for all, the myth of racial inferiority. In this chapter we take a closer look at the authors and texts read at Black colleges and universities during a roughly seventy-year period. The reading list reflects the works recommended by the American Philological Association for college-entrance and graduation requirements in the classical languages, published in 1928, but also encompasses recommendations made since 1899.[2] Course listings at

Black colleges and universities replicated those of White schools and illustrated a similar appeal of the classics among educated Americans: to illustrate a situation or to offer a historical parallel; to evoke the classical past as a model to emulate or, in some cases, to avoid; and generally to provide a cultural frame of reference. Additionally, the assigned texts emphasized valor and moral improvement; the fight against injustice, tyrants, and human vices; good rulers; a life of virtue; the study of oratory to communicate effectively; and the Greek New Testament for the training of ministers.

All in all, the sheer difficulty of the classical authors reveals at least something of the level of instruction and student preparedness. The inclusion of these authors in the surviving catalogs, often with the specific text to be assigned, speaks to the breadth and range of authors being studied. But beyond the challenges of being able to read an ancient text with increasing facility and ease, we must consider how the classical authors read by the students (and, inasmuch as it can be recovered, how they read them) broadened their horizons to more open, more self-affirming ways of being and acting. William Sanders Scarborough's Greek grammar illustrates how he, as a man of color, had achieved, through careful study and experience, the level of authority required to teach Greek to others. In so doing, Scarborough kept the Greek language and its syntax from being the exclusive prerogative of Whites.

Texts for classics students were printed in attractive cloth-bound editions and were readily available for the classroom market.[3] Those textbooks in Albert Harkness's Standard Latin series, published by the American Book Company, sold, according to an 1878 ad appended to the back of Harkness's edition of Cicero's select orations, for between $0.87 and $3.50. The majority retailed for $1.00 to a $1.50. An 1878 dollar had the approximate purchasing power of $26.00 in 2020, so these texts were not inexpensive, especially for students of limited means. That being the case, a likely scenario is that books (or perhaps a single book) were shared by the small number of students, if indeed they had not purchased their own new (or used) copy, and that the instructor applied the text's lessons through the time-honored method of class recitation and repetition. In the preface to his Greek grammar, Scarborough states that "the use of the blackboard cannot be too highly recommended. In my own classes I have found its daily use indispensable."[4]

Black colleges and universities made extensive use of Thomas Chase and George Stuart's classical series of Greek and Roman authors, as they were the most readily available. The front matter for Chase and Stuart's *Six Books of the Aeneid of Virgil* (1875) reflected the progressivism in teaching methods evident in the late nineteenth and early twentieth centuries in the United States: it takes pains to declare its accuracy, clarity, and help to the student. Bowing to the new philological methods promulgated first in Germany and exported to the United States by Basil Lanneau Gildersleeve and others, it states, "Points of geography, history, mythology, and antiquities are explained in accordance with the views of the best German scholars." Textbooks of the time prided themselves on how they were "humanizing" the teaching of Greek and especially Latin. Indeed, this new humanism at times might even frown on the teaching of Latin simply for ethical training.[5] Rather, Latin, with its broad curricular applications and its importance for the study of modern European languages, provided useful preparation for a modernizing, secular world. However, given the widespread idea of the classics as the traditional staples, no good instructor could fail "to call to the reader's attention that the traditional six orations of Cicero are *materia politica*, the Manilian Law a treatise on citizenship and character, the poetry of Vergil a plea for patriotism and piety."[6]

The textbooks regularly touted their usefulness for the student. For example, Harkness's *A Complete Latin Grammar* is described as a "model for perspicuity of statement and clearness of arrangement." Similarly, the preface to Scarborough's *First Lessons in Greek* emphasizes its usefulness—namely, to provide "*a clear and concise statement of the rudimentary forms of the language.*"[7] The goal of this, no less than that of the other beginning grammars, was to prepare the student, under the teacher's guidance, to appreciate the finer points of grammar and syntax, to memorize select passages, and thus to acquire at least a degree of fluency in the language. This was to be achieved, Scarborough states in the preface to his Greek text, through recitation, repetition, use of the blackboard, grammatical instruction, and memorization—lessons Scarborough himself acquired in his learning and teaching.

All in all, the college catalogs we have examined present a daunting list of authors and works. The classical curriculum and the authors taught were fairly consistent across schools. There were, however, idiosyncrasies at individual institutions, which attests to professors' preferences in light of changing times. For example, Spelman College in Atlanta favored poetry over philosophy, history, and rhetoric. Johnson C. Smith University, founded as the Biddle Memorial Institute, in Charlotte, North Carolina, appeared to have the most idiosyncratic list, with its course offerings in Greek tragedy, late Roman history, Pliny's letters, and Roman Republican poetry. Morris Brown's academic course included Caesar, Cicero's orations, Vergil's *Aeneid* in Latin, and, in Greek, Xenophon's *Anabasis* and James Hadley and Frederic de Forest Allen's *Greek Grammar for Schools and Colleges*.

A passage from Morris Brown University's 1923–24 catalog helps illustrate the tenor and goals of classical instruction. Stress is laid on "systematic study,"

80 CHAPTER THREE

the principles of prosody, and the practice of scansion and metrical reading, with collateral reading in mythology. Textbooks named include Minnie L. Smith's *Elementary Latin*, Ernst Riess and Arthur L. Janes's *Caesar's Gallic War*, and Robert W. Tunstall's *Eleven Orations of Cicero, with Introduction, Notes, and Vocabulary*. Beyond the more canonical authors, selections from Ovid provide for a "careful study of verse and Mythology with practice in reading at sight short extracts of poetry and prose." The text used here is Clarence W. Gleason's *A Term of Ovid: Stories from the* Metamorphoses *for Study and Sight Reading*. The textbooks used were the course in most cases: both instructors and students would follow the text and review its lessons in class during a semester.[8]

The classical course listing in the Atlanta University 1882–83 catalog is full: first-year students studied (in Greek) Hadley and Allen's *Grammar*, James Robinson Boise's *First Lessons in Greek*, and three books of Xenophon's *Anabasis* and (in Latin) Cicero's *De senectute (On Old Age)* and *De amicitia (On Friendship)*, Thomas Chase's selections from Livy's *History*, and Elisha Jones's *Exercises in Latin Prose Composition*. Sophomores read (in Greek) three books of Xenophon's *Anabasis* and *Cyropaedia (The Education of Cyrus)* and selections from Homer's *Odyssey* and (in Latin) Livy's *History*, Tacitus's *Germania* and *Agricola*, and Horace's *Odes*. Juniors studied (in Greek) Demosthenes's *Olynthiacs* and *Philippics*, orations of Lysias, and Plato's *Gorgias* and (in Latin) Cicero's *Tusculan Disputations* (in Chase and Stuart's classics series).[9] No classics were offered in senior year.

The Fisk classical course at the common normal level consisted of Harkness's *A Complete Latin Grammar* and, at the higher normal level, Harkness and selections from Caesar and Cicero. The classical course at the college level consisted of, in Latin, Harkness's Latin grammar and *A Latin Reader* and, at the higher levels, Vergil, Horace's *Odes* and *Satires*, Livy's *History*, Cicero's select orations and the *De senectute*, Quintilian, Tacitus's *Germania* or *Agricola*, and Elisha Jones's *Exercises in Latin Prose Composition*. The beginning Greek level used Boise's *First Lessons in Greek* or Hadley and Allen's *Greek Grammar* and, at the higher levels, taught Xenophon's *Anabasis* and *Memorabilia*, Plato's *Phaedo*, the Greek New Testament, the *Iliad*, Demosthenes's *On the Crown*, Sophocles's *Antigone*. Euripides's *Iphigenia in Tauris*, Charles Alan Fyffe's *History of Greece*, book 7 of Thucydides's *History*, and Greek prose composition. In addition to the classical languages, courses in both German and French were required. These courses, for the major in classics, held, with some variation in authors and readings, throughout the first half of the twentieth century, although by the 1920s the classical languages were no longer required for admission to the college course.

The college program at Alcorn University, located in Lorman, Mississippi, was fully devoted to the liberal arts: first-year students studied, in Latin, Cicero's dialogues *De senectute* and *De amicitia*, prose composition, Livy, and Henry George Liddell's *A History of Rome*. Sophomores read Horace's *Odes*, *Epistles*, and *Satires*; Tacitus's *Histories*; the *Iliad*; William Smith's *A History of Greece*; and Ernst F. Bojesen's *Manual of Greek and Roman Antiquities*. Juniors read, in Latin, Tacitus's *Germania* and *Agricola*, Quintilian, and Juvenal's *Satires* and, in Greek, Demosthenes's *On the Crown*, Plato's *Gorgias*, and Aeschylus's *Prometheus*. No classics courses were offered senior year; instead, students could take such courses as Human Intellect and Moral Philosophy.

While day-to-day instruction in the classroom cannot be recovered, much can be gleaned about pedagogical method from the grammars and editions available at the time. The texts themselves could buttress both a conservative and expansionist reading and appreciation of the classics: conservative in that classical pedagogy involved the centuries-old tradition of rote memorization and mastery of grammar and syntax, and expansionist in that mastery of the classical languages imparted broad knowledge, dignity, and self-worth. To assess their relative value in the formation of African American students, we have broken down the different subject areas of the classical curriculum into philosophy, history, poetry, rhetoric, and readings in secondary sources.

Philosophy

As our survey of Black colleges and universities' curriculums and texts indicates, the classics taught were about more than declensions and conjugations. They were about forming the whole human being. Such formation would have benefited from Cicero's philosophical works. Often assigned were his *De amicitia* and the *De senectute*, dealing with friendship and old age, respectively; the *Tusculan Disputations*; and those others on the nature of the soul and on the emotions. Cicero's philosophical works were treatises on virtuous living, which, according to Cicero, depended on no frivolous outward show; nor was there any need to fear death because it is either a cessation of consciousness or else a shaking off of the body's shackles and a release to immortality. These pagan philosophical convictions, based on both Epicurean and Stoic principles, noble as they are, would nonetheless have clashed at times with the Christian ethos of the colleges and the students, which must have provided some spirited classroom discussion. Other assigned Greek and Roman philosophers and texts included Plato's dialogues *Phaedo* (on the nature of the soul), *Euthyphro* (on piety), and *The Republic* (on the ideal form of government); Lucretius's *De rerum natura* (*On the Nature of the Universe*); and Cicero's *De natura deorum* (*On the Nature of the Gods*).

Cicero's *De amicitia* and *De senectute*, among the perennial staples taught at Black colleges and universities for their moral lessons, often appear together in teaching texts. Their themes are universal: friendship (*amicitia*) is rare and can be between only good men; wrongdoing cannot be condoned even if undertaken on a friend's behalf. *De senectute* examines old age and its problems, which all human beings must face. Cicero's *Tusculan Disputations* are concerned with controversies between the two main schools of philosophy: Stoicism, on patient endurance of hardship, and Epicureanism, which preached freedom from anxiety and mental pain, and with that the enjoyment of moderate pleasures. In these works Cicero sought to establish a viable Roman philosophy.

The preface to Thomas Chase's edition of Cicero's *Tusculan Disputations* further emphasizes the value of the philological method then favored by Gildersleeve and other classical scholars who had been trained in Germany: "The high character of many of the editions of Greek and Roman authors which have lately appeared from the American press, indicates the rapid progress of classical scholarship in this country in the last few years. The light recent philological investigations have shed upon the history, structure, and significance of the ancient languages, and thus upon the science of language itself,—language, which is at once the great instrument of thought and the noblest production of mind,—adds a new dignity and value to even the most elementary processes in classical instruction."[10]

The Historians

Along with philosophy, Greek and Roman history imparted modes of behavior to emulate or avoid. The Fisk catalog for 1923–24 shows that the historians were read with an emphasis on rhetoric, history, and philosophy, since ancient historiography as a genre could encompass all these.[11] Among the most popular texts taught, as evidenced by several of the college catalogs, were those by Sallust, Livy, and Herodotus; Thucydides's *History of the Peloponnesian War*; and Tacitus's *Annales* and, even more, his *Germania* and *Agricola*. The *Agricola* was written in praise of Tacitus's father-in-law, Gnaeus Julius Agricola, during the latter's campaign in Britain, from where he was recalled by the despotic emperor Domitian (ruled 81–96 CE). Tacitus contrasts Domitian's tyranny and paranoia with Agricola's incorruptibility and virtue. The *Germania* is an ethnographic study that, read broadly, similarly contrasts virtue with corruption, in this case the monogamy, simplicity, bravery, and chastity of the German tribes against Roman immorality.

Both the *Germania* and *Agricola* were read in the college course at Wilberforce, beginning in the 1872–73 academic year; they appear in the extant course catalogs for Wilberforce not every year but with regularity thereafter, especially in the course listings from 1907–8 through 1912–13. Fisk University and Spelman classics students read both works in the late nineteenth and early twentieth centuries. The *Germania* and the *Agricola*, or the *Germania* alone, appear in course catalogs for Howard, Livingstone, Florida Memorial, Lincoln, Johnson C. Smith, and Simmons University. The texts mentioned (when indeed they are specified) are Chase and Stuart's classical series, available for $1.25 to $1.50 in the 1870s (used by Wilberforce, Howard, and Livingstone); W. S. Tyler's 1847 *Germania* and *Agricola* (Fisk), and William Allen's 1913 *Life of Agricola* (Fisk, Johnson C. Smith).

At one level the *Germania* and the *Agricola* may be read as other Roman histories, including Livy's *History of Rome* and Sallust's *Conspiracy of Catiline*, namely, as a contrast between virtue and vice. But this juxtaposition could be problematic. In the preface to his history of Rome from its foundation, Livy laments that the empire has reached such a point of crisis that "we can endure neither our vices nor their remedies." It will be beneficial, therefore, to look back to Rome's beginnings, before it became a world empire. Indeed, the very idea of empire is not monolithic but rather open-ended. The Germans described by Tacitus may be praised for their simplicity and for the importance they give to monogamy, in contrast to the Roman predilection for serial marriage; on the other hand, the Germans are castigated for their bibulousness and violence. In the end, they are better off under the yoke of empire, although they may be in a position of servitude within that empire.

One of the more startling episodes in the *Agricola*, as described by Richard Alston and Efrossini Spentzou in their study of Roman literature of the first century CE, is the speech of the British chieftain Calgacus (*Agricola*, secs. 30–32), in which he delivers "a thorough critique of Rome and Roman imperialism." He "accuses the Romans of a megalomaniacal desire for world conquest that pushes Roman power to its furthest limits." Agricola's victory over the Britons and their reduction to slavery, therefore, may be read as a vindication of Calgacus's charge: "Where they [i.e., the Romans] make a desert, they call it peace" (sec. 30). However, the multiple failings of the British tribes show that they cannot be used as models of the noble savage. Rather, they may be seen "as a savage who may, from time to time, do something noble."[12] Cornelius Nepos's *De viris illustribus* (*On Famous Men*), on the reading list of Morehouse, Fisk, and other colleges, similarly compared Romans and foreigners, including generals, kings, lawyers, orators, poets, historians, and philosophers, though Nepos's purpose was mainly eulogistic.

Other questions of empire, ethnicity, and what constitutes Romanness emerge in the *Agricola* and *Germania*. These are questions to be asked in light of how Roman historical texts, which often were concerned with manners and morals, were read in the late nineteenth and early twentieth centuries at Black colleges and universities in the United States, particularly against what was happening to African Americans at the time. This was a period, after all, of racial discrimination, exclusion, lynching, and other violence. Such life lessons might include questions like, How would African American teachers and their students have understood Tacitus's ambivalence toward Rome and its empire—corrupt in so many ways but the best in an essentially bad world? Would they have felt kinship with the barbarian, the outsider who, once amalgamated into the empire, would have acquired Romanness?

How subversive in fact was African Americans' reading? On one level it would have been subversive for the very reason that African Americans' reading such texts at all, and in the original languages, would have struck most Whites as outrageous and heterodox. William Wells Brown ([1814?]–84), for example, who was born a slave but who became a medical doctor and an abolitionist, found in his own reading of Roman history ample material to question the vaunted superiority of the Anglo-European. Indeed, he learned that the Romans resorted to the same arguments for racial inferiority as were used against African Americans in his own time:

> We all acknowledge the Anglo-Saxon to be the highest type of civilization. But from whence sprang this refined, proud, haughty, and intellectual race? Go back a few centuries, and we find their ancestors described in the graphic touches of Caesar and Tacitus. See them in the gloomy forests of Germany, sacrificing to their grim and gory idols; drinking the warm blood of their prisoners, quaffing libations from human skulls; infesting the shores of the Baltic for plunder and robbery; bringing home the reeking scalps of enemies as an offering to their king. . . .
>
> Caesar writing home, said of the Britons,—"They are the most degraded people I ever conquered." Cicero advised his friend Atticus not to purchase slaves from Briton [sic], "because," said he, "they cannot be taught music, and are the ugliest people I ever saw."[13]

Whites could therefore look on such an astute reading of classical sources by an African American as subversive and even dangerous, for it challenged the primacy of Anglo-European Whiteness.

Poetry

The chief poetic staples of the classics curriculum across Black colleges and universities were Vergil, Horace, Ovid, the Roman comic writers, and the Greek tragedians. Chief among them was Vergil's *Aeneid*, his epic poem on the founding of Rome. The *Aeneid* imparted lessons of piety and patriotism. But it would also have provided more sobering lessons on the dangers and pitfalls attending empire building.[14] Horace, author of the *Odes, Satires, Epistles,* and *Epodes*, was one of the most celebrated poets of imperial Rome. He wrote in praise of the simple life, love, and friendship and castigated human vices and foibles. Less taught was the late Republican lyric poet Catullus, although Catullus was offered at Wilberforce, Fisk, and Johnson C. Smith. The Greek comic playwright Aristophanes was taught at Wilberforce, as he was a specialty of William Sanders Scarborough's; in 1886 Scarborough delivered his scholarly study, "Birds of Aristophanes."[15]

Chase and Stuart's classical series includes the text of the Roman comic poet Terence's first and last attested plays, *Andria* (*The Girl from Andros*) and *Adelphoe* (*The Brothers*), taught at Wilberforce, Spelman, and elsewhere. The text as given assumes a good knowledge of Latin and also Greek, since Greek and Latin testimonies to the life of Terence in the notes are left untranslated. These plays were chosen as representative of Terence's style and that of Roman comedy generally; Terence was considered a better role model for students since he is less bawdy than Plautus. (School texts of the time were dedicated mostly to providing the most pious facts of the ancient poets' lives, based on available testimony.)

The biography of Terence in E. P. Crowell's edition of the *Andria* and *Adelphoe* would have been of interest to African American students. Although Crowell was not writing with them specifically in mind, he emphasizes Terence's African heritage and his manumission from slavery, his importance to the development of Latin literary style, and his esteem among the likes of Caesar and Cicero for his elegant Latinity. These qualities demonstrated that a man of color, and a former slave at that, could be a superb Latinist.[16]

Crowell's notes on meter and orthography, while helpful in explaining the text and offering necessary background, also are quite academic, which leads to the assumption that either the students were excellent and well prepared or their instructor gave them a great deal of help. In any event this edition is well within the tradition of nineteenth-century classical school texts, with the text and its notes to be used in conjunction with students' lexicons and grammars, as well as class lectures. Stress is laid on points of grammar and syntax. The students would laboriously progress through the text to work out parts of speech, helped by the explanatory notes, and then attend to the significance of what the words were saying. (It is useful to point out again the argument used repeatedly by defenders of the classical languages: that Greek and Latin aided in logical thinking and provided a sound foundation for mastery of English grammar, an argument that appears in the college catalogs.) The students would be further drilled by their teachers in points of grammar and syntax, including aids to memory as well as accurate translations.[17]

The Role of Classical Rhetoric in Framing African American Discourse

Of utmost importance was rhetoric, a staple of the traditional curriculum, especially because skill in speaking formed the core of effective communication for those who would be called on to address the aspirations of the race to the White public along with a plea for racial and social equality. Popular texts read across Black colleges were Cicero's orations against the conspirator Catiline (e.g., Wilberforce, North Carolina Agricultural and Technical, Fisk, Wiley); Demosthenes's *On the Crown* (e.g., Fisk, Howard, Livingstone, Simmons) and *Olynthiacs* (e.g., Howard, Florida Memorial); the speeches of the Greek orators Lysias (e.g., Florida Memorial, Oberlin), Aeschines (e.g., Johnson C. Smith, Oberlin), and Isocrates (e.g., Oberlin); and Quintilian's *Institutio oratoria*, or *Institutes of Oratory* (e.g., Simmons).

The African American classicist and educator George Morton Lightfoot (1868–1947) emphasized, as he put it, "How language is intimately connected with life": "Through the medium of language, we not only possess the power of communicating our thoughts and feelings in the daily intercourse with our fellow-men, but we enter into full heritage of all that is best in the vast accumulation of knowledge in the past; since whatever any particular age may produce in the realm of thought and feeling that is valuable, is through the vehicle of language transmitted to succeeding generations."[18] Although he was not addressing an exclusively African American audience, Lightfoot spoke, as an African American, to the importance of correct expression for a people long denied any voice at all beyond the way in which the Roman author Varro, author of the agricultural treatise *De re rustica*, designated the enslaved—that is, as an *instrumentum vocale*, or "speaking tool" (1.17), recoding Aristotle's own designation of the enslaved as a "living tool" (*empsychon organon*). Black teachers and students of rhetoric actively worked to reset the terms of those epistemic practices that had previously been responsible for such "toolsing" of human beings, turning them into inarticulate chattel.

Not only did speech have to be correct; it had to be powerful and persuasive. Indeed, oratory as a tool of social change was a staple of the early American republic, and it continued to flourish throughout the nineteenth century. Refuting a number of scholars who claimed that the status of rhetoric declined at this time, Nan Johnson, in her book *Nineteenth-Century Rhetoric in North America*, argues that

> the pedagogical, philosophical, and theoretical interests of the discipline were supported vigorously by the liberal arts curriculum which consistently affirmed the cultural function of rhetorical education. . . . Rhetorical education played a crucial role in bolstering the idealism of nineteenth-century liberal education, an enterprise that was committed to the development of an intellectually progressive and culturally enlightened society. From the perspective of nineteenth-century educators in the United States and Canada, only an education in the rhetorical arts could foster those virtues that every intelligent and civilized individual must possess: "the cultivation of . . . taste . . . the exercise of the imagination . . . the development of . . . intellectual traits and feelings . . . and clearness and power of expression."[19]

Several sourcebooks for aspiring orators were available, prominent among them Caleb Bingham's *Columbian Orator* (1797), which was a widely used and imitated textbook in secondary education in the first half of the nineteenth century. It went through more than twenty editions, for a total of two hundred thousand copies in print. Containing speeches from Greek, Roman, British, French, and American political history, it was cited by Frederick Douglass as the source of his oratorical skills. Bingham and other texts, says Granville Ganter, "universally declared their intent to train students in the ways of *virtue*."[20]

The speeches in Bingham's *Columbian Orator*, ranging from classical antiquity to the late eighteenth century and including excerpts from plays and poems, emphasized industry, eloquence, a distinctly stoical attention to duty, and moral probity. Rhetoric is directly tied to liberty, for only in free republics may men speak openly and with truth. In his introduction Bingham specifically adduces the Roman rhetorician Quintilian's call for the orator to be a *vir bonus*, or "good man." His introduction also emphasizes proper decorum and gestures that Bingham derives from classical sources. As Johnson further notes, the Roman handbooks' stress on good moral character was carried through nineteenth-century rhetorical training: "The importance that nineteenth-century rhetoricians awarded to prerequisite moral character in the speaker is confirmed by the view that oratory plays a crucial role in moral edification, civil education, and communal debate regarding social values."[21]

Nineteenth-century handbooks underlined the special role assigned to the rhetorician in the preservation of freedom and thus the promotion of

88 CHAPTER THREE

the common good. According to Edward T. Channing (1790–1856), Boylston professor of rhetoric and oratory at Harvard University: "You need not fill your imaginations with glorious forms of ideal perfection in the arts, only ask yourself what must be the power of an orator who is perfectly fitted for an age like this: of one thoroughly prepared to do all that eloquence can do among *the enlightened and free, I would set no bonds to his power*; it is only for truth and freedom and justice to do it."[22]

Orality, not to mention oratory, had long been a tradition in the African American community, beginning in the Black church, with its sonorous hymns and forceful preaching, which required both training and stamina. Nonetheless, a common charge brought against African Americans by Whites was that they could not speak, or speak properly. Caricatures of African Americans produced in quantity in the late nineteenth and early twentieth centuries often center on the mouth, which is exaggerated with enormously thick white or red lips set against a coal-black face. The mouth is normally overly large, often showing teeth and tongue. Despite the size of the mouth, however, the caricatured African American has no voice, or no voice that registers meaning. The mouth speaks in a broad Negro dialect, if it speaks intelligibly at all. Therefore, it should have come as no surprise to Mary Church Terrell, as she recounts in her 1940 autobiography, *A Colored Woman in a White World*, when, as a student at Oberlin, she was called on to read Greek before the visiting English school examiner Matthew Arnold (1822–88): "One day Matthew Arnold, the English writer, visited our class and Professor Frost asked me both to read the Greek and then to translate. After leaving the class Mr. Arnold referred to the young lady who read the passage of Greek so well. Thinking it would interest the Englishman, Professor Frost told him I was of African descent. Thereupon Mr. Arnold expressed the greatest surprise imaginable, because, he said, he thought the tongue of the African was so thick he could not be taught to pronounce the Greek correctly."[23] The power of Terrell's performance in Greek thus countered Arnold's racist conception of the Black body.

Among the more prominent Black rhetoricians in the nineteenth century were Sojourner Truth (1797–1883) and Frederick Douglass (1818–95), both of whom were similarly subject to the scrutinizing, but also marveling, White gaze. An arresting description of Truth is feminist and abolitionist Frances Gage's (1808–84) recollection of Truth's 1851 speech "Ain't I a Woman?": "She had taken us up in her strong arms and carried us safely over the slough of difficulty, turning the whole tide in our favor. I have never in my life seen anything like the magical influence that subdued the mobbish spirit of the day." Harriet Beecher Stowe's (1811–96) 1863 essay "Sojourner Truth, the Libyan

SURVEY OF THE CLASSICAL TEXTS **89**

Sibyl" also attests to Truth's power in a manner conjuring images of séances or other medium-inspired manifestations and betraying a hint of exoticism: "I do not recollect ever to have been conversant with anyone who had more of that silent and subtle power . . . than this woman. In the modern, spiritualistic phraseology, she would be described as having a strong sphere."[24] These descriptions include physical strength ("her strong arms"), a "magical influence," and a "subtle power." Both Gage and Stowe convey a forceful impression of what they heard and saw.

Sojourner Truth's rhetorical power belied the tradition of public speaking as the specific province of the male. Women were to be discouraged from public speaking since, by Victorian standards at least, it violated their delicate natures. They ought, rather, to devote themselves to "domestic science." This sexist orientation helps put in context the decidedly masculine description of Sojourner Truth. Sexism's relation to rhetoric and, more broadly, to the "hard sciences" is one reflected in the form of education recommended for African Americans—that is, one in which they keep their place, silently and obediently, as domestic servants or manual laborers and are therefore deprived of their autonomy and even masculinity. When read by Douglass and other African Americans, Bingham's *Columbian Orator*, with speeches invoking courage, self-reliance, and liberty, mustered its readers to courageous acts. In this context the person of Sojourner Truth as read by Gage and Stowe is downright transgressive. Indeed, a selection from the *Columbian Orator* titled "An Oration on the Powers of Eloquence, Written for an Exhibition of a School in Boston, 1794" directly ties rhetoric to liberty.[25]

Therefore, it is not surprising that Demosthenes, Cicero, Quintilian, and other ancient rhetoricians were a staple of the classics courses taught at Black colleges and universities, including Wilberforce, Fisk, Spelman, and Howard. The tropes of classical rhetoric informed the speech and arguments of African American public intellectuals; Cicero was praised above all for his usefulness. Cicero likewise provided a Roman example of the statesman who used his gift of speech to sway his listeners and to stand up against the growing tyranny of Julius Caesar and Marc Antony. The classics were essential for the training of effective rhetoricians. It was the case for White orators too, but it had special urgency for educated African Americans to speak out on behalf of the race. After graduation these students were expected to go out into the world and argue for their right to equality and full citizenship.

The reaction of a White reporter who attended an 1873 commencement ceremony at Lincoln College that included a Latin salutatory and a classical oration defending the classical curriculum illustrates the importance of oratorical exercises at Black colleges and universities. He was moved to write, "While so many white youths decry Latin, it is quite refreshing to hear a colored youth advocate its study."[26] Jarratt describes how, as an outgrowth of the students' rhetorical training and in concert with student declamations, student publications at three prominent Black colleges, Fisk, Atlanta, and Howard, discussed vital issues of the day and took stands that were controversial. Likewise, as Jarratt observes, the antebellum Black press, such as *Freedom's Journal* and abolitionist and journalist William Lloyd Garrison's (1805–79) *Liberator*, had itself demonstrated that "the endorsement of traditional rhetorical education can have radical implications."[27]

A strong proponent of classical rhetoric at Black colleges and universities was the poet and educator Melvin B. Tolson (1898–1966), who taught at Wiley College in Piney Woods, Texas, from 1923 to 1947. Tolson, the son of a Methodist minister educated at Kansas City's Lincoln High School and Lincoln College in Pennsylvania, had been thoroughly instructed in the liberal arts tradition, including classics, religion, language instruction, and oratory. Thus he understood rhetoric's transformative, even radical, power. An indefatigable teacher, Tolson drilled his students in the fundamentals of grammar, syntax, and logic, the building blocks of effective oratory.

Modeling himself on Diogenes and Socrates, Tolson sought the truth in ways that might be unsettling; as he said, "Nothing educates us like a shock."[28] Such power in speaking could then be used to speak out against racial injustice. David Gold, describing the popularity of debating clubs and intermural competitions at Black colleges and universities, states it well when he says, "At Wiley, as at other black colleges, debate was not merely a campus diversion. Rather, for both men and women, oratorical competition served, practically and symbolically, as a means of both individual and community achievement. Speakers and audiences alike saw themselves as stakeholders in a public—and publicly performed—enterprise of racial uplift."[29]

Students formed debating and literary societies with such classically derived titles as the Ciceronian Literary Society at Morehouse, the Young Ladies Lyceum at Fisk, and Athene at Atlanta University. These served as important social outlets for a student body with few occasions for socializing beyond the college campus, given the segregation and exclusion African Americans routinely faced in the greater community.[30] Students debated important issues of the day, such as the Spanish-American War and American colonialism. But there were also the traditional oratorical exercises, the *suasoriae* and *controversiae*, in which students took opposing sides to debate such questions as "Which is more important to a man, a horse or a cow?" and "Was Phillis Wheatley the greatest of African poets?"

Student publications, such as the *Fisk Expositor*, later renamed the *Fisk Herald*, also offered a platform for discussing points of view, informed by the students' classical reading, on a variety of local, national, and international concerns. Thus, says Jarratt, "the course of study seems to have contributed a sense of rhetorical enfranchisement for several generations of young writers and new citizens who, despite the flourishing of a black rhetorical culture in national and religious spheres, were after reconstruction barred from decision making in southern legislatures and courts, and from white public discourse more generally."[31]

William Sanders Scarborough on Frederick Douglass's Power of Speech

In 1893 Scarborough was asked to write an introduction to the book *Frederick Douglass: The Orator*, by James M. Gregory (1849–1915), professor of Latin language and literature at Howard University, whom Scarborough had called "a forcible writer, a fluent speaker, and an acceptable orator."[32] Gregory argued that the main purpose of his book was one of usefulness—that is, to become "instrumental in leading our youth to study the character of this remarkable man and to draw from it lessons that will urge them to high and noble effort."[33] Gregory emphasized the utility of Douglass's rhetorical power to move the race by quoting Cicero in *De oratore*: "The best orator is he that so speaks as to instruct, to delight, and to move the mind of his believers."[34]

Douglass's physical appearance and deportment certainly enhanced his rhetorical prowess, conforming to and even embodying the idealized, masculinist description of the orator found in classical sources. Their power is amply conveyed by the large number of photographs Douglass had made of himself during his lifetime.[35] When speaking, Douglass made a similarly profound impression. The journalist Ossilie Assing described in 1858 the physical presence of, and her attraction to, Douglass the man: "This excellent speaker knows how to electrify and captivate his audience. Something like a personal relationship develops between him and the listener and elicits their undivided sympathy, letting them experience the magic of amiability that wins the hearts of everyone who is fortunate enough to meet this vibrant and noble man."[36] Other eyewitness descriptions of Douglass attest to his physical beauty, his strength, his height, his eyes, and his face, but most fixate on the power of his voice and his graceful, elegant expression, which left an indelible impression.[37]

Roman oratory described various rhetorical styles and the uses for each but distinguished broadly between a "rugged" and a "smooth" style. Over-

92 CHAPTER THREE

indulgence in either might result in a charge of either effeminacy or incomprehensibility. However, the Romans encouraged a strong manly style of delivery (the type exemplified by Douglass and, in her own way, by Truth); for example, in his *De oratore*, Cicero recommends that the orator not indulge in stagey, theatrical gestures but instead throw his chest out manfully like a soldier or a wrestler. Since African Americans were being subjected to the painful scrutiny of the White gaze, the rhetorical style with which they hoped to curry favorable notice had to accord with the classical Greek ideal of appropriateness (*to prepon*) as well as to usefulness (*tê ôphelia*). This stress on deportment is reflected in the rhetorical handbooks of the time. Drawing on the influence of the classical orators, such as Cicero and Quintilian, Black nineteenth-century orators stressed not only proper articulation but also correct body language, including proper breathing, stance, gestures, and expression of the eyes and face.[38]

In his introduction to the life of Douglass, Scarborough makes several pertinent points about the quality of Douglass's oratory: "He is a brilliant orator, a fluent talker, and an interesting conversationalist. . . . The greatness of the man and the inspiration that comes from every word that he utters, makes one wonder how it was possible for such a remarkable character to have ever been a slave."[39] (We note how Scarborough describes the way in which Douglass transforms himself in a manner all but unbelievable: that he could rise from the degraded status of a slave to become such a great statesman and orator. But he was by no means a singular example. Scarborough, himself born a slave, threw off the yoke of servitude. Scarborough praises his parents for being virtuous and persevering, which are honorable and "freeborn" traits.)

Scarborough compares Douglass's eloquence to that of Demosthenes, who displayed a zeal similar to Douglass's in rousing his people against the dangers of Philip of Macedon and who was no doubt "the greatest of all Athenian orators."[40] According to the Greek historian and teacher of rhetoric Dionysius of Halicarnassus, Demosthenes provided the true substance of the hard-working farmer's well-tended plot and its luxuries.[41] Demosthenes was popular since he offered students an ideal yet achievable role model of the self-made man who overcame his stuttering and whose successes they could hope to emulate; a man who, after great personal sacrifice and hard work, became a powerful speaker and public benefactor, respected even by his enemies. Demosthenes's *On the Crown* was perennially popular across schools and periods; African American students also read the *Philippics* (against the imperialist ambitions of Philip of Macedon) and *Olynthiacs* (against the seizure by Philip of the powerful Greek city Olynthus), as well as the speeches of the Greek orators Aeschines and Lysias.

SURVEY OF THE CLASSICAL TEXTS   **93**

The speeches contained in Bingham's *Columbian Orator* called on students to act rationally and morally. The speeches reflected, once again, the Roman writer and rhetorician Quintilian's insistence on the orator as *vir bonus peritus dicendi*—that is, a good man skilled at speaking.[42] Within the context of this discussion, the study of ancient models was necessary to form an effective speaker. The number of courses at Black colleges and universities that used the texts by great orators such as Cicero are evidence of this strain of pedagogy.

Secondary Sources, Grammars, and the Moral Power of the Classics

In addition to the texts of the classical authors, whether in the original languages or in English translations, Black colleges and universities assigned survey courses that included histories of Greece and Rome, as well as modern works with classical themes. For example, Morris Brown University in the 1920s assigned W. E. B. Du Bois's "Of the Quest of the Golden Fleece" (1911), based on the Medea myth, which dealt with the relation between northern financing and southern politics and political corruption.[43] Charles Kingsley's *Heroes of Greek Mythology* (1889) and Robert Fowler Leighton's *A History of Rome* (1881) were among the secondary sources assigned at Wilberforce for the study of Greek myth and Roman history.

Such texts would likely have given rise to discussions of types of people: the hero, the tyrant, the coward, the martyr, both historical and mythological, as well as the master and the slave. Given the religious orientation of Wilberforce and the other church-affiliated Black colleges and universities, professors and students would have mined the classical texts and secondary readings for moral lessons and models for emulation, since the classics traditionally stood for "the best." Greek and Latin grammar and prose composition formed students' manners of speech and mental discipline. Scarborough's own *First Lessons in Greek* was a distillation of other grammars he had studied as well as the practical experience he had gained in his own teaching. As stated in the text's preface, Scarborough's pedagogical purpose was, once again, to provide "*a clear and concise statement of the rudimentary forms of the language.*"

In his own life, Scarborough's study of the classics made him a peer of other scholars, even though Scarborough himself did not have a doctoral degree. Among his published titles on classical philology are "The Theory and Function of the Greek Thematic Vowel" and "The Chronological Order of Plato's Writings." In their book titled *African American Writers and Classical Tradition*, William W. Cook and James Tatum speak to the essence of Scarborough the scholar: "For Scarborough, classics was as much a means to culture as a career based on the German model of scientific, professional scholarship. . . . He was a prolific writer, teaching and publishing on both Greek and Latin literature, not least because he could read German, the indispensable language for the international discipline that classics had become."[44]

Scarborough's classical scholarship was heavily marked by the traditional scientific classicism, or *Altertumswissenschaft*, first promulgated in Germany, with its stress on philology and textual criticism. As fellow Black classicist Richard T. Greener (1844–1922) said in a letter to Scarborough, "You may think you are doing little, but it is something worthwhile to have proved Calhoun's statement false, and by your philological success alone you have lifted us all out of the ditch where he proposed we should always lie."[45]

Scarborough's standing among other classicists helped buffer him in his own experiences of racial discrimination and emboldened him to speak out on behalf of justice and equality. He demonstrated both his classical learning and his claim to both racial and social equality when addressing the White audience gathered in the Rotunda Library of the University of Virginia in Charlottesville, the site of the 1892 meeting of the American Philological Association. As Scarborough recounts in his autobiography, he was preparing to deliver his paper on the "Chronological Order of Plato's Dialogues" when he felt the portraits of Jefferson Davis, Robert E. Lee, and other prominent southerners glowering at the sight of a Black man, who normally would not be allowed in except as a servant. "Every eye was fixed upon me, and a peculiar hush," he says, "seemed to pervade the room. It was a rare moment. Like a flash the past unrolled before my mind, my early Atlanta examinations, Calhoun's famous challenge, that no Negro could learn Greek." Scarborough recovered his composure, however, and presented his paper, which was received "with hearty applause," mixed, perhaps, with some incredulity that a Black man had delivered it.[46] Scarborough was able to demonstrate his ability to speak before a White audience as both a peer and an equal, without having to put his race on trial.

While the course lists and texts used at Black colleges and universities varied according to the philosophy and educational requirements of the individual institution, there was broad consensus across Black colleges and universities about which classical authors they taught: those who, after centuries of primacy in the Western canon, were regarded as "the best." As such, they provided models of speech and important tools to think clearly about such matters as good government, moral sobriety, religion, and human beings' relation to the divine. In the later nineteenth and twentieth centuries, as the traditional model of instruction was being replaced at other institutions of higher

SURVEY OF THE CLASSICAL TEXTS **95**

learning, Black colleges and universities were being forced to follow suit. The Black schools experienced the added pressure from donors and legislatures to discard classics altogether.

African American students, along with their parents and teachers, resisted the watering down of their education to suit the demands of those who thought that a classical liberal arts curriculum was ill-suited to creating obliging Black workers for their place in a racially stratified society, mandating practical instruction instead. Modes of resistance were various, ranging from dissimulation and passing (that is, feigning agreement with Whites' demands) to outright physical rebellion. This is the subject of chapter 4.

Fig. 1. Frederick Douglass. Portrait with facsimile signature, 1882. Small, Maynard, and Company, 1899. Courtesy of the Library of Congress, Washington, D.C.

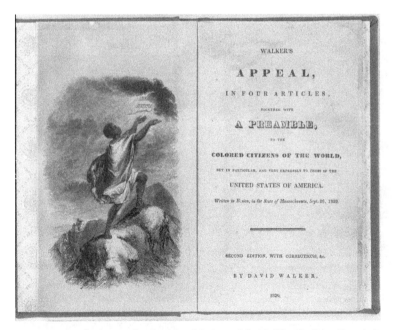

Fig. 2. David Walker's *Appeal to the Colored Citizens of the World*, 2nd edition. Frontispiece and title page, 1829. Courtesy of the Library of Congress, Washington, D.C.

Fig. 3. Fanny Jackson Coppin. Photomechanical print, ca. 1919. Courtesy of the Library of Congress, Washington, D.C.

Fig. 4. Anna Julia Cooper. C. M. Bell, photographer, ca. 1902. Courtesy of the Library of Congress, Washington, D.C.

Fig. 5. William Sanders Scarborough. C. M. Bell, photographer, ca. 1905. Courtesy of the Library of Congress, Washington, D.C.

Fig. 6. Edward Wilmot Blyden. L. L. D. Mauil and Company, Photographers and Miniature Painters, ca. 1860. Courtesy of the Library of Congress, Washington, D.C.

Fig. 7. Rev. Henry McNeal Turner, chaplain of the First U.S. Colored Regiment, 1863. Courtesy of the Library of Congress, Washington, D.C.

Fig. 8. From left to right: Robert C. Ogden, Senator William Howard Taft, Booker T. Washington, and Andrew Carnegie, at Tuskegee Institute's twenty-fifth anniversary celebration, 1906. Courtesy of the Library of Congress, Washington, D.C.

Fig. 9. Mary Church Terrell, ca. 1915. Courtesy of the Library of Congress, Washington, D.C.

Fig. 10. Charlotte Hawkins Brown (back row, center), with Palmer Memorial Institute faculty, 1907. Courtesy of the State Archives of North Carolina, Raleigh.

CHAPTER 4

The Classics as Tools of Empowerment and Resistance

If the Negro is given a chance and equal rights as a citizen he will eventually climb as high and accomplish as much as any race or people has accomplished. A college training is not bad for him nor does it unfit him for usefulness as is often said; but he is better able to meet the demands and responsibilities of the times.
—W. E. B. Du Bois and Augustus Granville Dill

How dare any man or set of men presume to limit us in our intellectual improvement—in the shaping of the highest faculties, unto which we have been endowed?
—*Fisk Herald*

Richard Wright Sr. (1855–1947), an influential classically trained Black educator of the post-Reconstruction era, recounts the following story: While a student at Atlanta University, he was once approached by a northern visitor who asked him what the freedmen had to say to their friends in New England. Young Wright's reply was, "Tell them we are rising."[1] Wright's own prodigious energy in learning and promoting the classics in his career exemplified the commitment that many African American teachers, administrators, students, and their parents brought to the classics classroom. They would use the cultural capital gained by study of the classics to fight oppression within the walls of their college or university, most notably efforts by the White power structure to water down the classical curriculum in favor of industrial education.

This chapter discusses the tools of dissimulation, resistance, and activism African American students and their teachers used to resist the degradation of the classical curriculum to suit the requirements of White power brokers. Often student resistance would be against the very officials of the college the students were attending. As Susan C. Jarratt states, the classical course "created a space for students to try on the ethos of the educated citizen, engaging in critical exchange about questions of collective concern."[2] Indeed, the *Altertumswissenschaft* practiced to such good effect by William Sanders Scarborough in his scholarly writing illustrates the extent to which African Americans' classical learning could serve as a means of self-empowerment. The classically educated Melvin Tolson regarded education itself as "fundamentally subversive." He celebrated the *hypokrisis* (related to the Greek *hypocrites*, or actor) of ancient Greek drama—that is, the actor's adopting a character's mask and voice.[3] Such Du Boisean double-voicedness learned in the classics classroom could therefore be one of the tools in the fight against the imposition of industrial education. Yet another tool of self-empowerment was provided by educated African American women, like Mary Church Terrell, who formed women's clubs to promote literacy and provide a sense of community for their Black sisters.

This was strikingly different from the motivation for education coming from the majority White power structure, which required a competent and complaisant Black workforce, and whose leaders decried the emphasis on classics as not useful for training African Americans, particularly in the Jim Crow South, for the lives they were expected to lead. Around the turn of the twentieth century, with the influx of immigrants from eastern and southern Europe to the United States, educators began to rethink the traditional nineteenth-century ideal of a common education for all. How, they wondered, could poor immigrants and African Americans migrating from the countryside to the city be expected to compete with the established White Anglo-Saxon population? How best to mold and train those destined to form a cheap and compliant source of manual labor?

Faced with African Americans' self-empowerment through the study of the classics, by the 1890s conservative voices in the White community, and even Black accommodationists, began calling for an end to classical liberal arts education in southern Black colleges.[4] The White power structure felt that such elite training would make African Americans "uppity" and unsuited for their "natural place" as manual laborers, housekeepers, and gardeners. Conservative African Americans opposed classical education for more complicated reasons. First, because of the intensity of the racial climate, college-educated African Americans were often the targets of racial attack simply for being educated. Second, given the prevailing racial attitude, African Americans, especially in the South, would find it almost impossible to get jobs commensurate with their training. Third, Black education, at all levels, but particularly at the college level, depended on White financial support, whether governmental, private, or philanthropic. All these forces worked to end what Whites saw as an education ill-suited to their racial and social inferiors. Thus the 1890s through the 1940s saw a continuous effort to eliminate classics for African Americans in the South, an effort that Bishop Henry McNeal Turner, a strident Black nationalist, felt, against all evidence, was teaching "Negro inferiority."[5]

Much of the literature on Black education in the Jim Crow era discusses how, for African Americans, particularly in the South, education was crafted as a tool of disempowerment. Says Johnetta Cross Brazzell, "Education could be used as a form of social control, defining the position of Blacks and Whites in the Southern racial harmony. For the Black masses, education would be used to train and socialize them for unskilled and semiskilled positions, such as household managers, sharecroppers, dressmakers, commercial cooks, chauffeurs, janitors, and laundry women." Any educational establishment for African Americans needed a list of such so-called practical courses to ensure White support, including from the John F. Slater Fund for the Education of Freedmen and various other financial bodies. While she is speaking particularly about Spelman, Brazzell does lay out a real problem for Black colleges and universities across the board: the necessity to accede to White demands for industrial education by teaching courses "in chamberwork, table-work, dishwashing, cooking, washing, ironing, and plain sewing. As an elective students could learn printing. Of the 836 students attending Spelman in 1892, 419 are listed in the Industrial Department and 44 in the Printing Department. This represented 55 percent of the total student body."[6] The irony in all this, according to the traditional histories of Black education, is that the White missionary teachers tried to offer literary instruction as well, even when doubtful of African Americans' abilities to handle college subjects.

The racial climate in the post–Civil War United States was far from pacific, and it would become more violent as the nineteenth century progressed. Maxine D. Jones, in her discussion of the American Missionary Association and the Beaufort, North Carolina, school controversy of 1866–67, describes the friction between the Black community and the White missionaries. White missionary teachers from the North regarded African Americans as resistant to the missionaries' efforts to "New Englandize" Blacks, who also were angry about being excluded from schools the missionaries had set up for poor Whites, because the larger White community had ridiculed them for attending school with freedmen.[7] The Black community regarded these separate schools for Whites as preferential treatment. The picture Jones paints, therefore, is one of fractiousness and divisiveness between the White and Black communities that was driven by White oppression and by the White teachers' impression that the Black community was equally prejudiced against Whites and generally ungrateful for the favors offered them.

This was why White power holders, particularly in the South in the late nineteenth and early twentieth centuries, wanted to deny the liberal arts to African Americans; they felt that such a training would spoil Blacks for the work they were supposed to do. Meant for lives as servants and manual workers, African Americans were deemed, against all evidence, too backward and undisciplined to bring an intelligent or effective reading to classical texts, which were regarded as the exclusive domain of Whites. This occurred, says Veronica T. Watson, during "a time when social Darwinists were still arguing that 'lesser' races should be allowed to 'naturally' decline so that the fitter Caucasian race could thrive . . . and scholars in the nascent field of sociology were classifying humankind into superior and, of course, inferior, races."[8] As Watson cogently argues, particularly in her chapter on the 1957 desegregation of Central High School in Little Rock, Arkansas, allowing the so-called lesser races to decline was necessary to keep Black students out of White-controlled spaces to maintain the fiction of White superiority. This vaunted superiority was threatened especially by the Little Rock Nine's traversing of Central High's corridors and classrooms, which would shatter any complacent notion of Whiteness.

Equally destabilizing to the fiction of Black inferiority and inherent difference was this elegant statement in Morehouse's 1898–99 catalog, which defined the aim of its classics course: "To give the student such a knowledge of these languages as will enable him to read them rapidly and accurately. . . . Stress is placed on these two particulars [i.e., translation of Greek and Latin into idiomatic English and the etymology of English words derived from Greek and Latin] in order that the student may gain from his study of Greek and Latin a higher appreciation of his own language and greater facility of expression in it."[9] Morehouse's 1902–3 catalog more or less repeated this mission statement: "To give the letter and spirit of the classics, and to improve English expression." *Sic transit* Black inferiority.

Industrial versus Liberal Arts Education

Industrial education was an idea that had been around for a long time. There were discussions of the suitability of industrial education for Black students even as early as the 1830s in the North. However, with the founding of Hampton Institute by the Civil War general Samuel Chapman Armstrong in 1868 and its great success in raising money, the predominantly White trustees of Black colleges throughout the South increasingly saw industrial education as a way to gain White approval and raise money. We should not quickly dismiss outright this notion of gaining White approval as merely an accommodationist tactic. Indeed, the very idea of an educated Negro in any capacity was inflammatory in a great many places in the South, and numbers of schools were burned and teachers and students attacked simply for advocating for an education of any kind. After all, it is rather difficult to teach and study when you fear for your life. The following letter by a student addressed to the Freedmen's Bureau from Forsyth, Georgia, dated July 22, 1867, illustrates the hostility to African American education during Reconstruction:

> Sir Sir [sic]: I write to inform you of a most Cowardly outrage that took place last Saturday night. Our teacher whom we have employed here was shot down by a crowd of Rebel Ruffians for no other cause than teaching School.
>
> General, this is the second teacher that has been assaulted. The Rebels make their brags to kill every Yankee teacher that they find. We do not know what we may do if the Military does not assist us. The Freedmen are much experienced at such an outrage.
>
> [signed] George H. Clower, William Wilkes &c, Freedmen.[10]

After the success of Hampton and then with the founding of Tuskegee by Armstrong's most famous protégé, Booker T. Washington, vocational and industrial education was an idea whose time had come. At Fisk the pressure to discontinue its classical curriculum, part of a national trend, was strong. As Joe M. Richardson notes, increasingly the thinking at Fisk was that "knowledge of Latin, Greek, and higher mathematics would be of little value in guiding a mule down cotton rows or in laying bricks."[11] However, the teachers at Tuskegee were usually from Fisk and Atlanta University. Indeed, as Du Bois noted in his essay "The Talented Tenth,"

> The demand for college-bred men by a school like Tuskegee, ought to make Mr. Booker T. Washington the firmest friend of higher training. Here he has as helpers the son of a Negro senator, trained in Greek and the humanities, and graduated at Harvard; the son of a negro congressman and lawyer, trained in Latin and mathematics, and graduated at Oberlin; he has as his wife, a woman who read Virgil and Homer in the same class room with me; he has as college chaplain, a classical graduate of Atlanta University; as teacher of science, a graduate of Fisk; as teacher of history, a graduate of Smith—indeed, some thirty of his chief teachers are college graduates, and instead of studying French grammars in the midst of weeds, or buying pianos for dirty cabins, they are at Mr. Washington's right hand helping him in a noble work. And yet one of the effects of Mr. Washington's propaganda has been to throw doubt upon the expediency of such training for Negroes, as these persons have had.[12]

With this statement Du Bois exposed the imposture of Tuskegee's mantra of practical and industrial education as the only fit training for African Americans at the dawn of the twentieth century.

CLASSICS AS TOOLS OF EMPOWERMENT **101**

A Challenge Overcome

The pressure for Fisk to change its curriculum came as early as the 1880s. As was the case for most cash-strapped institutions, the president of Fisk, George Augustus Gates (1851–1912), was on a continual hunt for funds. In that search he learned, as most Black college presidents of the era did, that fundraisers at Hampton and Tuskegee had already tied up almost all northern funds, private and philanthropic. In 1884 Gates accepted monies from the Slater Fund, in exchange for which he set up a workshop and some painting classes, but not much more. Gates's successor, James Griswold Merrill (1840–1920), also accepted Slater money and began a domestic science course for female students. The Slater Foundation wanted a bigger commitment and was willing to give Fisk $5,000. Merrill and the trustees accepted the money, but with the proviso that "Fisk did not expect to make farmers, carpenters, machinists, laundrywomen, dressmakers . . . but to teach [students] the underlying principles of chemistry and physics as applied to modern industry and agriculture."[13] Clearly, this stance adversely affected the board's fundraising for the next several years, but the trustees did not veer from their commitment to the classical curriculum. Throughout this time the American Missionary Association (AMA) and later the United Church of Christ maintained their commitment to funding Fisk as best they could, with no marked diminution in the liberal arts curriculum, even as it offered courses in agriculture and home economics among its college subjects, but with a view to training teachers in these subjects for colleges and universities.[14]

Tools of Nonviolent Resistance

The situation was a bit different at the Georgia State Industrial College, established outside Savannah in 1891. In fact, a great many things were different about Georgia State Industrial College. This school was actually the subject of a news story in the *Christian Observer* of December 28, 1904. Under the headline "Colored Evangelism," the paper asked, "Can the negro be educated?" The article recounted a visit to the school by the Reverend William E. Boggs, D.D. (1838–1920), the former chancellor of the University of Georgia. The article noted that "it was his privilege to visit, unannounced, that school each month. He said he saw, in his own words, their *black* negro teacher [original emphasis] put Greek exercises, involving fine points of the language on the board for the pupils. Doctor [Boggs] said he would not have undertaken to do the work without special preparation. He said those young negroes solved difficult problems in mathematics, necessitating the use of logarithms in or-

102 CHAPTER FOUR

der that the work might be reduced. He [Boggs] said, 'It is the gross moral and spiritual darkness that keeps them down.'"[15]

As future events would demonstrate, Boggs was something of a prophet or else just an objective observer of southern race relations. Georgia State Industrial College was founded because the state wanted to, and did, accept funds from the first Morrill Act of 1862, which was designed to create land-grant colleges. Because Georgia had no provision for creating a Black land-grant institution, it gave $8,000 of Morrill money to Atlanta University (a private church-supported school) to help educate Georgia's Black citizens. However, state legislators learned that some White students also were attending Atlanta University, since it had no race requirements for entry. This would not do. Therefore, the legislators cut off the Morrill money.[16]

However, to receive funds from the second Morrill Act of 1890, Congress required that southern states provide learning facilities for Black students, hence the creation of Georgia State Industrial College.[17] Its first president, Richard Wright Sr. (no relation to the novelist), though born a slave, was able, through the intervention of Gen. Oliver O. Howard (1830–1909), to receive his bachelor's degree from Atlanta University in 1876 and his law degree in 1879. With his appointment as president of Georgia State Industrial College, Wright became the first Black president of a Black college. In addition to his administrative duties, Wright taught Latin and Greek, which he had learned at Atlanta University and Wilberforce Divinity School.

At Georgia State Industrial College, the courses were agricultural, mechanical, normal, and classical. Its professors came from Atlanta University, Lincoln College in Pennsylvania, Oberlin College, MIT, and Florida A&M College. One of Georgia State's many classics professors was Loring B. Palmer (1875–1935), a graduate of Atlanta University and the son of Dr. Fred Palmer (1834–1919), the inventor of Palmer's Skin Whitener.[18] Things were progressing nicely at Georgia State until the state commissioners began to think about what was happening there. They had started this school so that they could receive "their" share of the Morrill dollars, but now it looked as if the students were getting a real liberal arts education, not just industrial training.

As Richard Wright Jr. (1878–1967) noted in his autobiography, *87 Years behind the Black Curtain* (1965),

> The main thing they [the state commissioners] wanted was a Negro-American school so as to enable the State of Georgia to get her share of the United States land grant fund. But they did not want to give Negro-Americans a "white man's education." The chair of the state commission at one commencement said, "I believe in educating you people. The state of Georgia needs intelligent Negroes

(pronounced 'Niggras'); but I do not believe in educating you people to want things you can never get. We must educate the Negro to be the best possible Negro and not a bad imitation of a white man."[19]

How to do that? Very simple: "Cut this Latin out and teach these boys to farm."[20] Wright recounts further,

> I shall never forget the profound impression made upon the students when President Wright [Wright Jr.'s father] told us the decision of the [state] commission to drop Latin and Greek. He begged us not to leave the college. The President stated that the teachers had agreed to give lessons in the forbidden courses at night and in the afternoon if we would remain. Consequently, for more than a year, I studied Calculus and the Greek and Latin poets, Sophocles, Homer, Horace, and Ovid, as extra-curricular activities, in the homes of my teachers, who taught outside of regular class hours and received no compensation.[21]

So surprised was the state commission at the sincere interest and persistence of both students and teachers that the classics were restored to the curriculum.

There is another way to interpret this event. When the classics courses were cut from the curriculum, the students threatened to leave. This was not an idle threat. All these first students at Georgia State Industrial College for Colored Youth were from Augusta and indeed from the same high school, the Asa Ware High School, where they had received classical training.[22] The only thing that kept most of them at Georgia State (although some did transfer to other Black colleges) was the faculty's willingness to keep teaching (for no compensation) the forbidden courses outside the classroom. With that threat to leave still hanging in the air, the students and their teachers persisted in reading the classics for more than a year.

The commission found itself in a catch-22 situation. If the students did leave, the state of Georgia would lose its share of the Morrill money, which would more than likely mean no new students would come to Georgia State Industrial College for Colored Youth (the small number of African Americans with a high school education in Georgia all knew what was happening there). This educational conflict did not take place in a vacuum. The year the state commissioners created Georgia State Industrial College for Colored Youth (1891) was the same year that the Georgia cities of Atlanta, Rome, and Augusta enacted their first segregation laws. This generation of college students was thus witnessing the hardening of the caste lines that would be constitutionalized in *Plessy v. Ferguson* (1896). They and their teachers knew what was at stake, but they also knew the powerful position they were in. As

African Americans would do first in the trolley-car boycotts from 1900 to 1906 and then during the bus boycotts of 1953–57, the Black students engaged in nonviolent resistance.[23] In the case of the Montgomery bus boycott, which began in December 1955, when Rosa Parks refused to give up her seat to a White passenger, Black residents walked or carpooled for more than a year, showing their determination to be treated with dignity and respect while financially crippling their oppressors.[24]

We suspect that the commissioners, like most White southerners, did not think that these students were serious about learning Greek and Latin. Rather, studying the languages was merely a game they were playing, and they ultimately would tire of it and stop. But when the students persisted in these studies for more than a year on an extracurricular basis, they demonstrated, as the Black citizens of Montgomery would, just how serious they were. Therefore, rather than lose the students and funds, the commission reinstated the courses. Nor was the faculty punished for circumventing the commission and providing the students with a "white man's education." Let us emphasize that we are not locating the origins of the civil rights movement in this protest. However, we do argue that the same passive nonviolent resistance was one of the many ways in which African Americans attempted to fight the onslaught of industrial education.

"Not in Healthy Sympathy with Industrial Education"

Another example of a school that faced an attack on its classical curriculum is Florida A&M College. The Florida Agricultural and Mechanical College (originally called the State Normal and Industrial School for Colored Students) opened in Tallahassee (on the site of what is now Florida State University) in October 1887, the same day as the State Normal School for White students.[25] The Florida Board of Education elected Thomas De Saille Tucker (1844–1903) as the first president of the State Normal School and Industrial School for Colored Students. But Tucker immediately frustrated the state board's expectations of creating a vocational curriculum. Actually, this was a case not so much of Black dissemblance as a lack of oversight by the board. The governor and former Confederate general Edward A. Perry (1831–89), who served on the board, had apparently failed to look into the educational background and educational philosophy of the man who had been recommended for the school's presidency. Tucker held a baccalaureate degree from Oberlin College and a law degree from Straight College (now Dillard University). He believed that African Americans should be trained in the liberal arts as well as in vocational skills. Thus Tucker and the people he hired, including

Ida Gibbs (1862–1957), another Oberlin graduate and a classics professor, set about creating their teacher-training program, which eschewed the Tuskegee model and embraced the liberal arts program.[26]

As Leedell Neyland and John W. Riley note in *The History of Florida Agricultural and Mechanical University,* "the normal courses consisted of Latin, higher mathematics, and natural, mental, and moral philosophy." During Tucker's tenure the school was designated a land-grant institution entitled to federal appropriations under the second Morrill Act of 1890. Tucker was thus able to acquire funds for teachers' salaries and teaching aids; however, the college's enhanced status also increased governmental pressure to replace the academic program with vocational training. Officials were already calling for Tucker's dismissal on the ground that he was "not in healthy sympathy with industrial education." However, Tucker did nothing to change the liberal arts curriculum: "The preparatory department gave instruction in elements of algebra and Latin and a thorough review of the common branches in addition to music, drawing, and bookkeeping."[27] Tucker adhered to this program until he was pressured to resign due to ill health and the repeated calls to replace the liberal arts curriculum. Tucker's intransigence came with consequences beyond his resignation. Construction of buildings was delayed and some were never completed, and the school never received all the meager funds it had been promised.

Tucker's successor, Nathan B. Young (1862–1933), who held a bachelor's degree in liberal arts from Talladega College and a master's in classics from Oberlin College, had been a protégé of Booker T. Washington and was a Tuskegee faculty member until he clashed with Washington regarding liberal arts versus vocational education. After his time at Tuskegee, Young taught at Georgia State Industrial College for Colored Youth, where he came under the mentorship of the senior Richard Wright.[28] Even while espousing the virtues of manual and industrial training, Young continued the liberal arts program at Florida A&M until 1923, when he too lost his job.[29] During Young's tenure, however, the institution had enhanced its status from a normal school to a college, with a change of name to the Florida Agricultural and Mechanical College. Nonetheless, even during a period of increasing racial tensions, Young had continued to champion a liberal arts curriculum, including classics, in direct defiance of White state officials.

In the wake of Young's forced departure, William H. Howard (b. 1872) was appointed president.[30] State officials opined that Howard would be more amenable to White demands for Black education. Howard had served as an aide to Young, who had promoted him to the rank of Smith-Hughes Professor of mechanical arts and dean of vocational studies, even though Howard held no college degree. The campus at large thought that Howard had been influential in the removal of President Young. Several faculty members resigned in protest of Howard's appointment. The General Alumni Association drew up and circulated a petition calling for Young's reinstatement but received no response from the board. In October 1923 the students drew up their own petition and sent it to the board, which the board filed without taking any action. The students next began boycotting their classes, demanding that the standards of the college not be lowered.[31] The chair of the board sent a note to Acting President Howard, instructing him "to permit no insubordination or 'striking' among the student body at A and M even if he had to expel the entire student body."[32]

Told they must stop the strike, students, being students, did exactly the opposite. This was followed by the burning of the college's main building, Duval Hall.[33] Howard had done exactly the wrong thing in asking the local White sheriff and his deputies to restore order because the deputies and Black students were in constant conflict. The board sent a representative to campus to investigate the possibility of closing the school for a year to let things cool down and to direct Howard to get tougher on the strikers. Howard duly began expelling the strikers, and after the eleventh student was dismissed, the strike collapsed.

But the fight was not over. In November Gibbs Hall, the women's dormitory, burned down. The school brought up on charges of arson three students who said that the burning was revenge for the expulsion of the eleven students earlier in the year. While the college could not produce any proof that these young men were involved, they were nonetheless expelled. Within three months of the Gibbs Hall fire, the hated Mechanical Arts Building burned down. This time no one was charged. Then Howard, continuing his string of bad decisions, hired White guards to patrol the campus and the men's dormitories. The students communicated to Black newspapers all over the South that there was "a reign of terror on the campus with white men standing over us with guns at their sides."[34]

This was finally enough for the board and they made arrangements to replace Howard. In retaliation for the disturbances caused at Florida A&M, the state legislature drastically reduced the school's already meager allotment. Howard's successor, John Robert Edward Lee (1864–1944), born of slave parents, was an honors graduate of Bishop College, founded in 1881 by the Baptist Home Mission Society in Marshall, Texas. Lee served as president of Florida A&M from 1924 to the year of his death, during which time Florida A&M rose from near anarchy to academic distinction. President Lee restored the classics curriculum but also acknowledged a role for industrial education. This latter move brought in much-needed funds from the General Education Board (a consortium of philanthropic groups that supported industrial education).[35]

In his 1902 study, *The Negro Artisan*, W. E. B. Du Bois noted that "the hundred schools giving industrial training have in the last twenty years sent one thousand actual artisans into the world," at a cost of "something between five and ten million dollars." As Francille Wilson observes, "this was less than half the number of black college graduates that negro colleges have produced, and with far fewer resources."[36] Du Bois laid out what he considered the inherent inefficiencies of industrial education. However, there may be an additional or alternate explanation for why it failed. Perhaps the schools were not doing what they said they were doing. Fisk, Georgia State Industrial College, and Florida A&M were examples of outright resistance and insurgency. However, other educators trained in the liberal arts used more subtle tools of resistance and subterfuge (that *hypokrisis*, or adoption of masks, that Tolson advocated) to promote racial uplift. These were the educators and institutions we discuss in the next section: Charles Ayer, president of Jackson College in Jackson, Mississippi; Charlotte Hawkins Brown of the Alice Freeman Palmer Memorial Institute in Sedalia, North Carolina; and the Reverend T. O. Fuller of Howe Institute in Memphis, Tennessee.

The Tools of Dissemblance and Subtle Resistance

Charles Ayer and Jackson College

By working together, the Baptist Home Mission Society and the Baptist Missionary Convention were able to secure funds to create the Natchez Seminary (now Jackson State University) in Natchez, the first capital of Mississippi, in 1877. The seminary began as a normal and theological school in an abandoned and dilapidated hospital, purchased, with its surrounding land, for $5,000. The campus was relocated to Jackson in 1883, and the institution was renamed Jackson College. The college's first president was Charles Ayer (1825–1901), a White northerner from Massachusetts classically educated at Amherst, Colgate, and Newton Theological Institution, whose appointment began on September 1, 1877, at the end of Reconstruction.[37] While Ayer clearly supported the mission of training teachers and ministers, he felt it was important that the students receive a classical education to better prepare them to meet the challenges of the world. With its strong emphasis on Greek and Latin, as well as French and German, the seminary caused great suspicion from the first. What were these Black students being educated to do? To allay these fears, Ayer spoke to the White community only of Jackson College's missionary training and not its normal school.[38]

Jackson College carried on its dual mission of training teachers and ministers from 1877 to roughly 1889, although, like most Black colleges and universities at the time, it struggled financially. In 1889 the John F. Slater Fund offered to make monies available on the condition it establish an industrial department, with courses in "sewing, cooking, carpentry, bricklaying, typewriting and tin work."[39] But there was no diminution in the college's liberal arts program. During Ayer's tenure, enrollment increased from a mere twenty in 1877 to more than one thousand in 1894, the year he retired for health reasons and ceded the presidency to Dr. Luther G. Barrett (1838–1932), who served from 1894 to 1911.[40]

Jackson College's troubles were not over, however. The sight of Black students riding to class on mules with "their greasy lunch bags" angered the college's White neighbors. Rather than counter their anger, Barrett withdrew from the scene of the conflict. In 1902 the college sold its north Jackson property to Millsaps College and took up quarters in west Jackson. There, despite continuing hostility from the White community and threats to Barrett's life, the campus rebuilt and grew, with the support of the American Baptist Home Mission Society. Between 1903 and 1908, the college spent more than $60,000 on the construction of new buildings. As a result of Barrett's negotiating skills and the tools of nonviolent resistance, the campus expanded and enrollment increased. An influx of new teaching faculty included Hubert D. Casey, instructor in natural sciences, literature, and Latin.[41]

Charlotte Hawkins Brown and the Palmer Memorial Institute

While not a historically Black college as such, Palmer Memorial Institute, which became the premier academy for young African Americans during the second third of the twentieth century, embodied high academic achievement. Its head, and tireless promoter, for more than half a century was Charlotte Hawkins Brown (1883–1961), who had been classically educated in the North and refused to accept that African Americans were in any way, intellectually or morally, inferior to Whites. Indeed, she embodied the liberating and equalizing power of a classical liberal arts education with her statement: "I sit in a Jim Crow car, but my mind keeps company with the kings and queens I have known. External constraints must not be allowed to segregate mind or soul."[42]

Brown, who was raised and studied classic American and English literature as well as Latin in Cambridge, Massachusetts, founded the Palmer Memorial Institute in Sedalia, North Carolina, in 1902. The school she began in a rundown building with missing window panes and holes in the roof grew into a nationally recognized preparatory school and junior college for African Americans. The school was named for Brown's mentor and friend Alice Freeman Palmer (1855–1902), the second woman president of Wellesley College and member of the Massachusetts Board of Education. The story of their meeting, which became the most-told anecdote of Brown's life, and one significant for our purpose, goes as follows: One day Palmer spotted Brown, still a teenager, while she was babysitting to earn some spending money. As Palmer put it, with one hand Brown was pushing the baby carriage and with the other was holding her Vergil, which she was reading in the original Latin. When Palmer asked Brown where she studied, Brown replied that she attended the Cambridge English High and Latin School.[43] Their first encounter thus ended. But Palmer inquired later at the school about the young girl reading Latin. Palmer offered financial assistance so that Brown could enter the state normal school for teachers. But before Brown could finish her studies, she accepted a teaching appointment at the AMA-founded Bethany Institute; when the AMA withdrew its support, Palmer took over the school and renamed it the Palmer Memorial Institute.[44] Through Brown's tireless campaigning, public speaking, and letter writing to raise money, the school gained a national and even international reputation and became the school of choice for the children of the cream of African American society before closing in 1971.

At Palmer, Brown developed a classical curriculum modeled on her New England educational experience. But to potential donors, especially at the school's beginning, when she desperately needed White support, she emphasized Palmer's agricultural and domestic training. Palmer did in fact raise livestock and grow its own fruits and vegetables, which were prominently displayed when White visitors came calling.[45] One mollified visitor wrote to Booker T. Washington in 1903 to describe the curriculum at Palmer as "an ordinary English education with a bit of Latin." To further curry White support, Brown even wrote a sentimental novel, *Mammy: An Appeal to the Heart of the South*, published in 1919. *Mammy* was intended to disarm Brown's racist neighbors in the segregated South and appeal to their best image of themselves by reflecting on the "good old days" of slavery. But in her letters of appeal for money, Brown used literature as a means of communicating that she was nonetheless a respectable lady of letters.[46] Her emphasis on deference and good manners was not only meant to promote a sense of self-worth; it was a means of presenting an acceptable Black face to the White majority. Brown told the press in 1921 that she was not interested in racial equality or in anything that might result in racial discord. Her one goal, she said, was

110 CHAPTER FOUR

to aid African Americans through education.[47] Whites applauded what they regarded as a safe objective.

But this accommodation was also a ruse to offset potential White hostility. As one former teacher at Palmer put it, "You would pretend to have a vocational school on the outside, and then you'd go in your classroom and teach [your students] French, or Latin and all the things you know."[48] Thus Latin, at least, was one of the adornments of Palmer Memorial Institute kept hidden from prying Whites' eyes, in rather the same way that Tuskegee's Carnegie Library's elegant classical portico turned inward, away from the main road.[49]

Brown understood that, in a segregated society, African Americans would need to comport themselves in a way that would be acceptable to Whites. She stressed the power of good manners, correct speech, and faultless grooming. In 1940 Brown self-published her second book, *The Correct Thing to Do, to Say, to Wear*, which contained instruction on the proper way to behave at school, at church, and at various social functions. She included "Earmarks of a Lady" and "Earmarks of a Gentleman," which advised, for example, that "a lady . . . does not mark tools, walls, or furniture" and that a gentleman "lets no opportunity whatsoever escape for improving himself." The book's purpose, Brown said, was to "shed any earmarks of color."[50] This stress on educating mind and manners and making oneself useful is one that appeared regularly in the brochures of the Black colleges and universities. But the advice Brown holds out about shedding "any earmarks of color" serves also to make being Black invisible.

Reverend T. O. Fuller and Howe Institute

One of the better-known and more prominent educators during the age of Jim Crow was the Reverend T. O. Fuller (1867–1942). Born the son of slaves in Franklinton, North Carolina, in 1867, Fuller attended Shaw University in North Carolina, where he received a classical and religious education under the tutelage of Dr. Thomas E. Skinner (1825–1905), a former slave owner and minister. In 1898 Fuller was the only African American elected to the North Carolina state senate. That election year was one of the most racially charged ever in North Carolina. Two days after the election a mob of Whites massacred twelve Black residents of Wilmington and burned down the Black newspaper's office. Fuller did serve out his term, which saw the almost total disenfranchisement of African Americans in North Carolina. He opposed it, but to no avail.[51]

In 1902 Fuller moved to Memphis to become minister of a large Black Baptist church and principal of Howe Institute, established in 1888 as Memphis's Baptist and Normal Institute. When Fuller took over Howe, the school offered religious training on the elementary and secondary levels and four years of Latin at the high school level. Although Whites strongly objected to the continuation of classical education for Black students in Memphis (they thought that a classical education would make the students unfit for labor and might even promote social equality), Fuller himself strongly believed that African Americans were equal to Whites based on his reading of the Bible. However, like Brown, Fuller was not a firebrand. He very much believed in interracial cooperation. In 1905, when African Americans throughout the South were boycotting the streetcars to protest the hardening segregation that was forcing Blacks to the rear of the trolleys and streetcars, Fuller refused to support the effort, stating in a letter published in the July 4, 1905, Memphis *Commercial Appeal*, that while he thought the law was wrong, it was still the law and the best way to change it was to bring about cooperation between the races.[52]

At the same time, Fuller did not cede to Whites in all racial matters. As principal, Fuller continued to offer Greek and Latin courses. He made it appear that he was going along with the industrial arts program, but he continued on his own course. In his interviews with reporters, Fuller maintained the same prudence with which he preached racial harmony by emphasizing Howe's industrial training, never its liberal arts program.[53] According to the Fuller biographer David Tucker, this was a deliberate strategy to gain support from Whites, who wanted Black cooks rather than scholars.[54] However, while Howe advertised itself as an industrial institution, it offered only cooking classes for girls and printing classes for boys. In 1906 the Memphis *Commercial Appeal* paid for the summer cooking classes for the city's Black cooks. This effort received wide publicity; again, nothing was said about the Greek and Latin and psychology courses being offered. Yet when one reads of the courses, the instructors, and the list of graduates of Howe, one is struck by the breadth and depth of advanced training.[55] Throughout its brief history, and despite publicity to the contrary, Howe offered four years of Latin and two years of Greek. All but three of the instructors employed at Howe were liberal arts graduates. And, most telling for the students for whom records survive, the majority went into teaching, preaching, and medicine.[56] But Howe's financial situation remained precarious: it had no endowment and was forced to rely on tuition and donations, which dried up during the Depression. Howe subsequently lost its autonomy and was merged with LeMoyne College in 1937.

112 CHAPTER FOUR

Black Women's Clubs

As a direct outgrowth of their liberal arts education, many Black women worked autonomously to promote the status of their sisters. They accomplished this by founding female academies and by speaking publicly. Other venues for combating racial stereotyping were the Black women's clubs and other self-help organizations founded and run by women. Prominent among them is Mary Church Terrell, classically educated at Oberlin and a former teacher at Wilberforce, who later took a position at the M Street Colored High School (known today as Dunbar High School) in Washington, D.C., and also served on the school board in the District of Columbia. Following her teaching career, Terrell spent two years in Europe. She returned to the United States with the express purpose of uplifting her race. In 1896 she cofounded and served as president of the National Association of Colored Women (NACW); its motto was "Lifting as We Climb." This and other Black women's clubs worked to combat stereotypes of Black women as promiscuous and incapable of monogamy. The clubs were strongly oriented to domesticity and dispensed advice on how to manage homes in ways that remind us of the domestic arts courses taught at Black colleges and universities.

But Terrell's strategy did not end with good housekeeping and mothering. As Beverly W. Jones reports, "Terrell used several strategies to create an interlocking network among Black women in the United States. First, she established communications by a monthly newsletter, the *National Notes*, to channel information about the programs and objectives of the organization. Each issue contained editorial comments from President Terrell inviting all existing clubs 'with well-defined aims for the elevation of the race for membership.'" Terrell also organized biennial conventions in cities outside Washington with large Black populations, including Nashville, Chicago, and Buffalo. These conventions showcased art exhibits and hosted lectures on maternity, proper dress, and care of the home but also on literary topics. By drawing ever more elite educated women of color into such organizations and creating local affiliates of the NACW, Terrell embraced Du Bois's "Talented Tenth" philosophy—that is, that a band of elite women would lift up the race.[57]

Like her Black counterpart Charlotte Hawkins Brown, founder of Palmer Memorial Institute, but also like Jane Addams (1860–1935), the founder of Hull House, Terrell "maintained that the female's monopoly on virtue obliged her to be the pivotal force in the advancement of society."[58] Even as they emphasized women's traditional gender and domestic roles, Terrell and other educated Black women were consciously subverting racial stereotypes and therefore challenging White women to rethink their opinions of their Black sisters as merely servants and caregivers. Important to this message of uplift was the promotion of selfhood through writing in the form of newsletters, memorials, scripts for plays, and yearbooks. Black women's clubs moved literacy beyond the confines of their individual organizations. They produced their own reports recounting their history and activities for dissemination among other women's clubs, both Black and White, without the restrictions of male-dominated publishing industries. Belying their pledge to "labor modestly," these Black women's groups strove to build up the image of their race and to argue as well for gender equality.[59]

In this discussion of literacy and advocacy, we cannot help but reflect on the ways in which the classical liberal arts education of Brown, Terrell, and other educated Black women—notably Anna Julia Cooper (1858–1964), classically trained teacher and scholar and Terrell's colleague at M Street High School—informed their sense of self-worth and their zeal to promote the interests of African American women and indeed all African Americans. This zeal to memorialize and celebrate Black women extended to the name of the Phillis Wheatley Home in Cleveland, Ohio, founded by Jane Edna Harris Hunter (1882–1971) in 1911 to help house and assist young working women of color who were excluded from the YWCA and similar White organizations.[60]

This chapter has described the various modes of dissemblance, passive resistance, and political activism practiced by scholars, students, clubwomen, and administrators who believed that the education they were providing, receiving, and administering was doing what a classical liberal arts education ought to do—that is, train individuals who could stand up and demand their rights as full citizens of the republic. Promotion of vocational and industrial education over the liberal arts was resisted by those very scholars and their students whom one would least expect to be social movers and shakers.

Nonetheless, all in the name of usefulness, White America continued to question the value of a classical education for African Americans, indeed for Americans generally, as a preparation for the roles they were expected to fill in the rapidly industrializing United States of the late nineteenth and early twentieth centuries. Black America countered by adducing its own reasons for retaining the classical curriculum, again in the name of usefulness. Despite this argument for utility, however, classics remained an area of contestation between White and Black America. This is the subject of the final chapter.

CHAPTER 5

Practicality and the End of Classics

From the point of view of the White man as well as the superior type of Negro it is a question still whether these universities founded by generous men or by generous religious communities are not too narrowed in usefulness by their imitation of eighteenth to nineteenth century English and Scottish Universities and Colleges. They still afflict the Negro and the coloured man . . . with an inordinate and wholly unnecessary amount of Greek and Latin grammar and literature.
—Sir Harry H. Johnston, *The Negro in the New World*

Latin is good, but it is not everything *at the present day.*
—J. Havens Richards, S.J.

In this chapter we examine further how both Black and White educators addressed the suitability of the classics for African Americans, following the rise of the research university and the expansion of the curriculum to include courses addressing the needs of a rapidly modernizing America. This development was occurring while African Americans were being subjected to greater degrees of racial violence and segregation in all areas of public life. Therefore, what practical good would a training in dead languages do, especially for a low caste, when the classical course was rapidly losing primacy in America at large?

The question of what constitutes practicality in education has been addressed several times in our nation's past. In the late nineteenth and early twentieth centuries, the question was often concerned with the value of an elitist education heavy in Latin and Greek language and literature, which was regarded as increasingly irrelevant at a time of growing industrialization and therefore a greater reliance on a suitably trained workforce that was more oriented to the future, not focused on the past.

In 1894 Charles W. Eliot (1834–1926), the influential president of Harvard University, introduced a college curriculum based on electives. With this came the dropping of the classical languages as a requirement.[1] This was a time also when the number of those attending White colleges was expanding to include working-class students, as well as women and minorities, thus exacerbating concerns about which courses best served this new diverse college population.

Classics, Black or White?

Two reports relevant to the continued role of classics for African Americans are *Higher Education of the Negro: Its Practical Value*, by Horace Bumstead (1841–1919), president of Atlanta University (1890), and *The Practical Value of Latin*, printed by the Classical Association of the Atlantic States (1915). These reports are particularly salient for the respective dates of their appearance, in that they encompass the period from Booker T. Washington's Atlanta Compromise speech, of 1895, to the premiere of that racist cinematic spectacle glorifying the Ku Klux Klan, *The Birth of a Nation*. While both reports address similar concerns about the goal of higher education, they define them in racially disparate ways.

Bumstead's report, surveying the twenty-five years that had elapsed since the end of the Civil War, points to education's need to address "the appalling illiteracy of the masses" of African Americans, their "criminal tendencies," and their crushing poverty. His narrative of the crippling effects of "savagery in Africa and slavery in America" recalls the "centuries of heathenism and slavery" decried by the Atlanta University catalog for 1882–83, which education needed to address and remedy. Subscribing to a form of social Darwinism, Bumstead identified several classes of Negroes. The task of education therefore was to discover those with exceptional ability. The work of the exceptional few among African Americans, says Bumstead, is "to help . . . stem the tide of animalism and materialism that is ever threatening to sweep them away."[2]

But what sort of education, specifically, does Bumstead recommend? "I mean," he says, "a curriculum in which the humanities are prominent, and in which intercourse with books and personal contact with highly educated teachers constitute the chief sources of power. Let us, furthermore, understand such a curriculum to be handled not in any dry-as-dust spirit, but with the most modern methods of teaching, and with the most direct and practical application to the needs of modern life as they will be encountered by the students pursuing it." Those subjects to be pursued are "the study of history, and science, and language, and philosophy, and mathematics" by exceptional Negroes for their own social uplift and that of the race. Indeed, when the college-educated Negro returns home, he makes his fellows "wise by proxy." This does not mean, however, that

> they are all going to learn Latin and Greek from their representative, or make him a little demi-god of culture for their worship. But it does mean this: That

in every community of Negroes it ought to be possible for the common people, occasionally at least, to look into the face of a college-bred man or woman of their own race, and catch something of inspiration from its high attainment. Currents of culture and progress are ever being set in motion among the masses of mankind by this sort of educational induction, even where no direct efforts are put forth to that end.

The uplift so fervently desired will be achieved by well-trained teachers. This, in short, is for Bumstead the practical end of a liberal arts education for men and women of color in the United States of the late nineteenth century, which is expressly to cancel out the doleful legacy of their African past.[3]

A quarter century after Bumstead came *The Practical Value of Latin,* geared to a very different audience from the one Bumstead was addressing. Whereas Bumstead's appeal was to both African American men and women and thus gender inclusive, this call to retain Greek and Latin in the curriculum addresses an audience overwhelmingly male and White. This audience needs to be swayed by the ability of classical study to increase their earning power, and thus their overall success, as well as to enhance their cultural cachet; for example, "The men trained by the study of Latin may be clerks, but they will be something more—, salesmen, but something more—, politicians, but skillful statesmen too—, merchants, but also cultivated gentlemen. This 'something more' is often the determining factor in success, in a way few young men pause to consider."[4]

The bulk of the report consists of testimonials by the elite: physicians, academics, lawyers, and politicians. The differences between this and Bumstead's work of 1890 are stark. The classical languages promote "manliness"; for President Woodrow Wilson (no champion of racial equality), classics "holds a sort of primacy in the aristocracy of natural selection." Says C. H. Grandgent, professor of romance languages at Harvard University, "Through the Classics the man of European stock, from ancient times, almost until our own day, has received his mental discipline; it is they that have taught him how to observe, how to discriminate, how to reason, how to remember. . . . They have cultivated the taste and broadened the horizon." *Practicality* is defined for their purposes as "knowing the best that has been thought and said by our greatest predecessors."[5] Thus the classically educated man (women are not included) will, even if in business, become a more well-rounded being and therefore more successful; he will develop into a natural aristocrat. And he will be White and of European descent.

Howard University's Statement on the Usefulness of a Classical Education for African Americans

The appeal to culture generally transcended the racial divide and became a powerful argument for the primacy of the classical curriculum. But for the Black community itself, culture went beyond mere window dressing. It was a call to a deeper, more profound humanity. In November 1907 Howard University held a celebration to mark its fortieth anniversary and the inauguration of its new president, Wilbur T. Thirkield (1854–1936), who championed higher education for African Americans. The program was full and included testimonials by alumni who had gone on to distinguish themselves in various professions, as well as by college faculty. Thirkield spoke eloquently to the changing face of modern education in his address, "The Meaning and Mission of Education." As Thirkield states, modern education

> has given true place to the modern sciences, history, economics, sociology, philosophy, literature, and physical training, along side of Latin, Greek and Mathematics, which once held exclusive sway. It has broken the tradition that education is for an aristocracy; has made education free and democratic; has made education not for luxury, but for life; not the badge of class distinction, but equipment for service. Education, then, makes its appeal not to the intellect alone, but to the entire man. A rounded personality, wit, foresight, insight, widesight, is the supreme outcome.
>
> What knowledge, then, is of most worth? We answer, the knowledge that can be wrought most effectively into the fabric of life; that will ennoble and strengthen character; that will develop personality; that will equip man for his place and part in the real work of the world.[6]

Such "real work of the world" is to be accomplished by an elite corps of Black men and women, whom Thirkield calls "the elect tenth" (a clear reference to W. E. B. Du Bois's "Talented Tenth"). The training for the uplift of the race—for that is the purpose of higher education for African Americans—includes manual and domestic training, in addition to modern education science, economics, and sociology. Indeed, the cause is a sacred one, described in language reminiscent of what we found in catalogs of other colleges, and a cause that needed to be trained on the southern United States, where the need was greatest. The address of the Honorable James Carroll Napier (1845–1940), businessman, lawyer, politician, and civil rights leader, on the occasion of Howard's fortieth anniversary is a direct appeal to its graduates to work with and for African Americans in the South:

118 CHAPTER FIVE

The work of the graduates of Howard University, as well as those of other like institutions, ought for years to come to be largely confined to the southern portion of our country. The so-called Negro problem is there to be wrought and *rightly* settled. The Negro himself must have [a] voice in its settlement; and who can do more to aid in the accomplishment of this end than the cool-headed, well-balanced Negro. The millions there are constantly crying out for you to come and help in the upward struggle. Will you not hear and answer the cry? Will you not come over into Macedonia and help us? It may require some sacrifice, but before the end comes the reward will doubtless be a rich one.[7]

Such is the goal of a practical education, realized once more as part of a messianic mission to uplift the race.

What, then, is the place of the Greek and Latin classics within higher education for African Americans at the dawn of the new century? George Morton Lightfoot, professor of Latin at Howard, in 1908 recommended a classical education as a stay against what he saw as the encroachment of materiality into modern life. While the humanities may at first glance seem irrelevant to the increasing call for a training that will outfit its graduates for a useful occupation, Lightfoot adduces reasons voiced by other classicists of the time to show why the classics ought to be retained, using the language of utility: "The aim of instruction in the departments of Classical languages is the same as that in all other departments of study in the University—viz., to assist in fitting young men and women for the higher duties of citizenship and to make them efficient members of society." The classical languages lay a firm foundation for English and offer insight and breadth of judgment. In short, classical study helps create leaders who will thrive in their respective professions and, in doing so, benefit the race.[8]

To Benefit the Race by Ending Classics

Ironically, political, social, and economic gains for African Americans during the twentieth century resulted in increasingly negative attitudes toward the study of the classics, which again was deemed not useful by its critics, including some African Americans themselves. In the words of one disgruntled exponent of the dilemma faced by modern Black intellectuals, "One need never have read the *Iliad* to function competently as a manager at Macy's."[9] By the turn of the twentieth century, especially by the time of World War I, there was an increasingly strong reaction against classics for African Americans as a mere parroting of the traditional White man's education, which did nothing to uplift the race. This was the argument brought by the classically trained

Carter G. Woodson (1875–1950), journalist and founder of the Association for the Study of African American Life and History. Classical education, Woodson argued, turned the Black reader away from developing an independent identity. Haroon Kharem, speaking in his own role as an educator (he is a professor at Brooklyn College), reiterates Woodson's argument: "He [Woodson] asserts African American children are educated not only to embrace a Eurocentric worldview, but also a pedagogy that disparages their own African American culture. African American heritage is either erased or disparaged, black children are given a curriculum on the preeminence of European culture and history. Woodson believes that American education not only colonizes but corrupts the minds and hearts of black children."[10]

In the view of Woodson and others, classical training was simply another tool of the dominant racial culture to encode and validate the superiority of Whiteness.[11] The retrenchment in the teaching of the classics was occurring even at elite White institutions. This was the result partly of the increasing emphasis on teaching the hard sciences and on "career-oriented" courses of study, as was happening at Harvard.[12] But in the case of Black colleges and universities, it was also the result of expanding the Hampton-Tuskegee model of industrial education for African Americans in preparation for the lives they were expected to lead in the strictly segregated United States. Classics as a course of study for African Americans was therefore viewed as merely impractical and even deleterious to their best interests. Even the classically influenced Frederick Douglass had himself advocated for a practical education for African Americans to alleviate what he described as the social diseases of "poverty, ignorance, and degradation." Those African Americans who have pursued a classical education, says Douglass in an 1853 letter to Harriet Beecher Stowe, "have found themselves educated far above a living condition, there being no methods by which they could turn their learning to account."[13]

Indeed, much of the twentieth-century literature on the state of education for African Americans reads as a chronicle of ill-preparedness, inadequate or inappropriate instruction, and economic hardship. A report titled *The College-Bred Negro American*, edited by W. E. B. Du Bois and Augustus Granville Dill, was published by Atlanta University Press, under the auspices of the Slater Fund, following the Fifteenth Annual Conference for the Study of the Negro Problems, held at Atlanta University on May 24, 1910. The report was based on "college catalogs, letters of officials and the reports of 800 Negro graduates." It is both an uplifting and dispiriting document: uplifting in that it praises Black colleges and universities for educating the overwhelming majority of African American college graduates at a time of entrenched racial disharmony and exclusion; dispiriting in its assessment of how Black colleges and universities had to be more like high schools than institutions of higher learning, given the dearth of secondary schools for African American children in the South.[14]

The estimated number of class hours devoted to "Ancient Languages," accounting for variables across institutions, ranged from 10 to 23 percent of total class hours. Slightly more than half of those men and women who did receive a college degree (53.8 percent) were engaged as teachers, one of the few elite occupations open to them. In light of their limited resources and the need for graduates to be trained for jobs they could fill, the report states, under the heading "Resolutions of the Fifteenth Atlanta Conference": "We believe the amount of Greek and Latin in college should be gradually reduced"—a not-surprising outcome, given the Slater Fund's funnelling of what monies were available into practical instruction for African Americans.[15] As a result, as gleaned from the catalogs themselves, the number of class hours devoted to classics instruction at Black colleges and universities began to decline.

Efforts by Black colleges and universities to retain the classical curriculum, even after it was falling out of favor at White colleges, was criticized by educators such as Thomas Jesse Jones (1873–1950), whom Du Bois called "that evil genius of the Negro race" but who was in fact White.[16] In his book *Negro Education: A Study of the Private and Higher Schools for Colored People in the United States*, published in 1917, Jones states, "The colleges have been . . . handicapped by the tenacity with which they have clung to the classical form of the curriculum. They have had an almost fatalistic belief not only in the powers of the college, but in the Latin and Greek features of the course. The majority of them seem to have more interest in the traditional forms of education than in adaptation to the needs of their pupils and their community. Ingenuously, some of their leaders have been urging secondary schools to prepare their pupils for college rather than life."[17]

A study titled *General Education in the Negro College*, by Irving Anthony Derbigny (1899–1957), published in 1947 but based on data on twenty Black colleges collected before World War II, spoke especially to a lack of resources: "The Negro college, that queer child of fate and circumstance in a democracy, began its group existence less than a century ago. . . . In comparison with American colleges generally, the Negro college is not a well-to-do institution. Its strength is rather a rugged leanness and an indomitable will to survive, held firm by the belief that the future perhaps can scarcely be more hazardous than the past."[18]

Derbigny's report cited as a chief inadequacy the emphasis on classics and its inability to furnish a proper training for African Americans in the midtwentieth century: "To center all or even a great part of the student's learning upon the remote past, with only passing reference to present-day conditions, is to prepare him for life in a civilization which has long ago passed away. Or to expect the adolescent to transfer, without considerable aid, the insights obtained from a study of the golden age of Pericles to the solution of the problems of municipal government in the city of Chicago is indeed to tempt the gods. All studies show that where direct learning is possible it is greatly to be preferred."[19]

In 1965 Earl J. McGrath (1902–93) published *The Predominantly Negro Colleges and Universities in Transition*, his own disparaging assessment of the current curriculum at Black colleges. In it McGrath voiced similar concerns about the dearth of scientific courses and what he considered the colleges' overemphasis on the humanities:

> In sum, the curricula of the predominantly Negro colleges, although varying widely from institution to institution, are heavily weighted in favor of the humanities and reciprocally reduced in the natural and social sciences. This curricular imbalance accentuates—and if allowed to persist, will perpetuate—academic and vocational deprivation among Negro youth. The predominantly Negro colleges need to strengthen their programs, in part by enriching existing courses, in part by adding completely new instruction. These additions and expansions are needed at once to extend educational opportunity for the individual Negro student and to make his full potential services available to American society as a whole.

To alleviate such stagnation in the curriculum, McGrath pointed to the need to hire additional faculty in the sciences. The broadening of course offerings would attract more young men and rectify the lopsidedness in the gender makeup of the student body—that is, the far greater number of women students pursuing careers in primary and secondary education (which McGrath recognized as still one of the few white-collar professions open to African Americans at the time). McGrath, then, paints a picture of dearth, of lack, and of the danger of low expectations. Negro institutions, as he calls them, "are inadequate to meet the needs of many young people. . . . The most disturbing disclosure is the complete lack in many colleges of majors in such fields as physics, mathematics, and economics. . . . *The curricular options in the predominantly Negro colleges must be expanded if many Negroes are not to be kept in low economic and social status by narrow curricular options.*"[20]

122 CHAPTER FIVE

This question of the relevance of the classics to the lives of African Americans and, more broadly, the role of the liberal arts in today's academy is one still being asked, as Black colleges face continued challenges. Recently, Black colleges and universities have begun to receive increased appropriations from the federal government, private philanthropists, and their own alumni. This, combined with increased enrollments, is allowing these institutions to envision a brighter economic path forward.[21] But with these resources being relegated to the hard sciences, the liberal arts have seen further cutbacks. Howard University's once thriving classics program—indeed, the last at a historically Black college—was closed in the spring of 2021. Only the four tenured members of the department were retained and then were relocated to other departments.[22] The classics department's closure attracted widespread and heated media coverage, stating that this move "buys into White supremacist narratives over what kind of education Black people should have. And it denies the crucial role the Black-centered study of classics has played in the Black experience in America."[23]

Bias lingers against the very idea of classically educated African Americans, particularly those of prominence and accomplishment who are thought to pose a danger to the racially entrenched status quo—which is precisely why African Americans continue to push back by employing the classics in their arsenal of tools of greater inclusion and resistance to entrenched racism.

EPILOGUE

Bridging Two Worlds

Throughout the history of the United States, but particularly after the Civil War, African Americans have had to bridge two worlds. Helene Cooper, writing in the *New York Times* in 2009, described the then middle-aged Black children of 1969 who attended elite colleges and who went on to assume prominent places in business, the law, and politics. Without naming him, the article adduced W. E. B. Du Bois's "double consciousness," which he described first in an 1897 *Atlantic Monthly* article and republished as an essay in The *Souls of Black Folk*. There Du Bois defined "double consciousness" for African Americans as an awareness both of oneself and of how one is perceived by others. For the children of 1969, as Cooper called them, it meant a sometimes uneasy movement "between the world their skin color bequeathed them and the world which their college degree opened up for them."[1] A special case in point is President Barack Obama, whose rise engendered an especially corrosive and polarizing political rhetoric, in part for his appropriation of classical culture.

We turn our attention to an article by Philip Kennicott, published in the *Washington Post* after then presidential candidate Obama's historic acceptance speech at the conclusion of the Democratic National Convention in Denver in 2008. Obama spoke outdoors at Invesco Stadium before a crowd of eighty thousand people. To give his podium scale in such a large arena, it was flanked by Doric pillars and an entablature. This setting, reminiscent of many classical buildings in the United States, England, and elsewhere, brought derision from conservative commentators who mocked it as "the temple of Obama" and "Barackopolis." Kennicott placed this whole conservative backlash within the context of the recent U.S. culture wars and conservatives' defense of the "pure classics" against what they see as the onslaught of multiculturalism.[2]

But it goes beyond multiculturalism and extends to the issue of Whiteness. The question Kennicott asks, more salient for our purposes, is this: "Is race involved in the criticism of Obama's 'temple'?" The debate, he rightly points out, was about whether Obama could lay claim not only to a classical architecture but also to a classical culture that remains deeply encoded as European and White. In an op-ed that appeared in the *Columbus* (Ohio) *Dispatch* just days after Obama's inauguration in January 2009, Victor Davis Hanson, a senior fellow at the Hoover Institution and himself a classicist, voiced his own disparagement of what he regarded as candidate Obama's grandiosity by resorting to classical tropes: "He [Obama] adopted Greek temple sets at the Democratic convention. And like Zeus on Mt. Olympus, he talked about making the planet cool and the oceans recede." Beyond the dispute over his claims of kinship with classical culture, such racist rhetoric sought to delegitimize Obama's right to claim the office of the presidency, because he had (mis) appropriated the trappings of Whiteness.[3] Despite, then, the progress African Americans have made in all areas of American intellectual life and their ascension to high political office, misconceptions about African Americans' intellectual capacity continue, instigated by lingering prejudice even among those who may profess to be unbiased. Animosity toward educated and successful African Americans, particularly when it comes to positive associations with the classical world, remains rife in American thought.

Little or nothing demonstrates Cooper's "uneasy movement" more than the hostility historically faced by African American teachers and students of the liberal arts, the classics especially, as we have demonstrated in this book. For Du Bois himself, as for William Sanders Scarborough, Mary Church Terrell, and others, the classical liberal arts education he received was truly transformative and thus unnerving to the White establishment, because it enabled him to consort with the greatest minds of the ages, not as a racial inferior but as a welcome colleague. This recalls Charlotte Hawkins Brown's oft-repeated statement about the self-empowerment of a classical liberal arts education: "I sit in a Jim Crow car, but my mind keeps company with the kings and queens I have known. External constraints must not be allowed to segregate mind or soul." Thus do both Du Bois and Brown call on a lineage based not on biological race but rather on a direct descent from learned ancestors going back to antiquity.

Says Du Bois:

I sit with Shakespeare and he winces not. Across the color line I move arm in arm with Balzac and Dumas, where smiling men and welcoming women glide in gilded halls. From out of the caves of evening, that swing between the strong-limbed earth and the tracery of the stars, I summon Aristotle and [Marcus] Aurelius and what soul I will, and they come all graciously with no scorn nor condescension. So, wed with truth, I dwell above the veil. Is this the life you begrudge us, O knightly America? Is this the life you long to change into the dull red hideousness of Georgia? Are you so afraid lest peering from this high Pisgah, between Philistine and Amalekite, we sight the Promised Land?[4]

In opposition to the proponents of industrial education, who thought that it would take generations of manual labor before African Americans could hope to ascend to anything like equality, Scarborough and Du Bois argued that the Black race deserved the right to full civic engagement through Africa's historical link with the classical world. In 1918 Du Bois penned an unsigned article in the NAACP's magazine, the *Crisis*, titled "A Philosophy in Time of War." In it Du Bois extended the scope of history to include all human history. African Americans "are a symbol of antiquity, justice, and redemption. Compared to that, the pretensions of White Europe and America are small indeed."[5] The following excerpt from Du Bois's article may serve to recapitulate what we have been discussing in regard to educated African Americans' link to both Africa and the classical world and Black agency as a result of their being "the first civilization":

> Calm and with soul serene, unflurried and unafraid we send a hundred thousand black sons and husbands and fathers to the Western Front and behind them rank on rank stand hundreds of thousands more.
>
> We are the Ancient of Days, the First of Races and the Oldest of Men. Before Time was, we are. We have seen Egypt and Ethiopia, Babylon and Persia, Rome and America, and for that Flaming Thing. [sic] Crucified Right, which survived all this staggering and struggling of men—for that we fight today in and for America—not for a price, not for ourselves alone, but for the World.[6]

In closing, we must ask ourselves, in this politically and culturally fraught moment, whether the lessons of inclusion and equality that the study of the classics fostered will prevail. With the hardening of the racial divide, the hazards of double consciousness remain only too real. For African Americans the trick, traditionally, has been to keep one foot in their African heritage while negotiating with a dominant and often hostile White culture intent on co-opting the classics for its own racist purposes.[7] This negotiation includes the right to embrace the cultures of Greece and Rome, which educated African Americans saw as their rightful legacy. Classics teachers and their students formed manners of thinking and speaking through their acquaintance with the languages and literatures of ancient Greece and Rome. By their rigorous study of grammars and texts, African Americans of all socioeconomic levels became fuller participants in the republic of ideas.

The White majority historically has regarded classically educated African

Americans as chimaeras, freaks, seeking a foothold in a civilization that had nothing to do with them. Yet despite the unremitting forces in league against it—those calls for a training fitted to "hewers of wood and drawers of water"—African America continues to stake its claim to the classical world. To do so and succeed is the truest test of its Africanness and, with that, its full humanity.

NOTES

Introduction. Our Heritage Too

1. Jarratt, "Classics and Counterpublics"; Goings and O'Connor, "Black Athena before *Black Athena*"; Goings and O'Connor, "Lessons Learned"; Malamud, *African Americans and the Classics*.

2. For a broad discussion of the literature on Black education from 1890 to the 1980s, see Butchart, "Outthinking and Outflanking."

3. Kiwanda and Zap, letters to the editor, *Chronicle of Higher Education*, March 4, 2012; Carlson, "Future of American Colleges."

4. Gilpin Faust, "University's Crisis of Purpose," 19.

5. Ibid.

6. See Barnard, *Empire of Ruin*, 120.

7. Joshua 9:21 (King James Version).

8. This move was not limited to Black colleges and universities, as parents across the board began to insist on an education that would prepare their children for jobs in an America rapidly industrializing after 1865. Even Jesuit-founded colleges, such as the College of the Holy Cross in Worcester, Massachusetts, reluctantly added commercial courses such as bookkeeping and basic math. Mahoney, *Catholic Higher Education*, 68.

9. Jewell, *Making of a Middle Class*, 9.

10. This was the traditional philosophy of Jesuit colleges. Mahoney writes, "One of the fundamental tenets of humanist educational theory—that study and mastery of the literary texts of antiquity fostered individual virtue and the development of upright character—dovetailed neatly with the Jesuits' commitment to 'help souls.'" *Catholic Higher Education*, 41. There was thus a distinctly religious incentive to study the classics.

11. Such passive and submissive behavior is accepted even by so recent a study, excellent as it is, as Hager's *Word by Word*.

12. Ronnick, *Autobiography of William Sanders Scarborough*; Scarborough, *Works of William Sanders Scarborough*.

13. Hairston, *Ebony Column*, 20n45.

14. See, for example, Goings and Smith, "'Unhidden' Transcripts."

15. Jarratt says, "Access to the classical curriculum was a mark of acceptance into full personhood—a transcendence of the veil of racism, in [W. E. B.] Dubois's terms." "Classics and Counterpublics," 142.

16. On the classics as a disciplinary formation, see, for example, Harloe, *Winckelmann*.

17. For more on this, see Rankine, "Community-Engaged or Public Scholarship."

18. "Letter to James Madison," April 27, 1809, cited in Barnard, *Empire of Ruin*, 2n7.

19. Gates, *Figures in Black*. See also Bok, *Secrets*; and Bok, *Lying*. In *Methodology of the Oppressed*, Sandoval discusses the adoption of masks as exposing White postures as ar-

129

tifacts (that is, social constructions), whereas the White power structure regarded masks as natural.

20. Gundaker, "Hidden Education," 1605, 1599.

21. See Geiger, *American College*, 160.

22. This dispute between the liberal arts and practical instruction is still ongoing. According to Price, training for a profession is contributing to the continuing decline of Black America. Black colleges and universities should, rather, concentrate on training public intellectuals with a liberal education. See "Historically Black University." Price's jeremiad against what he considers the base motives of historically Black colleges and universities in promoting vocational training at the expense of the *artes liberales* completely ignores the fact that Black colleges have historically had to embrace at least some practical instruction to receive critical funding.

23. These statistics were provided by M. Anderson, "Look at Historically Black Colleges"; and Bridges, "African Americans."

24. Edgcomb, *From Swastika to Jim Crow*, 57.

25. Jarratt, "Classics and Counterpublics," 135.

26. Hairston, *Ebony Column*, 2.

27. Jarratt, "Classics and Counterpublics," 140.

Chapter 1. Formative Influences of Classical Culture

1. See Span, From *Cotton Field to Schoolhouse*.

2. V. Franklin, *Black Self-Determination*. See also Cornelius, *Read My Title Clear*, 2.

3. Cornelius, *Read My Title Clear*, 9; McCoskey, "Subjects of Slavery,"104–73.

4. See Williams, *Self-Taught*, 18.

5. Gundaker, "Hidden Education," 1592–93.

6. Says the historian Derrick Bell, commenting on the unquestioned appropriation of White supremacy, "Even those whites who lack wealth and power are sustained in their sense of racial superiority and thus rendered more willing to accept their lesser share, by an unspoken but no less certain property right in their 'whiteness.' This right is recognized and upheld by courts and the society like all property rights under a government created and sustained primarily for that purpose." "White Superiority in America," 139. See also Harris, "Whiteness as Property," which examines how Whiteness, originally constructed as a form of racial identity, evolved into a form of property, historically and presently acknowledged and protected in American law. After the end of slavery, Whiteness became the basis of racialized privilege, providing societal benefits not available to people of color.

7. Jefferson, *Life and Selected Writings*, 243.

8. Immerwahr, "Hume's Revised Racism," 481.

9. *Dred Scott v. Sandford*, 60 U.S. 393 (1857).

10. Cook, "Ultimate Meaning and Significance," 18, emphasis added.

11. Gundaker, "Hidden Education," 1593.

12. Douglass, "Mrs. Auld," 275.

13. Burton, *Personal Narrative*, 112, 114.

14. Said, *Orientalism*, 204, emphasis added. In *Souls of White Folk* (1920), Du Bois addresses the continuance of the racist imperialism of European colonialism following World War I: "How many of us today fully realize the current theory of colonial expan-

sion, of the relation of Europe which is white, to the world which is black and brown and yellow? Bluntly put, that theory is this: It is the duty of white Europe to divide up the darker world and administer it for Europe's good." In Roediger, *Black on White*, 192.

15. The concept of the "West" and "Western culture," "to name a heritage and object of study," as Appiah describes it in his book *Lies That Bind*, "doesn't really emerge until the 1880s and 1890s, during a heated era of imperialism, and gains broader currency only in the twentieth." The idea, however, that the cultures of Greece and Rome were a direct inheritance to Christian Europe dates to the Middle Ages. The link only grew in the Renaissance, when lost works of antiquity were being rediscovered and disseminated (200, 196).

16. Said, *Culture and Imperialism*, 9, 50.

17. Van Steen, *Liberating Hellenism*, 107–8, 18.

18. Nelson, *Color of Stone*, 59. See also Ceserani's *Italy's Lost Greece*.

19. Nelson, *Color of Stone*, 104.

20. Hairston, *Ebony Column*, 36; Koch and Peden, *Life and Selected Writings*, 240. Ronnick cites a passage from Hume's essay "Of National Characters" (1753) that similarly derides the classical learning of the Jamaican-born Black Francis Williams, who had studied Latin and mathematics at Cambridge University: "About Williams, Hume said, 'tis likely he is admired for very slender accomplishments, like a parrot who speaks a few words plainly.'" Ronnick, "Racial Ideology," 170. See also Ronnick, "Francis Williams," 19–29.

21. We must acknowledge here as well the writings of Jupiter Hammon (1711–1805), a Black slave belonging to the Lloyd family of Long Island, New York. The circumstances of his life were similar to Wheatley's: a precocious child whose talents were recognized by a kindly master, who in turn educated him and gave him access to the master's library. The first published Black American slave, Jupiter Hammon wrote poems on various subjects and essays. Coincidentally, he published a eulogistic poem in 1778 titled "An Address to Phillis Wheatley, Ethiopian Poetess, in Boston." See Brucia, "African-American Poet."

22. Hairston provides a more extensive discussion of Phillis Wheatley's education in *Ebony Column*, 25–30.

23. Phillis Wheatley, "To Maecenas," line 40, in Wheatley, *Complete Writings*.

24. While flattered by Wheatley's celebratory poem, Washington was unsure how to respond. As Hairston describes it, "Struggling to find an appropriate form of address for an African woman slave who had provided 'new evidence of [her] genius,' Washington settled on a compromise between the uncomfortably genteel and the awkwardly racist: 'Miss Phillis.'" Hairston, *Ebony Column*, 36.

25. Barnard, *Empire of Ruin*, 42.

26. Wheatley, *Complete Writings*, xxxv.

27. Barnard, *Empire of Ruin*, 57.

28. Barnard, *Empire of Ruin*, 57, 25. For the work by classicists and scholars, see, for example, Spigner, "Phillis Wheatley's Niobean Poetics."

29. In her book of poems engaging with the life and work of Phillis Wheatley, Jeffers explores the questions of who gets to write poetry and why the treatment of Wheatley as both a poet and a Black woman still resonates today. *Age of Phillis*. See also Greenwood, "Politics of Classicism."

30. Kaesser, "Rudolf Pfeiffer." The same scholarly rigor would be applied as well to the study of scripture. See Gura, *American Transcendentalism*, 99.

31. On the "godlike" Greeks and the racializing arguments of Müller and others, see Konaris, *Greek Gods in Modern Scholarship*.

32. Bernal, *Fabrication of Ancient Greece*, 309–10. See also Richard, *Golden Age of the Classics*, 190, for a willful misreading of Herodotus on racist grounds by the Southerner John C. Calhoun. Whereas Calhoun states that Herodotus says nothing about "wooly-headed" Africans, Herodotus does in fact refer to the Ethiopians, "a people he admired." Wolf himself restricted the study of antiquity to the Greco-Roman world. Theodor Bergk (1812–81), in his own contribution to *Altertumswissenschaft*, published in the *Zeitschrift für die Althertumswissenschaft*, dismissed any claims of Egyptian influence on classical culture. See Whitaker, "*Alterthumswissenschaft* at Mid-Century," 137.

33. Bernal, *Fabrication of Ancient Greece*, 293. Adler provides a good overview of the backlash, by Mary Lefkowitz and other critics, against this and other statements by Bernal. *Classics*, 113–71. In "Proof and Persuasion," Blok highlights what Lefkowitz sees as Bernal's misstatements about perceived racism and anti-Semitism in Müller's scholarship. But see Young on the Aryanization of not only Greece but also Egypt and with that the denial by European and American racists in the nineteenth century of Africa in the formation of classical culture. "Afterlives of *Black Athena*," 174–88. For more on the Aryanization of Greek civilization during the nineteenth century, see Said, *Culture and Imperialism*, 15–16. See also Appiah's discussion of nineteenth-century classifications of intellectual and morphological differences among the so-called White, Yellow, and Black races, as in Arthur de Gobineau's influential 1855 *Essay on the Inequality of the Human Races*. Gabineau, credited with developing the theory of the Aryan master race, influenced prominent nineteenth-century anti-Semite Richard Wagner and, later, leaders of the Nazi party. Appiah, *Lies That Bind*, 113.

34. For the mapping of social hierarchies and transgression, see, for example, Pile, *Body and the City*; and Stallybrass and White, *Politics and Poetics*. Such social coding is of course nothing new; several classical examples may be adduced, among them, Plato (*Timaeus* 69c–70a, 90a), Cicero (*De officiis* 1.150–52), and Seneca (*Epistles* 88.21). Cicero, for example (*Letters to Atticus* 1.16.1), refers condescendingly to Rome's lower classes as *sordem urbis et faecem*—that is, "the filth and dregs [or, more graphically, shit] of the city." It is not inconceivable that educated Whites in the United States were drawing, even indirectly, from such ancient texts. Even if they were not, they had inherited social and racial attitudes that were current in antiquity and reinforced in subsequent centuries. For other analyses of racist associations between Black bodies and dirt, see Thomas, "Strange Fruit," 385; and Markovitz, *Legacies of Lynching*, 99.

35. Page, *Rebuilding of Old Commonwealths*, 132–33. The African American novelist, essayist, and journalist George S. Schuyler (1895–1977) offered his own bemused appraisal of Whites' opinions of the Black mind: "The amazing ignorance of whites—even Southern whites—about Negroes is a constant source of amusement to all Aframericans. White men who claim to be intelligent and reasonable beings persist in registering surprise whenever they hear of or meet a Negro who has written a novel, a history, or a poem, or who can work a problem in calculus." "Our White Folks," 80.

36. For more on the link between the influence of Greek civilization in modern America and the strict maintenance of White racial purity, see Ronnick, "Politics of Classical Education," 61–62.

37. Aristotle, *Politics* 1254b 16–21.

38. Calhoun, "Speech on the Reception." Malamud cites another proslavery advocate, William John Grayson, who praised Aristotle's *Politics*, stating, "A complete household or community is one composed of freemen and slaves." Malamud, *African Americans and the Classics*, 129. Grayson's understanding of *household* is that of the Greek *oikos* and the Roman *familia*, which would have included slaves as well as parents and children—that is, everyone living in the household.

39. See Barnard, *Empire of Ruin*, 142, 119.

40. Richard, *Golden Age of the Classics*, 189–90.

41. Crummell, "Attitude of the American Mind."

42. See Gura, *American Transcendentalism*, 31.

43. Briggs, *Soldier and Scholar*, 18–19.

44. Ibid., 291–94. See also Lupher and Vandiver, "Yankee She-Men."

45. See Durrill, "Power of Ancient Words."

46. For Gildersleeve's articles, see Briggs, *Soldier and Scholar*, 361–88, 389–413. Malamud writes that Gildersleeve "proudly fought on the side of the Confederacy, and viewed what he and other Southerners called the 'War Between the States' through the lens of the Peloponnesian War." *African Americans and the Classics*, 142.

47. For further background on African Americans' drive for literacy and self-empowerment in the antebellum period, see, for example, Goings and O'Connor, "Lessons Learned"; and Hall, *Faithful Account*, chap. 1. See Malamud, *African Americans and the Classics*, 19–22, for educational efforts by antebellum Blacks to establish schools and academies to teach Greek and Latin; for example, the Watkins Academy for Negro Youth, founded in 1820 in Baltimore by William Watkins, who was not only an educator but an active member of the American Moral Reform Society as well as an outstanding antislavery advocate.

48. Raboteau, *Fire in the Bones*, 43; Barnard, *Empire of Ruin*, 82.

49. In his still controversial book, *Stolen Legacy* (1954), George James, professor of logic and Greek at Livingstone College, argues that the Egyptians and not the Greeks were the primary sources of Greek philosophy, which the Greeks appropriated, often without acknowledgment.

50. Malamud, *Ancient Rome and Modern America*, 1.

51. Schueller, introd. to Dorr, *Colored Man Round the World*, xxix–xxx.

52. Hall, *Faithful Account*, 30, 34, 62.

53. Ibid., 65.

54. Richard, *Golden Age of the Classics*, 194–95.

55. See H. Wilson, "Edward Wilmot Blyden."

56. Ronnick, "Latin Quotations," 101; July, "Nineteenth-Century Negritude," 74.

57. July, "Nineteenth-Century Negritude," 83.

58. "Princes shall come out of Egypt: Ethiopia shall soon stretch out her hands unto God." Psalms 68:31 (KJV).

59. Hall, *Faithful Account*, 168. The more religiously oriented Black colleges and universities would especially stress piety and truth.

60. McHenry, *Forgotten Readers*, 50.

61. Jarratt, "Classics and Counterpublics," 140.

62. McHenry, *Forgotten Readers*, 340n48. The nexus between African American publications and reading rooms was clear: both encouraged literacy and self-help. Indeed,

NOTES TO CHAPTER ONE **133**

Charles B. Ray, a minister and managing editor of the *Colored American*, and Samuel Cornish, founder of *Freedom's Journal, Rights of All, and Colored American*, established reading rooms and libraries as well as lecture series. See Hall, *Faithful Account*, 37–38; and Jarratt, "Classics and Counterpublics," 140.

63. Samuel Cornish, *Rights of All*, September 18, 1829, in Glaude, *Exodus*, 28. The brackets are Glaude's.

64. Nathaniel Paul, "An Address Delivered on the Celebration of the Abolition of Slavery in the State of New York, July 5, 1827," *Freedom's Journal*, August 10, 1827, reprinted in Woodson, *Negro Orators and Their Orations*, 76.

65. Barnard, *Empire of Ruin*, 85.

66. Hinks, introd. to Walker, *Appeal*, xli.

67. Walker, *Appeal*, 3, emphasis in the original.

68. Koch and Peden, *Life and Selected Writings*, 241.

69. Walker, *Appeal*, 15, 18.

70. Ibid., 22.

71. Ibid., 17–18.

72. Hinks, *To Awaken My Afflicted Brethren*, xxvii.

73. In "Nero, the Mustard," Williamson draws on evidence from the Anglophone Antilles.

74. For the names of classical authors cited by other prominent African Americans in the antebellum United States, see Malamud, "Classics and Race."

75. Malamud, *African Americans and the Classics*, 67.

Chapter 2. Founding of Black Colleges and Universities

1. Quoted in J. Anderson, *Education of Blacks*, 5.

2. Geiger, *American College*, 140.

3. J. Anderson, *Education of Blacks*, 5, 134.

4. See, for example, Drago, *Politicians and Reconstruction*; R. Morris, *Reading, Writing, and Reconstruction*; and Richardson, *Christian Reconstruction*.

5. Williams, *Self-Taught*, 1.

6. Richardson, *History of Fisk University*, 7.

7. Fisk University, "First Annual Catalogue," 1867, 19, emphasis in the original.

8. Such gradation was by no means confined to Black schools; it was widespread among denominational colleges. At Boston College in the 1880s, with its seven-year course of study, students at the lower levels made up 60 percent of the total student body. In the 1890s only 35 percent of Boston College's students actually began college work. Moreover, the overall number of enrollees remained small. Mahoney estimates that colleges in 1890 averaged only 106 students. Mahoney, *Catholic Higher Education*, 122, 133. See also Geiger, *American College*, 147.

9. Anderson and Moss, *Dangerous Donations*, 23.

10. Fisk University, "Catalogue of the Officers and Students," 1912–13, 26.

11. Simmons College of Kentucky, Kentucky Normal and Theological Institute, catalog, 1881–82, 26, under "Aims and Methods."

12. Morris Brown University, catalog, 1883–84, 11.

13. Hankins, *Second Great Awakening*, 106.

14. See Gura, *American Transcendentalism*, 157, 159.

15. Geiger, *American College*, 142–43. As documented by Du Bois and Dill, by the first decade of the twentieth century, White student attitudes at Oberlin had hardened against African American students, who were being denied membership in campus clubs. *College-Bred Negro American*, 42–43. For instances of discrimination against Black students after Reconstruction, see Waite, "Segregation of Black Students."

16. Fairchild, *Oberlin*, 19.

17. Mahoney provides a good example of such strict discipline at the Jesuit-founded Boston College: "As in other Catholic institutions, students at Boston College began each day with mass, with some of their number being pressed into service as altar boys. Traditional devotional practices punctuated the rest of the day. . . . Students lined up and marched between classes and events. Gentlemanly conduct was expected, while smoking and boisterous behavior were prohibited." *Catholic Higher Education*, 119–20. See also Geiger, *American College*, 132. Harvard's move in the 1880s to make chapel attendance voluntary was seen as a step toward godlessness.

18. Oberlin College students read Arthur J. Macleane's edition of works by the lyric poet and satirist Horace, with notes in English, according to the course catalog for 1864–65 and thereafter. Others included later were the Roman lyric poet Catullus, the satirist Juvenal, and the comic playwrights Plautus and Terence, though in expurgated editions.

19. Fairchild, *Oberlin*, 55, emphasis in the original.

20. Ibid., 145.

21. Scarborough, *Autobiography of William Sanders Scarborough*, 46; Lawson and Merrill, "Antebellum 'Talented Thousandth,'" 148.

22. See McGinnis, *History and an Interpretation*, 139–55, on the Wilberforce faculty and their alma maters.

23. Fairchild, *Oberlin*, 72.

24. Strictly speaking, there were no Black universities until 1957, when Howard graduated its first doctoral student. Edgcomb, *From Swastika to Jim Crow*, 89.

25. Edgcomb, *From Swastika to Jim Crow*, x.

26. In *College-Bred Negro American*, Du Bois and Dill provide a table (14–15) listing thirty-two Black colleges that cumulatively had 1,131 students taking college classes, as well as 3,896 students in high school for the academic year 1909–10. The ratio, then, is roughly three to one, at least for these particular institutions. Geiger estimates that in 1890 the average collegiate enrollment at Black colleges was 26 students. *American College*, 135.

27. Richardson, *Christian Reconstruction*, 135; Polt, "Anti-Catholicism."

28. Schools founded by the AMA include Arkansas Baptist College (1884), Atlanta University (1865), Avery Normal Institute (1865), Barber-Scotia College (1867), Benedict College (1870), Bennett College (1873), Bethune Cookman (1904), Bishop College (1881), Claflin University (1869), Clark College (1865), Concordia College (1922), Fisk University (1866), Florida Memorial University (1879), Guadalupe College (1884), Johnson C. Smith University (1867), Knoxville College (1875), Leland University (1870), LeMoyne Normal and Commercial School (1870), Morris College (1908), Oakwood University (1896), Paine College (1882), Philander Smith College (1877), Rust College (1866), Saint Augustine's College (1867), Saint Paul's College (1888), Saint Philip's College (1898), Selma University (1878), Shaw University (1865), Straight College (1869), Talladega College (1867), Texas College (1894), Tillotson Collegiate and Normal Institute (1881), Tou-

galoo College (1869), Virginia Union University (1865), Virginia University of Lynchburg (1886), Vorhees College (1897), and Wiley College (1873).

29. Campbell and Rogers, *Mississippi*, xiv.

30. Richardson, *History of Fisk University*, 40–41.

31. DeBoer, *His Truth Is Marching On*, 366.

32. McPherson, "White Liberals and Black Power," 1358–59. This paternalistic and racist sentiment of southern education was expressed in starker terms in 1908 by Charles Dabney, president of the University of Tennessee until 1904, later professor of chemistry at the University of North Carolina and director of the Southern Education Board's propaganda division. The board's purpose was to keep African Americans subordinated by promoting industrial arts over a liberal arts education. Said Dabney, "The Negro is a child race, at least two thousand years behind the Anglo-Saxon in its development." Dennis, "Schooling along the Color Line," 144; Dennis, "Skillful Use of Higher Education," 116.

33. McPherson, *Abolitionist Legacy*, 203–24.

34. Richardson, *Christian Reconstruction*, 44. For example, in Fisk University's "Catalogue of the Officers and Students," 1894–95, the fees range from $3.50 to $5.00 per term, depending on discipline, for day students. Combined tuition and board cost $12.00 per month, which included "furnished room, heat, light and washing" (57).

35. Flemming, "Effect of Higher Education," 209.

36. Benedict College, catalog, 1917–18, 12.

37. Simmons College of Kentucky, State University, catalog, 1919–20, 43, under "Dress"; 1910–11, 22, under "Regulations"; M. Jones, "Student Unrest," 73. In his essay "Diuturni silenti" (1924), Du Bois inveighed against the draconian rules in force at Black colleges. Using Fisk as an example, he states, "The temptation and the tendency is to cramp self-expression, reduce experiment to the lowest terms and cast everything in an iron mould. College women are put in uniforms in a day when we reserve uniforms for those who are organized to murder for lackeys and for insane asylums and jails. Not only is the system of uniforms at Fisk ineffective and wasteful, but its method of enforcement is humiliating and silly" (47).

38. See Jewell, *Making of a Middle Class*, 108–9. Tuskegee Institute demanded similarly strict dress codes. Its "Twenty-Fourth Annual Catalogue," 1904–5, mandated "simplicity and economy in dress," with uniform dresses for women and uniforms, complete with military-style caps, for men (21).

39. Bartlett revisits the dress code in a 2009 article notable for its rhetoric. It focuses on the all-male Morehouse College's "Operation Pull Up Your Pants," whose ostensible purpose was to forbid the wearing of saggy pants that drop well below the waist but adding as well strictures against (repeat, male) students "wearing women's clothes, including dresses, tunics and pumps," which critics called "intolerant, even homophobic." The caption beneath a waist-down photo of three students in loose droopy slacks reads, "Historically black colleges are cracking down on 'unbridled' personal expression, like saggy pants." The use of the loaded word *unbridled* especially suggests lewdness and impropriety, thereby reviving racial stereotypes. See "Black Colleges React."

40. The average age of Fisk students in 1883 was twenty-six. Richardson, *Christian Reconstruction*, 126.

41. See, for example, Benedict College, "Tenth Annual Catalogue," 1891–92.

42. Anderson and Moss, *Dangerous Donations*, 4–5, 85–108, 155–90. See also Dennis, "Skillful Use of Higher Education," 117.

43. Atlanta University, "Catalogue of the Officers and Students," 1882–83, 27–28, under "Concerning Endowments." About fifty years later, in 1923, Fred L. Brownlee, the AMA secretary, was touting the successes of the AMA: "In less than a century, an enslaved race, ministered to by such agencies as the A.M.A., has passed from barbarism to a race of noble, cultured, intelligent Christian men and women." Drago, *Initiative, Paternalism, and Race Relations*, 140. Kharem regards this as typical of the White colonialist attitude regarding African Americans: "White people were always characterized as civilized while nonwhite people were labeled 'savage.' . . . The mythical image of the wild man/woman created by European superstitions was perceived to lack any social or linguistic abilities, yet possesses extraordinary sexual prowess and physical strength, walks around naked, and resorts to cannibalism." *Curriculum of Repression*, 37.

44. The *Atlanta University Bulletin*, ser 2, no. 1 (1910), under the heading "The Educational Need of American Negroes," speaks to the nobility of work for African Americans in a graded racist society: "We must have in this world hewers of wood and drawers of water. We want somebody to hoe corn and pick cotton and cook and look after the children. But while we must have these, we ought not to have *mere* hewers of wood and drawers of water. . . . Just as in a household we would like the cook to realize that if she cooks well, putting a spirit of high service into her work, she is to that extent the partner of the master of the house, who may be pleading for justice in the court or preaching the gospel in the church, so we want all sections of human society to realize the truth that each in his place is a part of the whole" (8).

45. Tougaloo College, catalog, 1918–19, 23.

46. Ibid., 28. This was part of a move during the 1920s toward courses "dealing with the Negro." It was meant to be a form of curricular innovation, both at Tougaloo and at other Black colleges. Morris Brown University's 1931–32 catalog lists, under "Social Sciences," a section on Negro history, including a course called "Negro Problems": "The aim of this course is to acquaint the students with the social, economic, political and religious forces, which enter into the relations between the races of America" (29). There is also a Negro history course covering slavery and Reconstruction, "racial adjustment, and the struggle of the Negro for social justice" (29). White colleges viewed such courses negatively because they were marked with a so-called Negro identity. See Renker, *Origins of American Literature Studies*, 92.

47. Tougaloo College, catalog, 1931–32, 25.

48. Influential in Avery's founding was Francis Lewis Cardozo, a prominent member of Charleston's African American community and superintendent of AMA work in Charleston, who had been classically educated at the University of Glasgow. He was hired as a professor of Latin at Howard University in 1881. DeBoer, *His Truth Is Marching On*, 181, 196.

49. Drago, *Initiative, Paternalism, and Race Relations*, 82–83.

50. Avery Institute, "Circular of Information," 1882–83, 7–8.

51. Drago, *Initiative, Paternalism, and Race Relations*, 85, 96, 95; Anderson and Moss, *Dangerous Donations*, 29–30.

52. Drago, *Initiative, Paternalism, and Race Relations*, 71.

53. Ibid., 223, 96.

54. Campbell and Rogers, *Mississippi*, xiv.

55. Driskell, *Schooling Jim Crow*, 10–11.

56. See Du Bois and Dill, *College-Bred Negro American*, 17.

57. *Atlanta University Bulletin*, ser 2, no. 1 (1910): 8.

58. Atlanta University, "Catalogue of the Officers and Students," 1894–95, 39; Morris Brown University, catalog, 1913–14, 58.

59. Atlanta University, "Catalogue of the Officers and Students," 1879, 19; 1883–84, 21. On the 1884 catalog, see Bacote, *Story of Atlanta University*, 34.

60. Atlanta University, "Catalogue of the Officers and Students," 1885–86, 21; 1882–83, 29; 1888–89, 33, under "Government."

61. Ibid., 1872–73, 15.

62. Atlanta University, "Report of the Board," 1884, 30, emphasis added.

63. *Atlanta University Bulletin*, ser. 2, no. 1 (1910): 8; no. 4 (1911); no. 7 (1912); Atlanta University, "Catalogue of the Officers and Students," 1894–95, 35, 36.

64. Atlanta University, "Catalogue of the Officers and Students," 1922, 17.

65. Richardson, *History of Fisk University*, 57.

66. Ibid., 15.

67. Anna Julia Cooper, born a slave, recounts how, to gain admission to Oberlin College in 1879, she had studied, while at Saint Augustine's Normal School and Collegiate Institute in Raleigh, North Carolina, "beside the English branches, Latin: Caesar, seven books; Virgil's Aeneid, six books; Sallust's Cataline [sic] and Jugurtha; and a few orations of Cicero;—Greek: White's first lessons; Goodwin's Greek Reader, containing selections from Xenophon, Plato, Herodotus and Thucydides; and five or six books of the Iliad;—Mathematics: Algebra and Geometry entire." Gabel, *From Slavery to the Sorbonne*, 19.

68. Richardson, *History of Fisk University*, 15.

69. Said Chapman in 1881, speaking of the evangelism of the AMA: "Here is our work—to prevent [the emancipated African American] becoming worse than he was before—there is great danger of it. Latin and Greek are not the cure; we must build up character, habits of thinking; the work is mainly intellectual and moral now—to teach the Freedman to see; to get him in his right mind." DeBoer, *His Truth Is Marching On*, 275.

70. Engs, *Educating the Disenfranchised*, 88–114; Meier, *Negro Thought in America*, 85–99.

71. J. Anderson, *Education of Blacks*, 247, 248. In "Schooling along the Color Line," Dennis offers a broader history of the moves in the early twentieth century by so-called progressives in the South to enforce strict school segregation and industrial training for African Americans, all in an effort to maintain White supremacy. See also Dennis, "Skillful Use of Higher Education."

72. J. Anderson, *Education of Blacks*, 247, 248; Meier, *Negro Thought in America*, 89–90.

73. Hampton University, "Catalogue of the Hampton Normal," 1909, 34; 1911, 78.

74. Tuskegee Institute, "Twenty-Fourth Annual Catalogue," 1904–5, 12.

75. Adler, *Classics*, 58; Geiger, *American College*, 153.

76. Nash, "Entangled Pasts," 439.

77. Geiger, *American College*, 162; McMillan, "Negro Higher Education," 13.

78. George Boyer Vashon (1824–78) was a professor of Latin and Greek at Alcorn from 1874 to 1878. Logan and Winston, *American Negro Biography*.

79. Alcorn State University, "Officers and Students of Alcorn University," 1873, 3.

80. Alcorn State University, "Alcorn A. and M. College," 1887–88, 13.

81. Alcorn State University, "Alcorn Agricultural and Mechanical College," 1912–1913, 47; 1914–15, 40–41, 48.

82. Alcorn State University, "Alcorn Agricultural and Mechanical College," 1921–22, 45.

83. Florida Agricultural and Mechanical University, "College Courses of Study," 1915–16, 41, under "Courses for Teachers."

84. Ibid., 1929–30, 65.

85. Alabama Agricultural and Mechanical College, "College of Alabama for Negroes." 1905–6, 26–27.

86. Daniel B. Williams (1861–95), the first Black classicist hired by the state of Virginia, served as an instructor and later a professor of ancient languages at Virginia Normal and Collegiate Institute (now Virginia State University), a land-grant college founded in 1882. Williams's innovative teaching was denigrated by the all-White state board of supervisors, one of whose members, state delegate Paul Cabell, remarked that he saw "Negro scholars in luxuriously equipped quarters and lecture rooms, learning, or pretending to learn, chemistry, Latin and Greek." Cabell duly called for a halt to, in his words, "such nonsense." Becker, "Daniel B. Williams," 95.

87. North Carolina Agricultural and Technical, "Catalogue of the North Carolina State," 1919–20, 20.

88. For the *Commentaries*, see Bennett, *Caesar's Gallic War*.

89. DeBoer, *His Truth Is Marching On*, 153–54.

90. R. Logan, *Howard University*, 13.

91. Howard University, "Catalogue of the Officers and Students," 1890–91, 32.

92. McPherson, *Abolitionist Legacy*, 268.

93. AME schools were Wilberforce University, Morris Brown College, Allen University, Paul Quinn College, Edward Waters College, Kittrell College, and Shorter College. The AME Zion college was Livingstone College. The Colored Methodist Episcopal Church founded Lane Institute and Paine Institute (both later became colleges), Miles College, and Texas College. Negro Baptist colleges were Arkansas Baptist College, Selma University, Natchez College, Shaw University, and Virginia College and Seminary.

94. Tanner, *Apology for African Methodism*, 16, 17. Both Frederick Douglass, the orator and social activist, and Harriet Tubman, the great abolitionist, were members of the AME Church: both embodied the church's activist nationalist ethos.

95. J. Anderson, *Education of Blacks*, 67. Citing an article by Robert Scherer, Anderson notes that "Booker T. Washington was virtually alone in urging that prime emphasis be put in industrial education rather than classical liberal education." Rather, Washington, in conjunction with the industrial philanthropists, was acting as the official mouthpiece of what was actually a larger educational movement.

96. The Cincinnati Conference committee had originally planned to name the new institution the Ohio African University. The members later resolved to name it after Bishop Wilberforce. McGinnis, *History and Interpretation*, 33.

97. Scarborough, *Works of William Sanders Scarborough*, 56; Gerber, "Segregation, Separatism, and Sectarianism," 3.

NOTES TO CHAPTER TWO **139**

98. McGinnis, *History and an Interpretation*, 44.

99. Wilberforce University, "Triennial Catalogue of Wilberforce University," 1872–73, 18–19.

100. Terrell, *Colored Woman*, 61–62.

101. Lewis, *W. E. B. Du Bois*, 153.

102. McGinnis, *History and Interpretation*, 146.

103. Lewis, *W. E. B. Du Bois*, 153; Weisenburger, "William Sanders Scarborough," 220.

104. Ronnick, "William Sanders Scarborough," 1787–93.

105. Weisenburger, "William Sanders Scarborough"; Scarborough, "Educated Negro and Menial Pursuits," 205.

106. Ronnick, "William Sanders Scarborough," 1791. The eminent American historian John Hope Franklin, in his essay "Dilemma of the American Negro Scholar," recounted a similar tale of exclusion in the mid-1940s. When doing research at the Library of Congress in Washington, D.C., Franklin was denied access to the common reading rooms; special accommodations had to be made for him to exclude him from Whites. He was likewise barred from area restaurants. But he took it in good stride, assuring a friend that "for a Negro scholar searching for truth, the search for food in the city of Washington was one of the *minor* inconveniences" (73, emphasis in original). A *New York Times* article eulogizing Professor Franklin shortly after his death in 2009 describes how his peerless scholarship opened up avenues of inquiry not only to African Americans but to other hitherto marginalized groups—namely, women, gays and lesbians, and Hispanics: "Dr. Franklin accomplished this not through advocacy but rather through the traditional means of scholarly inquiry." Applebome, "Scholar and Witness," 5.

107. Du Bois, *Autobiography of W. E. B. Du Bois*, 191. After returning from Germany to the United States or, as he put it, to "'nigger-hating' America!" Du Bois was hired to replace Scarborough. With his dapper cane and white gloves, Du Bois looked out of place in rural Xenia. He described himself as "innocent, arrogant, and dedicated to pedagogical standards that were no more useful" to the people then in power at Wilberforce "than the declensions found in Professor Scarborough's Greek textbook." Lewis, *W. E. B. Du Bois*, 153. Du Bois quickly awakened to the Machiavellian forces that would later drive him from the campus. His tenure at Wilberforce lasted only two years. Du Bois's unwillingness to take part in daily prayers and chapel services rankled the Wilberforce administration. His efforts to build up the library were met with fierce resistance, and his attempt to stage Shakespeare's comedy *A Midsummer Night's Dream* in a picturesque ravine on campus, with student players, ended in failure. (The ravine was later filled in.) Du Bois, *Autobiography of W. E. B. Du Bois*, 190–91.

108. Litwack, *Trouble in Mind*, 78. On efforts in the South by the General Education Board (a nongovernmental organization of wealthy philanthropists supporting higher education) to circumvent racial prejudice and the politics of Jim Crow by appealing to local interest and educational groups, see Malczewski, "Weak State, Stronger Schools."

109. Wilberforce University, catalogs, 1915–16; 1916–17.

110. See Renker, *Origins of American Literature Studies*, 93.

111. Gerber, "Segregation, Separatism, and Sectarianism," 13.

112. "Wilberforce University Annual Report," 1910, 21, in Renker, *Origins of American Literature Studies*, 74.

113. Renker, *Origins of American Literature Studies*, 94.

140 NOTES TO CHAPTER TWO

Chapter 3. Survey of the Classical Texts

1. Jarratt, "Classics and Counterpublics," 140, 135.

2. Fromm, "College Entrance," 187.

3. The following is a sample list of texts and primers available in the late nineteenth and early twentieth centuries for use in the classics classroom. They usually provided vocabulary and notes for the aid of students: Charles E. Bennett, *M. Tulli Ciceronis: "Cato Maior de Senectute," with Notes*, rev. ed. (1897) (this text was part of the Students' Series of Latin Classics); Bennett, *New Latin Grammar* (1895); Bennett, *Caesar's Gallic War* (1903); Bennett, *Cicero's Selected Orations* (1904); Thomas L. Chase, *Selections from Horace, with Notes and a Vocabulary*, revised by Francis H. Lee (1892); Benjamin L. D'Ooge and Frederick C. Eastman, *Caesar in Gaul, with Introduction, Review of First-Year Syntax, Notes, and Vocabularies* (1917); Louis Dyer, ed., *Plato* (1890); Henry S. Frieze, *The Tenth and Twelfth Books of the* Institutions *of Quintilian, with Explanatory Notes* (1865); Basil Lanneau Gildersleeve and Gonzalez Lodge, *Gildersleeve's Latin Grammar* (1895); William Watson Goodwin, *The First Four Books of Xenophon's* Anabasis: *With Notes Adapted to the Revised and Enlarged Edition of Goodwin's Greek Grammar* (1896); Albert Harkness, *Select Orations of Marcus Tullius Cicero, with Explanatory Notes, and a Special Dictionary* (1878); Richard Claverhouse Jebb, *Homer: An Introduction to the* Iliad *and* Odyssey (1898); Harold Whetstone Johnston, *The Private Life of the Romans* (1903); Charles Knapp, ed., *The* Aeneid *of Vergil* (1900); E. P. Morris, ed., *The* Captives *and* Trinummus *of Plautus* (1898); *Pearson's Essentials of Latin* (1908); Clifton Price, ed., *M. Tulli Ciceronis* Laelius de Amicitia (1902); George Stuart, ed., *The* Germania, Agricola *and* Dialogus de oratoribus *by Tacitus* (1875); Frank B. Tarbell, ed., *The* Philippics *of Demosthenes* (1896); John Williams White, *The First Greek Book* (1896).

4. Scarborough, *First Lessons in Greek*, iv.

5. See, for example, White, "Humanizing the Teaching of Latin."

6. White, "Latin and the Reconstructionists," 272; for comparison, see Fisk University, "Catalogue of the Officers and Students," 1912–13, 57. The Lex Manilia, enacted in 66 BCE, awarded supreme military power to Pompey in his battle against Mithridates VI, king of Pontus and Armenia Minor in northern Anatolia (now Turkey). The popular assembly, with the support of some members of the aristocracy, had put this law through against the desires of the aristocracy, at a time when Pompey's popularity with the people was at its peak.

7. Scarborough, *First Lessons in Greek*, iii, emphasis in original.

8. Morris Brown University, catalog, 1923–24, 46–47.

9. For the Chase and Stuart edition of *Tusculan Disputations*, see Chase, *Marcus Tullius Cicero*.

10. See Chase, *Marcus Tullius Cicero*.

11. Fisk University, "Fisk University Annual Catalog," 1923–24, 62.

12. Alston and Spentzou, *Reflections of Romanity*, 214.

13. W. Brown, "On Race and Change," 56.

14. The *Aeneid* had been a staple of classical reading from the early days of the American colonies, either in the original Latin or in a popular translation by John Ogilby (originally published in London in 1644; revised and reprinted in 1654, 1666, and 1675). See Brucia, "African-American Poet," 520.

15. Scarborough read "Birds of Aristophanes" at the American Philological Association in 1886 before it was published as a pamphlet titled *The Birds of Aristophanes*. Even so, the inclusion of Aristophanes in the Wilberforce classics curriculum is somewhat curious, especially for a religiously affiliated institution of the time, in that his plays are thoroughly scabrous, indulging as they do in sexual double entendres and scatology. Aristophanes's comedies are at the same time sharp rebukes of contemporary political figures and Athens's lengthy war with Sparta.

16. Crowell, Andria *and* Adelphoe *of Terence*. But see McCoskey on how slavery was treated in select nineteenth-century Latin grammars printed both before and after the Civil War. Sentences for students to translate, from Latin to English or English to Latin, reveal the vexed attitudes about the behavior and treatment of slaves in such examples as "The master praises his slaves" and "The master flogs his slaves." Although meant as grammar- and vocabulary-building exercises, the master-slave relationships depicted in these sentences, McCoskey says, "reflect the complicated and anxiety-ridden ways slaves were cast as the foil of free Americans, subjects against whom the American project was being written." "Subjects of Slavery," 109–10. Some of these texts, such as Harkness's *Complete Latin Grammar*, were used at Black colleges and universities, where exercises featuring the interrelation between masters and slaves would have aroused a comparable anxiety, though most likely of a different sort, than that aroused among White students.

17. Often these aids to learning grammar and syntax were in the form of rhymes, such as this one to help recall Latin verbs that are followed by the dative case: "A dative put—remember pray— / After envy, spare, obey, / Persuade, believe, command; to these / Add pardon, succor and displease," etc. White, "Humanizing the Teaching of Latin," 515.

18. Lightfoot, *Latin Element*, 1.

19. Johnson, *Nineteenth-Century Rhetoric*, 16.

20. Ganter, "Active Virtue," 464.

21. Johnson, *Nineteenth-Century Rhetoric*, 166.

22. Channing, *Lectures Read to the Seniors*, 25, emphasis added.

23. Quoted in Hairston, *Ebony Column*, 9. See also Jarratt, "Classics and Counterpublics," 143.

24. Both quoted in S. Logan, "Black Speakers, White Representations," 21–22.

25. Bingham, *Columbian Orator*, 246–52.

26. Bond, *Negro Education in Alabama*, 421.

27. Jarratt, "Classics and Counterpublics," 140.

28. Gold, "Nothing Educates Us," 236.

29. Gold, *Rhetoric at the Margins*, 43.

30. See Little, "Extra-Curricular Activities."

31. Jarratt, "Classics and Counterpublics," 140.

32. Scarborough, *Works of William Sanders Scarborough*, 53.

33. Gregory, *Frederick Douglass*, 13.

34. Cicero, *De oratore* 2.310.

35. These photographs range from the first daguerreotypes of 1841 to the photos taken of Douglass the year of his death, in 1895. They are beautifully presented in Stauffer, Trodd, and Bernier, *Picturing Frederick Douglass*.

36. S. Logan, "Black Speakers, White Representations," 22. Margaret Malamud discusses the power of oratory and its link to freedom in the life and work of William G. Allen, who was influential in his lifetime, though a lesser-known orator than Douglass. In 1852 Allen, who had been educated at the Oneida Institute in New York, delivered a speech later distributed in a pamphlet titled *Orators and Oratory*. In it he cited the greatest speakers of antiquity, including Demosthenes and Cicero. After marrying a White woman, Allen narrowly escaped being lynched by a White mob and had to flee to England, where he and his wife died in poverty. See Malamud, *African Americans and the Classics*, 98–102.

37. Douglass's powerful oratory in defense of the liberation of Blacks in America fostered comparisons with Patrick Henry and his famous line, "Give me liberty or give me death." Says Barnard, "In his preface to the first edition of the *Narrative of the Life of Frederick Douglass, an American Slave*, William Lloyd Garrison attested that, upon hearing Douglass speak at an antislavery convention, he felt sure that 'Patrick Henry, of Revolutionary fame, never made a speech more eloquent in the cause of liberty.'" This trope of liberty versus death had been popularized by Joseph Addison's play *Cato: A Tragedy* (1713), which was widely read and performed in North America during the early republic. Barnard, *Empire of Ruin*, 62, 60. The historical Cato the Younger (95–46 BCE) committed suicide rather than submit to the growing tyranny of Julius Caesar.

38. An abridged version of Quintilian's *Institutio oratoria*, in Henry S. Frieze's 1865 edition, was one of the assigned texts at some Black colleges and universities.

39. Scarborough, *Works of William Sanders Scarborough*, 54.

40. Ibid., 55.

41. Dionysius, *On the Admirable Style of Demosthenes*, sec. 32.

42. Quintilian, *Institutio oratoria*, sec. 12, para. 1.1. Quintilian himself borrowed this phrase from *Ad filium (To His Son)*, the didactic treatise of Cato the Elder (also known as Cato the Censor). There Cato expands his meaning of *vir bonus* to include excellence in agriculture: "Vir bonus est, Marce fili, colendi peritus cuius ferramenta splendent" (an honorable man, son Marcus, is skilled in cultivating, and his instruments shine). Says Sciarrino, "In fact, we are not dealing here with two separate precepts, one about oratory and another about agriculture. Critics have long pointed out that the latter expresses the same preoccupations with the definition of the *vir bonus* that we find in the Preface to the *De Agricultura* [*On Agriculture*]; what has gone unnoticed is that agricultural and oratorical themes belong to the same sphere of activities. As the *De Agricultura* teaches us, speaking authoritatively is the same as caring for one's farm since what the latter ultimately means is to exercise one's control over the weave of constraints and possibilities that inform power relations." *Cato the Censor*, 158.

43. "Of the Quest of the Golden Fleece" is chapter 8 in Du Bois, *Souls of Black Folk*.

44. Cook and Tatum, *African American Writers*, 101. See pages 103–4 for a more complete description of Scarborough's painstaking scholarship, based on the best philological methods.

45. Ibid., 96. Calhoun had been overheard as saying "that if he could find a Negro who knew the Greek syntax, he would then believe that the Negro was a human being and should be treated as a man."

46. Scarborough, "Chronological Order." See also Malamud, *African Americans and the Classics*, 18–19.

Chapter 4. Classics as Tools of Empowerment

1. J. Anderson, *Education of Blacks*, 29.
2. Jarratt, "Classics and Counterpublics," 141.
3. Gold, "Nothing Educates Us," 230. Hine, writing about the powerlessness of Black women, describes African Americans' "dissemblance" as an act that "involved creating the appearance of disclosure, or openness about themselves and their feelings, while actually remaining an enigma." "Rape and the Inner Lives," 294.
4. Goings and O'Connor, "Tell Them We Are Rising."
5. Litwack, *Trouble in Mind*, 78.
6. Brazzell, "Brick without Straw," 30, 41.
7. M. Jones, "American Missionary Association."
8. Watson, *Souls of White Folk*, 21.
9. Morehouse College, catalog, 1898–99, 21–22.
10. Sterling, *Trouble They Seen*, 297–98.
11. Richardson, *History of Fisk University*, 55.
12. Du Bois, "Talented Tenth," 45.
13. Richardson, *History of Fisk University*, 61.
14. See, for example, Fisk University, ""Fisk University Annual Catalog," 1923–24, 46, 59–60.
15. Lynn, "Colored Evangelism."
16. Wright, *Behind the Black Curtain*, 33.
17. Ibid.
18. Ibid.
19. Ibid., 35.
20. Wolters, *New Negro on Campus*, 197.
21. Wright, *Behind the Black Curtain*, 36.
22. Wright Sr. "was asked to set up and direct Ware High School in Augusta, Georgia, which became the state's first public high school for blacks." Richings, "Richard R. Wright, Sr."
23. Meier and Rudwick, "Boycott Movement," 757.
24. A. Morris, *Origins*, 51–63.
25. Neyland and Riley, *History of Florida*, 10.
26. Ellis, "Nathan B. Young," 156.
27. Neyland and Riley, *History of Florida*, 14, 41, 14.
28. Several letters in the Booker T. Washington papers outline the conflict between the two educators (Young simply refused to endorse the industrial education model) that would ultimately lead to Young's dismissal from Tuskegee. Given Young's unwillingness to bend, even for Washington, on the liberal arts question, one wonders why Washington decided to recommend him to the Florida Higher Education Commission. See Harlan, *Booker T. Washington Papers*, 68–69, 89–90, 133–34, 145–48, 209–10.
29. Ellis, "Nathan B. Young," 168.
30. Neyland and Riley, *History of Florida*, 78.
31. Wolters, *New Negro on Campus*, 198–201.
32. Neyland and Riley, *History of Florida*, 79.
33. Ibid., 81.
34. Wolters, *New Negro on Campus*, 201.
35. Neyland and Riley, *History of Florida*, 81–88.

36. Du Bois, *Negro Artisan*, 78–79; F. Wilson, *Segregated Scholars*, 37.

37. Charles Ayer's birth and death dates courtesy of Jackson State University.

38. Rhodes, *Jackson State University*, 24, 18.

39. Ibid., 32.

40. Luther G. Barrett's birth and death dates courtesy of Jackson State University.

41. Rhodes, *Jackson State University*, 40–41.

42. Marteena, *Lengthening Shadow*, 92.

43. Ibid., 19.

44. Wadelington and Knapp, *Charlotte Hawkins Brown*, chaps. 1–3; see also Charlotte Hawkins Brown Museum, *Brief History*.

45. DeBerry, "Study of the History."

46. Hoffman, "Minding and Marketing Manners," 25, 24.

47. Wadelington and Knapp, *Charlotte Hawkins Brown*, 96.

48. See interviews of Ruth Totten and Glenda Gilmore, in Wormser, Jersey, and Pollard, *Rise and Fall*.

49. Grandison notes that not only were Black colleges and universities built on the worst scrubland in the area but also that Black college campuses were frequently laid out backward, with the best, often classically inspired, facades turned away from the main road to evade White scrutiny. See "Negotiated Space."

50. Wadelington and Knapp, *Charlotte Hawkins Brown*, 174.

51. For a more detailed description of his life, see Fuller, *Twenty Years in Public Life*.

52. Meier and Rudwick, "Boycott Movement," 769.

53. A. Cooper, *Between Struggle and Hope*, 72.

54. Tucker, *Black Pastors and Leaders*, 60–66.

55. A. Cooper, *Between Struggle and Hope*, 72–73; Powell, "History of Negro Educational Institutions."

56. Fuller, *Twenty Years in Public Life*, 273–77; Powell, "History of Negro Educational Institutions," 25–44.

57. B. Jones, "Mary Church Terrell," 25, 26.

58. Ibid., 26.

59. For a good description of how gendered literacy worked in the struggle for racial uplift, see Gere and Robbins, "Gendered Literacy."

60. *Encyclopedia of Cleveland History*, s.v. "Hunter, Jane Edna (Harris)," accessed June 14, 2023, https://case.edu/ech.

Chapter 5. Practicality and the End of Classics

1. See Polt, who argues that this was a move by Eliot and the Protestant majority to distance American higher education from the traditional Jesuit *Ratio studiorum*, with its emphasis on Greek and Latin, as practiced at Boston University and other Catholic Jesuit colleges. "Anti-Catholicism."

2. Bumstead, *Higher Education*, 3, 13.

3. Ibid., 7, 9–10. Bumstead's argument for the liberal arts as the ideal training for African Americans would be taken up a century later by Price in his response to the emphasis on training for a specific profession that is currently the goal of most colleges and universities. As he states, "Notwithstanding the dignity and worth of vocational pursuits, the creation of a class of HBCU [historically Black colleges and universities]-ed-

ucated black intellectuals ought to be the first priority of HBCUS. . . . It is ultimately black intellectuals, weaned on the insights of the great texts, that initiate and provide the discourse that constitutes a valid intellectual culture." "Historically Black University," 107.

4. Classical Association, *Practical Value of Latin*, 2.

5. Ibid., 21, 31, 36.

6. Thirkield, "Meaning and Mission of Education," Howard University, 6.

7. Napier, "Address of the Hon. J. C. Napier," Howard University, 13, emphasis in original.

8. Lightfoot, "Classical Languages," 4. This echoes the address to utility voiced by another classicist, Charles Elliott, professor of Greek at Miami University in Oxford, Ohio. In a speech of 1850, Elliott stated, "Should the utilitarian, then, ask what advantage there is in spending six or seven years in the study of the classics and other things which cannot be turned into immediate practical use, the answer is; that it forms habits which are necessary to success and usefulness in the world." McCoskey, "Subjects of Slavery," 93–94n19.

9. Watts, "Dilemmas of Black Intellectuals," 502.

10. Woodson, *Mis-education of the Negro*; Kharem, *Curriculum of Repression*, 29.

11. Woodson, *Mis-education of the Negro*, 2–5, 13–15. Jewell discusses the tradition of Eurocentric education at Black colleges and universities, which he sees as biased against African Americans, as it seeks to recolonize the discipline as a White privilege only. This seems to be playing into the victimization model. Though they come to it from different angles, Woodson's jeremiad against classics as anti-African is reflected in the argument in favor of the essential Europeanness of classical antiquity embraced by the recent generation of conservative scholars and belletrists who invoke the classics to uphold their traditionalist Christian values and who promote the *Altertumswissenschaft*, or "science of antiquity," model. "To Set an Example," 16. Two examples from the publisher ISI Books are Kopff, *Devil Knows Latin*; and Simmons, *Climbing Parnassus*. See also Kopff, "Traditional Liberal Arts Curriculum." These apologias are in turn descendants of a classic historical study, Cochrane's *Christianity and Classical Culture*. Cochrane's book, incidentally, was greatly admired by the Anglo-American poet W. H. Auden.

12. Polt, "Anti-Catholicism."

13. Malamud, *African Americans and the Classics*, 27.

14. Du Bois and Dill, *College-Bred Negro American*, 5. Later Du Bois and Dill write, "The report of the United States Commissioner of Education for the year ending July, 1909, showed that in the whole South there were but one hundred and twelve high schools for Negroes. Even the larger cities which provide something of primary and grammar school education for Negroes make little or no provision for their high school training. The results here are two: first, Negro children graduating from the grammar school are unable to find public instruction in high school work; and second, the Negro colleges are without public feeders. To meet this situation the Negro colleges have been compelled to provide in large part their own feeders." (17–18).

15. Ibid., 7.

16. Kliebard, "Evil Genius," 5.

17. T. Jones, *Negro Education*, 56.

18. Derbigny, *General Education*, v.

19. Ibid., 61–62.

20. McGrath, *Predominantly Negro Colleges*, 89, 74–75, emphasis in original.

21. Century Foundation, "Achieving Financial Equity and Justice."

22. This information about the state of Howard's classics program was provided by Howard University professor Norman Sandridge in an email exchange in February 2022.

23. See Kennedy and Murray, "Classics." See also West and Tate, "Howard University's Removal." The department's closure also spurred an online petition begun by student Sarena Straughter, which was signed by thousands, including students who had taken classics courses. Despite the loss of the department, however, Latin and Greek will still, as of this writing, be taught, and some classics material will be fused into an interdisciplinary major. Saunders, "Classics Department Cut."

Epilogue. Bridging Two Worlds

1. Du Bois, "Strivings of the Negro People," 194; H. Cooper, "Meet the New Elite," 6.

2. Kennicott, "Obama amid the Pillars," c01. One example of this antagonism is provided by the late classicist Hugh Lloyd-Jones. In a 2003 article in the conservative journal *Chronicles*, Lloyd-Jones takes special aim at women's studies, gay studies, and Black studies, programs he derides as preaching "a collectivism [with echoes of Hitler and Stalin] that takes the form of an extreme preoccupation with the grievances of certain groups, particularly women, Blacks, and homosexuals." This is done all in the name of—another shibboleth—"political correctness." Lloyd-Jones thus mistakes positive self-identity for persecution mania. "Notes on American Education," 14–15.

3. Hanson, "Rhetoric Won't Keep Nation Safe," A9. His temerity seemingly undiminished, Obama spoke in Athens in November 2016, shortly before the end of his presidency. In his speech to the Athenian citizens, the president celebrated Greek democracy within an African American context: "It was here, twenty-five centuries ago, in the rocky hills of this city, that a new idea emerged. *Demokratia*. . . . *Kratos*—the power, the right to rule—comes from *demos*—the people. The notion that we are citizens—not servants, but stewards of our society. The concept of citizenship—that we have both rights and responsibilities. The belief in equality before the law—not just for a few, but for the many; not just for the majority, but also the minority. These are all concepts that grew out of this rocky soil." Obama, "Remarks by President Obama."

4. Du Bois, *Souls of Black Folk*, 87.

5. Strauss, "Black Phalanx," 49, 54.

6. Du Bois, "Philosophy in Time of War."

7. We write in the wake of the armed insurrection that took place at the U.S. Capitol on January 6, 2021. Among the guns, stakes, and Confederate symbols were such classical reminders as Greek helmets; T-shirts emblazoned with a golden eagle on a fasces, or a bound bundle of rods (symbols of Roman law and governance); and flags embroidered with the classical Greek phrase *molon labe,* or "Come and take them," uttered by the Spartan king Leonidas when the king of Persia ordered him to lay down his arms. This phrase has now become a slogan of American gun rights activists. See Poser, "Iconoclast."

BIBLIOGRAPHY

College Catalogs

Listings of single years refer to courses of study, not complete catalogs, as the catalogs for those years have not survived.

Alabama Agricultural and Mechanical College. I. E. Drake Memorial Library Archives, Normal, Ala.

"Agricultural and Mechanical College of Alabama for Negroes," catalogs, 1896–99, 1905–6.

State Agricultural and Mechanical Institute, annual catalog, 1923–24.

State Colored Normal and Industrial School, catalog, 1895–96.

Alcorn State University. J. D. Boyd Library Archives, Lorman, Miss.

Announcements, Alcorn, Mississippi, 1929–30.

"Catalogue of the Officers and Students, Alcorn A. and M. College," Rodney, Miss., 1887–88.

"Catalogue of the Officers and Students of Alcorn Agricultural and Mechanical College," Alcorn, Mississippi, 1912–15, 1921–25, 1928–29.

"Catalogue of the Officers and Students of Alcorn University," Oakland, Miss., 1872–73.

Atlanta University. University Center. Robert W. Woodruff Library Archives Department, Atlanta.

"Catalogue of the Officers and Students of Atlanta University," 1872–73, 1879, 1882–83, 1883–84, 1885–86, 1888–89, 1894–95, 1922, 1925, 1931.

"Report of the Board of Examiners," June 12, 1884.

Avery Institute. Avery Research Center for African American History and Culture. College of Charleston, Charleston, S.C.

"Circular of Information," Avery Normal Institute, 1882–83.

Benedict College. Benjamin F. Payton Learning Resources Center, Columbia, S.C.

Catalog, 1917–18.

"Tenth Annual Catalogue of the Officers and Students," 1891–92.

Fisk University. John Hope and Aurelia E. Franklin Library. Special Collections and Archives, Nashville, Tenn.

"Catalogue of the Officers and Students of Fisk University," 1894–95, 1912–13.

"First Annual Catalogue of the Fisk University and Normal School," 1867–68.

Fisk Graduate Studies, the College, the Department of Music, the High School, the Elementary School, announcements, 1924–25.

"Fisk University Annual Catalog," 1923–24.

Florida Agricultural and Mechanical University. Samuel H. Coleman Library. Heritage Room, Tallahassee, Fla.

"Florida Agricultural and Mechanical College Courses of Study," 1894–95, 1909–10, 1915–16, 1929–30.

Hampton University. Hampton University Archives, Hampton, Va.

"Catalogue of the Hampton Normal and Agricultural Institute," 1893–94, 1894–95, 1909, 1911, 1922–23, 1924–25, 1925–26, 1926–27, 1929–30.

Howard University. Founders Library Archives, Washington, D.C.

"Catalogue of the Officers and Students," 1890–91.

Napier, J. C. "Address of the Hon. J. C. Napier, at the Fortieth Anniversary." Great Alumni Reunion, November 1907.

Thirkield, Wilbur T. "The Meaning and Mission of Education." Great Alumni Reunion, November 1907.

Jackson State University. University Archives. H. T. Sampson Library, Jackson, Miss.

Morehouse College. Atlanta University Center. Robert W. Woodruff Library Archives Department, Atlanta.

Catalogs, 1898–99, 1902–3.

Morris Brown University. Atlanta University Center. Robert W. Woodruff Library Archives Department, Atlanta.

Catalogs, 1883–84, 1913–14, 1923–24, 1931–32.

North Carolina Agricultural and Technical State University. Ferdinand D. Bluford Library, Greensboro, N.C.

Announcements, 1938–39.

"Catalogue of the North Carolina State Colored Normal and Industrial School," 1916–17, 1919–20, 1937–38.

"Catalogue of the North Carolina State Normal School," 1907–8.

Oberlin College. Mary Church Terrell Main Library. College Archives, Oberlin, Ohio.

Catalog, 1864–65.

Simmons College of Kentucky. Library Archives, Louisville.

Kentucky Normal and Theological Institute, catalog, 1881–82.

State University (formerly the Kentucky Normal and Theological Institute), catalog, 1883–84,

State University catalogs, 1910–11, 1919–20.

Tougaloo College. L. Zenobia Coleman Library. College Archives, Tougaloo, Miss.

Announcements, 1937–38.

Catalogs, 1901–2, 1905–6, 1912–13, 1916–17, 1918–19, 1923–24, 1931–32, 1936–37.

Tuskegee Institute. Tuskegee University Archives Repository, Tuskegee, Ala.

"Twenty-Fourth Annual Catalogue," 1904–5.

Wilberforce University. Stokes Library Archives, Wilberforce, Ohio.

"Annual Catalogue of Wilberforce University," 1912–13.

Catalogs, 1915–16, 1916–17.

"Triennial Catalogue of Wilberforce University," 1872–73.

Books and Articles

Adler, Eric. *Classics, the Culture Wars, and Beyond.* Ann Arbor: University of Michigan Press, 2016.

Alexander, Elizabeth. "'We Must Be about Our Father's Business': Anna Julia Cooper and the In-Corporation of the Nineteenth-Century African-American Woman Intellectual." *Signs* 20, no. 2 (1995): 336–56.

Allen, William Francis, ed. *The Life of Agricola and the Germania.* New York: Ginn, 1913.

Alston, Richard, and Efrossini Spentzou. *Reflections of Romanity: Discourses of Subjectivity in Imperial Rome.* Columbus: Ohio State University Press, 2011.

Anderson, Eric, and Alfred A. Moss Jr. *Dangerous Donations: Northern Philanthropy and Southern Black Education, 1902–1930*. Columbia: University of Missouri Press, 1999.

Anderson, James. *The Education of Blacks in the South, 1860–1935*. Chapel Hill: University of North Carolina Press, 1988.

Anderson, Monica. "A Look at Historically Black Colleges and Universities as Howard Turns 150." *Pew Research Report*, February 28, 2017, nytnews@nytimes.com.

Appiah, Kwame Anthony. *The Lies That Bind: Rethinking Identity*. London: Profile, 2019.

Applebome, Peter. "Scholar and Witness: John Hope Franklin Reshaped the Study of Black History in America." *New York Times*, March 29, 2009.

Atlanta University Bulletin. Ser. 2, no. 1 (1910); no. 4 (1911); no. 7 (1912).

Bacote, Clarence A. *The Story of Atlanta University: A Century of Service, 1865–1965*. Atlanta: Atlanta University, 1969.

Barnard, John Levi. *Empire of Ruin: Black Classicism and American Imperial Culture*. Oxford: Oxford University Press, 2018.

Bartlett, Thomas. "Black Colleges React to Low Point in Fashion." *Chronicle of Higher Education* 56, no. 12 (2009): A1, A20–21.

Becker, Trudy Harrington. "Daniel B. Williams." *Classical Outlook* 76, no. 3 (1999): 94–95.

———. "A Source for Ideology: The Classical Education of Martin Luther King, Jr." *Classical Bulletin* 76, no. 2 (2000): 191–200.

Bell, Derrick. "White Superiority in America: Its Legal Legacy, Its Economic Costs." In Roediger, *Black on White*, 138–50.

Bennett, Charles E. *Caesar's Gallic War*. Vols. 1–4. Boston: Allyn & Bacon, 1903.

Bernal, Martin. *The Archaeological and Documentary Evidence*. Vol. 2 of *Black Athena: The Afroasiatic Roots of Classical Culture*. New Brunswick, N.J.: Rutgers University Press, 1991.

———. *The Fabrication of Ancient Greece, 1785–1985*. Vol. 1 of *Black Athena: The Afroasiatic Roots of Classical Culture*. New Brunswick, N.J.: Rutgers University Press, 1987.

———. *The Linguistic Evidence*. Vol. 3 of *Black Athena: The Afroasiatic Roots of Classical Culture*. New Brunswick, N.J.: Rutgers University Press, 2006.

Bingham, Caleb, ed. *The Columbian Orator*. Edited by David W. Blight. New York: New York University Press, 1998. First published 1797 by Manning and Loring (Boston).

Blok, Josine H. "Proof and Persuasion in *Black Athena*: The Case of K. O. Müller." *Journal of the History of Ideas* 57, no. 4 (1996): 705–24.

Boise, James Robinson. *First Lessons in Greek, Adapted to the Grammar of Goodwin, and to That of Hadley as Revised by Frederic D. Forest Allen*. Chicago: Griggs, 1893.

Bojesen, Ernst Frederik. *Manual of Greek and Roman Antiquities*. New York: Appleton, 1854.

Bok, Sissela. *Lying: Moral Choice in Public and Private Life*. New York: Vintage, 1989.

———. *Secrets: On the Ethics of Concealment and Revelation*. New York: Vintage, 1983.

Bond, Horace Mann. *Negro Education in Alabama: A Study in Cotton and Steel*. Tuscaloosa: University of Alabama Press, 1994. First published 1939 by Associated Publishers (Washington, D.C.).

Brazzell, Johnetta Cross. "Brick without Straw: Missionary-Sponsored Black Higher Education in the Post-Emancipation South." *Journal of Higher Education* 63, no. 1 (1992): 26–49.

Bridges, Brian. "African Americans and College Education by the Numbers." United Negro College Fund. November 29, 2018. https://uncf.org/the-latest/african-americans-and-college-education-by-the-numbers/.

Briggs, Ward W., Jr., ed. *Soldier and Scholar: Basil Lanneau Gildersleeve and the Civil War.* Charlottesville: University Press of Virginia, 1998.

Brown, Charlotte Hawkins. *The Correct Thing to Do, to Say, to Wear.* Boston: Christopher, [1941?].

——. *Mammy: An Appeal to the Heart of the South.* Boston: Pilgrim, 1919.

Brown, William Wells. "On Race and Change." In Roediger, *Black on White*, 56–66.

Brucia, Margaret A. "The African-American Poet, Jupiter Hammon: A Home-Born Slave and His Classical Name." *International Journal of the Classical Tradition* 7, no. 4 (2001): 515–22.

Bumstead, Horace. *Higher Education of the Negro: Its Practical Value.* Atlanta: Atlanta University, 1890.

Burton, Sir Richard. *Personal Narrative of a Pilgrimage to al-Madinah and Meccah.* Edited by Isabel Burton. 2 vols. London: Tylston & Edwards, 1893.

Butchart, Ronald E. "'Outthinking and Outflanking the Owners of the World': A Historiography of the African American Struggle for Education." *History of Education Quarterly* 28, no. 3 (1988): 333–66.

Calhoun, John C. "Speech on the Reception of Abolition Petitions." February 1837. In *Speeches of John C. Calhoun: Delivered in the Congress of the United States, 1811 to the Present Time*, 222–25. New York: Harper & Brothers, 1845.

Calloway-Thomas, Carolyn, and Deborah Atwater. "William G. Allen, on 'Orators and Oratory.'" *Rhetoric Society Quarterly* 16, nos. 1–2 (Winter–Spring 1986): 31–42.

Campbell, Clarice T., and Oscar Allan Rogers Jr. *Mississippi: The View from Tougaloo.* 2nd ed. Jackson: University Press of Mississippi, 2002.

Carlson, Scott. "The Future of American Colleges May Lie, Literally, in Students' Hands." *Chronicle Review*, February 5, 2012. https://www.chronicle.com/article/the-future-of-american-colleges-may-lie-literally-in-students-hands/.

Century Foundation. "Achieving Financial Equity and Justice for HBCUs." September 14, 2021. https://org/content/achieving-financial-equity-justice-hbcus/.

Ceserani, Giovanna. *Italy's Lost Greece: Magna Graecia and the Making of Modern Archaeology.* Oxford: Oxford University Press, 2012.

Channing, Edward T. *Lectures Read to the Seniors in Harvard College.* Boston: Ticknor & Fields, 1856.

Charlotte Hawkins Brown Museum. *A Brief History of the Charlotte Hawkins Brown Museum.* Gibsonville, N.C., n.d.

Chase, Thomas, ed. *The History of Livy (Selections).* Philadelphia: Eldredge, 1872.

——. *Marcus Tullius Cicero.* Chase and Stuart Classical Series. Philadelphia: Eldridge, 1873.

——. *Six Books of the* Aeneid *of Virgil.* Philadelphia: Eldredge & Brother, 1875.

Classical Association of the Atlantic States. *The Practical Value of Latin.* Ann Arbor: University of Michigan Library, 1915.

Cochrane, Charles Norris. *Christianity and Classical Culture: A Study of Thought and Action from Augustus to Augustine.* Oxford: Clarendon, 1940.

Collar, William Coe, and Moses Grant Daniell. *The First Latin Book.* Boston: Ginn, 1902.

Cook, Samuel DuBois. "What Are the Ultimate Meaning and Significance of *Brown v. Board of Education*? A Note on Justice, Constitutionalism, and the Human Person." In *The Promise of Justice: Essays on* Brown v. Board of Education, edited by Mac Stewart, 15–27. Columbus: Ohio State University Press, 2008.

Cook, William W., and James Tatum. *African American Writers and Classical Tradition*. Chicago: University of Chicago Press, 2010.

Cooper, Arnold. *Between Struggle and Hope: Four Black Educators in the South, 1894–1915*. Ames: Iowa State University Press, 1989.

Cooper, Helene. "Meet the New Elite, Not Like the Old." *New York Times*, July 26, 2009.

Coppin, Fanny Jackson. *Reminiscences of School Life, and Hints on Teaching*. Edited by Henry Louis Gates Jr. African American Women Writers, 1910–1940. 1913. Reprint, Boston: Hall, 1995.

Cornelius, Janet Duitsman. *When I Can Read My Title Clear: Literacy, Slavery and Religion in the Antebellum South*. Columbia: University of South Carolina Press, 1991.

Crowell, E. P., ed. *The* Andria *and* Adelphoe *of Terence*. Chase and Stuart Classical Series. Philadelphia: Eldridge, 1880.

Crummell, Alexander. "The Attitude of the American Mind toward the Negro Intellect." 1898. *In Black Scholars on the Line: Race, Social Science, and American Thought in the Twentieth Century*, edited by Jonathan Scott Holloway and Ben Keppel, 45–56. Notre Dame: University of Notre Dame Press, 2007.

DeBerry, Charles U. "A Study of the History and Development of Palmer Memorial Institute: With Special Reference to the Community in Which It Is Located." Master's thesis, New York University, 1939.

DeBoer, Clara Merritt. *His Truth Is Marching On: African Americans Who Taught the Freedmen for the American Missionary Association, 1861–1877*. New York: Garland, 1995.

Dennis, Michael. "Schooling along the Color Line: Progressives and the Education of Blacks in the New South." *Journal of Negro Education* 67, no. 2 (1998): 142–56.

———. "The Skillful Use of Higher Education to Protect White Supremacy." *Journal of Blacks in Higher Education*, no. 32 (2001): 115–23.

Derbigny, Irving Antony. *General Education in the Negro College*. Stanford, Ca.: Stanford University Press, 1947.

Douglass, Frederick. "Mrs. Auld." 1845. In Roediger, *Black on White*, 274–77.

———. *Narrative of the Life of Frederick Douglass, an American Slave*. Boston: Anti-slavery Office, 1845.

Drago, Edmund L. *Initiative, Paternalism, and Race Relations: Charleston's Avery Normal Institute*. Athens: University of Georgia Press, 1990.

———. *Politicians and Reconstruction in Georgia*. Baton Rouge: University of Louisiana Press, 1982.

Drewry, Henry N., and Humphrey Doermann. *Stand and Prosper: Private Black Colleges and Their Students*. Princeton, N.J.: Princeton University Press, 2001.

Driskell, Jay Winston, Jr. *Schooling Jim Crow: The Fight for Atlanta's Booker T. Washington High School and the Roots of Black Protest Politics*. Charlottesville: University of Virginia Press, 2014.

Du Bois, W. E. B. *The Autobiography of W. E. B. Du Bois: A Soliloquy on Viewing My Life from the Last Decade of Its First Century*. New York: International, 1971.

——. "Diuturni silenti." 1924. In Du Bois, *Education of Black People,* 41–60.

——. *The Education of Black People: Ten Critiques, 1910–1960.* Edited by Herbert Aptheker. Amherst: University of Massachusetts Press, 1973.

——. *The Negro Artisan: Report of a Social Study Made under the Direction of Atlanta University; Together with the Proceedings of the Seventh Conference for the Study of the Negro Problems, held at Atlanta University of May 27, 1902.* Atlanta: Atlanta University Press, 1902.

——. "A Philosophy in Time of War." *Crisis* 16 (1918): 164–65.

——. *The Souls of Black Folk.* Greenwich, Conn.: Fawcett, 1961.

——. *Souls of White Folk.* 1920. In Roediger, *Black on White,* 184–200.

——. "Strivings of the Negro People." *Atlantic Monthly* 79, no. 471 (1897–1901): 194–98.

——. "The Talented Tenth." In *Du Bois: Selected Essays,* 26–46. 1903. Reprint, Praha, Czech Republic: Madison & Adams Press, 2018.

Du Bois, W. E. B., and Augustus Granville Dill, eds. *The College-Bred Negro American.* Atlanta: Atlanta University Press, 1910.

Durrill, Wayne K. "The Power of Ancient Words: Classical Teaching and Social Change at South Carolina College, 1804–1860." *Journal of Southern History* 65, no. 3 (1999): 469–98.

Edgcomb, Gabrielle Simon. *From Swastika to Jim Crow: Refugee Scholars at Black Colleges.* Malabar, Fla.: Krieger, 1993.

Ellis, Reginald. "Nathan B. Young: Florida A&M College's Second President and His Relationships with White Public Officials." In *Go Sound the Trumpet: Selections in Florida's African American History,* edited by David H. Jackson Jr. and Cantor Brown Jr., 153–72. Tampa, Fla.: University of Tampa Press, 2005.

Engs, Robert Francis. *Educating the Disenfranchised and Disinherited: Samuel Chapman Armstrong and Hampton Institute, 1839–1893.* Knoxville: University of Tennessee Press, 1999.

Fairchild, James H. *Oberlin: The Colony and the College, 1833–1883.* Oberlin, Ohio: Goodrich, 1883.

Fanon, Frantz. *Black Skin, White Masks.* Translated by Charles Lam Markmann. New York: Grove, 1967.

Flemming, Cynthia Griggs. "The Effect of Higher Education on Black Tennesseans after the Civil War." *Phylon* 44, no. 3 (1983): 209–16.

Franklin, John Hope. "The Dilemma of the American Negro Scholar." In Hill, *Soon, One Morning,* 62–76.

Franklin, Vincent P. *Black Self-Determination: A Cultural History of the Faith of the Fathers.* Westport, Conn.: Greenwood, 1984.

Fromm, Aloysius. "College Entrance and Graduation Requirements in the Classical Languages." In Kirsch and Deferrari, *Classics,* 187.

Fuller, Thomas O. *Twenty Years in Public Life, 1890–1910.* Nashville: National Baptist Publishing Board, 1910.

Fyffe, Charles Alan. *History of Greece.* New York: American Book, 1890.

Gabel, Leona C. *From Slavery to the Sorbonne and Beyond: The Life and Writing of Anna Julia Cooper.* Smith College Studies in History. Vol. 49. Northampton, Mass.: Department of History of Smith College, 1982.

Gannett, William Channing, and Edward Everett Hale. "The Education of the Freedmen." *North American Review* 101 (October 1865): 528–49.

Ganter, Granville. "The Active Virtue of *The Columbian Orator.*" *New England Quarterly* 70 (1997): 464–76.

Gasman, Marybeth, and Nelson Bowman III. *A Guide to Fundraising at Historically Black Colleges and Universities: An All-Campus Approach.* New York: Routledge, 2012.

Gates, Henry Louis, Jr. *Figures in Black: Words, Signs, and the "Racial" Self.* New York: Oxford University Press, 1989.

Geiger, Roger, ed. *The American College in the Nineteenth Century.* Nashville: Vanderbilt University Press, 2000.

Gerber, David A. "Segregation, Separatism, and Sectarianism: Ohio Blacks and Wilberforce University's Effort to Obtain Federal Funds, 1891." *Journal of Negro Education* 45, no. 1 (1976): 1–20.

Gere, Anne Ruggles, and Sarah R. Robbins. "Gendered Literacy in Black and White: Turn-of-the-Century African-American and European-American Club Women's Printed Texts." *Signs* 21, no. 3 (1996): 643–78.

Gilpin Faust, Drew. "The University's Crisis of Purpose." *New York Times Book Review,* September 6, 2009.

Glaude, Eddie S., Jr. *Exodus! Religion, Race, and Nation in Early Nineteenth-Century America.* Chicago: University of Chicago Press, 2000.

Gleason, Clarence W. *A Term of Ovid: Stories from the* Metamorphoses *for Study and Sight Reading.* New York: American Book, 1920.

Goings, Kenneth W., and Eugene O'Connor. "Black Athena before *Black Athena:* The Teaching of Greek and Latin at Black Colleges and Universities during the Nineteenth Century." In Orrells, Bhambra, and Roynon, *African Athena,* 90–105.

———. "Lessons Learned: The Role of the Classics at Black Colleges and Universities." *Journal of Negro Education* 79, no. 4 (2010): 521–31.

———. "My Name Is 'Nobody': African-American and Classical Models of the Trickster in Ralph Ellison's *Invisible Man.*" *LIT: Literature Interpretation Theory* 1, no. 3 (1990): 217–27.

———. "'Tell Them We Are Rising': African Americans and the Classics." *Amphora* 4, no. 2 (2005): 6–7, 12–13.

Goings, Kenneth W., and Gerald Smith. "'Unhidden' Transcripts: Memphis and African American Agency." *Journal of Urban History* 21, no. 3 (1995): 372–94.

Gold, David. "'Nothing Educates Us Like a Shock': The Integrated Rhetoric of Melvin B. Tolson." *College Composition and Communication* 55, no. 2 (2003): 226–53.

———. *Rhetoric at the Margins: Revising the History of Writing Instruction in American Colleges, 1873–1947.* Carbondale: Southern Illinois University Press, 2008.

Grandison, Kendrick. "Negotiated Space: The Black College Campus as a Cultural Record of Postbellum America." *American Quarterly* 51, no. 3 (1999): 529–79.

Greenwood, Emily. "The Politics of Classicism in the Poetry of Phillis Wheatley." In *Ancient Slavery and Abolition: From Hobbes to Hollywood,* edited by Richard Alston, Edith Hall, and Justine McConnell, 153–80. Oxford: Oxford University Press, 2011.

Gregory, James M. *Frederick Douglass: The Orator.* Springfield, Mass.: Wiley, 1893.

Gundaker, Grey. "Hidden Education among African Americans during Slavery." *Teachers College Record* 109, no. 7 (2007): 1591–612.

Gura, Philip F. *American Transcendentalism: A History.* New York: Hill & Wang, 2007.

Hadley, James, and Frederic de Forest Allen. *A Greek Grammar for Schools and Colleges.* New York: Appleton, 1884.

Hager, Christopher. *Word by Word: Emancipation and the Act of Writing.* Cambridge, Mass.: Harvard University Press, 2013.

Hairston, Eric Ashley. *The Ebony Column: Classics, Civilization, and the African American Reclamation of the West.* Knoxville: University of Tennessee Press, 2013.

Hall, Stephen G. *A Faithful Account of the Race: African American Historical Writing in Nineteenth-Century America.* Chapel Hill: University of North Carolina Press, 2009.

Hankins, Barry. *The Second Great Awakening and the Transcendentalists.* Westport, Conn.: Greenwood, 2004.

Hanses, Matthias. "W. E. B. Du Bois's *De senectute* (1948)." *Classical Receptions Journal* 11, no. 2 (2019): 117–36.

Hanson, Victor Davis. "Rhetoric Won't Keep Nation Safe." *Columbus Dispatch,* January 23, 2009.

Harkness, Albert. *A Complete Latin Grammar.* New York: American Book, 1898.

———. *A Latin Reader, Intended as a Companion to the Author's Latin Grammar.* New York: Appleton, 1875.

Harlan, Louis, ed. *The Booker T. Washington Papers.* Vol. 4, *1895–1898.* Urbana: University of Illinois Press, 1972.

Harloe, Katherine. *Winckelmann and the Invention of Antiquity: History and Aesthetics in the Age of* Altertumswissenschaft. Oxford: Oxford University Press, 2013.

Harrington, J. Drew. "Classical Antiquity and the Proslavery Argument." *Slavery and Abolition* 10, no. 1 (1989): 60–72.

Harris, Cheryl I. "Whiteness as Property." *Harvard Law Review* 106, no. 8 (1993): 1707–91.

Hill, Herbert, ed. *Soon, One Morning: New Writing by American Negroes, 1940–1962.* New York: Knopf, 1963.

Hine, Darlene Clark. "Rape and the Inner Lives of Black Women in the Middle West: Preliminary Thoughts on the Culture of Dissemblance." In *Unequal Sisters: A Multicultural Reader in U.S. Women's History,* edited by Ellen Carol DuBois and Vicki L. Ruiz, 292–97. New York: Routledge, 1990.

Hinks, Peter P. Introduction to Walker, *Appeal,* xi–xliv.

———. *To Awaken My Afflicted Brethren: David Walker and the Problem of Antebellum Slave Resistance.* University Park: Pennsylvania State University Press, 1997.

Hoffman, Lydia Charles. "Minding and Marketing Manners in the Jim Crow South: Dr. Charlotte Hawkins Brown and the Alice Freeman Palmer Memorial Institute." Master's thesis, University of North Carolina, Chapel Hill, 1997.

Holmes, Dwight Oliver Wendell. *The Evolution of the Negro College.* New York: Arno, 1969. First published 1934 by Teachers College (New York).

Hume, David. "Of National Characters." 1753. In *David Hume: Selected Essays,* edited by Stephen Copley and Andrew Edgar, 13–25. Oxford: Oxford University Press, 1993.

Immerwahr, John. "Hume's Revised Racism." *Journal of the History of Ideas* 53, no. 3 (1992): 481–86.

James, George G. M. *Stolen Legacy: Greek Philosophy Is Stolen Egyptian Philosophy.* New York: Philosophical Library, 1954.

Jarratt, Susan C. "Classics and Counterpublics in Nineteenth-Century Historically Black Colleges." *College English* 72, no. 2 (2009): 134–59.

Jeffers, Honorée Fanonne. *The Age of Phillis*. Middletown, Conn.: Wesleyan University Press, 2020.

Jefferson, Thomas. *The Life and Selected Writings of Thomas Jefferson, Including the Autobiography, the Declaration of Independence, and His Public and Private Letters*. Edited by Adrienne Koch and William Peden. New York: Random House, 1944.

———. *Notes on the State of Virginia*. Philadelphia: Prichard and Hall, 1785.

Jewell, Joseph O. *Race, Social Reform, and the Making of a Middle Class: The American Missionary Association and Black Atlanta, 1870–1900*. Lanham, Md.: Rowman & Littlefield, 2007.

———. "To Set an Example: The Tradition of Diversity at Historically Black Colleges and Universities." *Urban Education* 37, no. 1 (2002): 7–21.

Johnson, Nan. *Nineteenth-Century Rhetoric in North America*. Carbondale: Southern Illinois University Press, 1991.

Johnston, Sir Harry H. *The Negro in the New World*. London: Methuen, 1910.

Jones, Beverly W. "Mary Church Terrell and the National Association of Colored Women, 1896–1901." *Journal of Negro History* 67, no. 1 (1982): 20–33.

Jones, Elisha. *Exercises in Latin Prose Composition*. Chicago: Scott, Foresman, 1898.

Jones, Maxine D. "The American Missionary Association and the Beaufort, North Carolina School Controversy, 1866–67." *Phylon* 48, no. 2 (1987): 103–11.

———. "Student Unrest at Talladega College, 1887–1914." *Journal of Negro Education* 70, nos. 3–4 (1985): 73–81.

Jones, Thomas Jesse, ed. *Negro Education: A Study of the Private and Higher Schools for Colored People in the United States*. Washington, D.C.: Government Printing Office, 1917.

July, Robert W. "Nineteenth-Century Negritude: Edward W. Blyden." *Journal of African History* 5, no. 1 (1964): 73–86.

Kaesser, Christian. "Rudolf Pfeiffer: A Catholic Classicist in the Age of Protestant 'Altertumswissenschaft.'" Princeton/Stanford Working Papers in Classics. September 2009. http://www.princeton.edu/~pswpc/pdfs/kaesser/090906.pdf.

Kennedy, Rebecca Futo, and Jackie Murray. "Classics Is Part of Black Intellectual History: Howard Needs to Keep It." *Undefeated*, June 4, 2021. http://theundefeated.com.

Kennicott, Philip. "Obama amid the Pillars of an Ancient Culture." *Washington Post*, August 30, 2008.

Kharem, Haroon. *A Curriculum of Repression: A Pedagogy of Racial History in the United States*. New York: Lang, 2006.

Kingsley, Charles. *Heroes of Greek Mythology*. New York: Macmillan, 1889.

Kirsch, Felix M., and Roy J. Deferrari, eds. *The Classics: Their History and Present Status in Education. A Symposium of Essays*. Milwaukee: Bruce, 1928.

Kliebard, Herbert M. "'The Evil Genius of the Negro Race': Thomas Jesse Jones and Educational Reform." *Journal of Curriculum and Supervision* 10, no. 1 (1994): 5–20.

Konaris, Michael D. *The Greek Gods in Modern Scholarship: Interpretation and Belief in Nineteenth and Early Twentieth Century Germany and Britain*. Oxford: Oxford University Press, 2016.

Kopff, E. Christian. "The Classics and the Traditional Liberal Arts Curriculum." *Modern Age* (1992): 136–42.

———. *The Devil Knows Latin: Why America Needs the Classical Tradition.* Wilmington, Del.: ISI Books, 2001.

Lawson, Ellen N., and Marlene Merrill. "The Antebellum 'Talented Thousandth': Black College Students at Oberlin before the Civil War." *Journal of Negro Education* 52, no. 2 (1983): 142–55.

Leighton, Robert Fowler. *A History of Rome.* New York: Clark and Maynard, 1881.

Lewis, David Levering. *W. E. B. Du Bois: Biography of a Race, 1868–1919.* New York: Holt, 1993.

Liddell, Henry George. *A History of Rome, from the Earliest Times to the Establishment of the Empire.* London: Murray, 1862.

Lightfoot, George Morton. "The Classical Languages." *Howard University Record* 2, no. 4 (1908): 3–5.

———. *The Latin Element in English Speech.* Washington, D.C.: Howard University, 1920.

Little, Monroe E. "The Extra-Curricular Activities of Black College Students, 1868–1940." *Journal of Negro History* 65, no. 2 (1980): 135–48.

Litwack, Leon. *Trouble in Mind: Black Southerners in the Age of Jim Crow.* New York: Knopf, 1998.

Lloyd-Jones, Sir Hugh. "Notes on American Education: Following Marx's Road Map." *Chronicles: A Magazine of American Culture* (September 2003): 14–15.

Logan, Rayford W. *The Betrayal of the Negro: From Rutherford B. Hayes to Woodrow Wilson.* New York: Collier, 1965.

———. *Howard University: The First Hundred Years, 1867–1967.* New York: New York University Press, 1969.

Logan, Rayford W., and Michael R. Winston, eds. *Dictionary of American Negro Biography.* New York: Norton, 1982.

Logan, Shirley Wilson. "Black Speakers, White Representations: Frances Ellen Watkins Harper and the Construction of a Public Persona." In *African American Rhetoric(s): Interdisciplinary Perspectives,* edited by Ronald L. Jackson II and Elaine B. Richardson, 21–36. Carbondale: Southern Illinois University Press, 2007.

Lovinggood, Reuben S. *Why Hic, Haec, Hoc for the Negro? Or, Did Our Northern Friends Make a Mistake?* Marshall, Tex.: Students of Wiley University, 1900.

Lupher, David, and Elizabeth Vandiver, "Yankee She-Men and Octoroon Electra: Basil Lanneau Gildersleeve on Slavery, Race and Abolition." In *Ancient Slavery and Abolition: From Hobbes to Hollywood,* edited by Richard Alston, Edith Hall, and Justine McConnell, 319–52. Oxford: Oxford University Press, 2011.

Lynn, L. R. "Colored Evangelism." *Christian Observer,* December 28, 1904.

Macleane, Arthur John. *The Works of Horace.* Boston: Allyn & Bacon, 1895.

Mahoney, Kathleen A. *Catholic Higher Education in Protestant America: The Jesuits and Harvard in the Age of the University.* Baltimore: Johns Hopkins University Press, 2003.

Mailloux, Steven. *Disciplinary Identities: Rhetorical Paths of English, Speech, and Composition.* New York: Modern Language Association, 2006.

Malamud, Margaret. *African Americans and the Classics: Antiquity, Abolition and Activ-*

ism. London: Tauris, 2016.

———. *Ancient Rome and Modern America*. West Sussex, U.K.: Wiley-Blackwell, 2009.

———. "Classics and Race in the Early American Republic." Unpublished paper delivered at the College Language Association meeting, University of Maryland Eastern Shore, March 25–28, 2009.

Malczewski, Joan. "Weak State, Stronger Schools: Northern Philanthropy and Organizational Change in the Jim Crow South." *Journal of Southern History* 75, no. 4 (2009): 963–1000.

Markovitz, Jonathan. *Legacies of Lynching: Racial Violence and Memory*. Minneapolis: University of Minnesota Press, 2004.

Marteena, Constance. *The Lengthening Shadow of a Woman. A Biography of Charlotte Hawkins Brown*. New York: Exposition, 1977.

McCoskey, Denise Eileen. "The Subjects of Slavery in 19th-Century American Latin Schoolbooks." *Classical Journal* 115, no. 1 (2019): 88–113.

McGinnis, Frederick A. *A History and an Interpretation of Wilberforce University*. Blanchester, Ohio: Brown, 1941.

McGrath, Earl J. *The Predominantly Negro Colleges and Universities in Transition*. New York: Institute of Higher Education, 1965.

McHenry, Elizabeth. *Forgotten Readers: Recovering the Lost History of African American Literary Societies*. Durham, N.C.: Duke University Press, 2002.

McMillan, Lewis K. "Negro Higher Education as I Have Known It." *Journal of Negro Education* 8, no. 1 (1939): 9–18.

McPherson, James M. *The Abolitionist Legacy: From Reconstruction to the NAACP*. Princeton, N.J.: Princeton University Press, 1975.

———. "White Liberals and Black Power in Negro Education, 1865–1915." *American Historical Review* 75, no. 5 (1970): 1357–86.

Meier, August. *Negro Thought in America, 1880–1915*. Ann Arbor: University of Michigan Press, 1963.

Meier, August, and Elliott Rudwick. "The Boycott Movement against Jim Crow Streetcars in the South, 1900–1906." *Journal of American History* 55, no. 4 (1969): 756–75.

Morris, Aldon. *The Origins of the Civil Rights Movement: Black Communities Organizing for Change*. New York: Free Press, 1984.

Morris, Robert. *Reading, Writing, and Reconstruction: The Education of Freedmen in the South, 1861–1870*. Chicago: University of Chicago Press, 1981.

Müller, Karl Otfried. *Geschichten hellenischer Stämme und Städte: Orchomenos und die Minyer* [History of Greek tribes and cities: Orchomenos and the Minyans]. Breslau: Max, 1820.

Nash, Margaret A. "Entangled Pasts: Land-Grant Colleges and American Indian Dispossession." *History of Education Quarterly* 59, no. 4 (2019): 437–67.

Nelson, Charmaine A. *The Color of Stone: Sculpting the Black Female Subject in Nineteenth-Century America*. Minneapolis: University of Minnesota Press, 2007.

Neyland, Leedell W., and John W. Riley. *The History of Florida Agricultural and Mechanical University*. Gainesville: University of Florida Press, 1963.

Obama, Barack. "Remarks by President Obama at Stavros Niarchos Foundation Cultural Center in Athens." White House. Accessed January 19, 2017. https://www.whitehouse.gov/the-press-office/2016/11/16/remarks-president-obama-stavros.

Orrells, Daniel, Gurminder K. Bhambra, and Tessa Roynon, eds. *African Athena: New Agendas*. Oxford: Oxford University Press, 2011.

Page, Walter Hines. *The Rebuilding of Old Commonwealths: Being Essays toward the Training of the Forgotten Man in the Southern States*. 1902. New York: AMS, 1970. First published 1902 by Doubleday, Page (New York).

Pile, Steve. *The Body and the City: Psychoanalysis, Space, and Subjectivity*. New York: Routledge, 1996.

Polt, Christopher. "Anti-Catholicism, Classical Curriculum, and the Beginning of Latin Drama in the United States." *Society for Classical Studies Newsletter*, July 2019.

Poser, Rachel. "The Iconoclast: Dan-el Padilla's War for the Future of Classics." *New York Times Magazine*, February 7, 2021, 36–45.

Powell, Marie. "The History of Negro Educational Institutions Sponsored by the Baptists of Tennessee from 1864–1934." Master's thesis, Tennessee Agricultural and Industrial State University, Nashville, 1953.

Price, Gregory N. "The Idea of a Historically Black University." *Negro Educational Review* 51, nos. 3–4 (2000): 99–113.

Raboteau, Albert J. *A Fire in the Bones: Reflections on African-American Religious History*. Boston: Beacon, 1995.

Rankine, Patrice D. "The Classics, Race, and Community-Engaged or Public Scholarship." *American Journal of Philology* 140, no. 2 (2019): 345–59.

Reinhold, Meyer. *Classica Americana: The Greek and Roman Heritage in the United States*. Detroit: Wayne State University Press, 1984.

Renker, Elizabeth. *The Origins of American Literature Studies: An Institutional History*. Cambridge: Cambridge University Press, 2007.

Rhodes, Lelia Gaston. *Jackson State University: The First Hundred Years, 1877–1977*. Jackson: University Press of Mississippi, 1979.

Richard, Carl C. *The Golden Age of the Classics in America: Greece, Rome, and the Antebellum United States*. Cambridge, Mass.: Harvard University Press, 2009.

Richardson, Joe M. *Christian Reconstruction: The American Missionary Association and Southern Blacks, 1861–1890*. Athens: University of Georgia Press, 1986.

———. *A History of Fisk University, 1865–1946*. Tuscaloosa: University of Alabama Press, 1980.

Richings, G. F. "Richard R. Wright, Sr., 1902." *Goin' North*. Accessed July 10, 2023. https://goinnorth.org/items/show/452.

Riess, Ernst, and Arthur L. Janes. *Caesar's Gallic War*. New York: American Book, 1914.

Roediger, David R., ed. *Black on White: Black Writers on What It Means to Be White*. New York: Schocken, 1998.

Ronnick, Michele Valerie, ed. *The Autobiography of William Sanders Scarborough: An American Journey from Slavery to Scholarship*. Detroit: Wayne State University Press, 2005.

———. "Francis Williams: An Eighteenth-Century Tertium Quid." *Negro History Bulletin* 61 (1998): 19–29.

———. "The Latin Quotations in the Correspondence of Edward Wilmot Blyden." *Negro Educational Review* 46, nos. 3–4 (1994): 101–6.

———. "Racial Ideology and the Classics in the African American Educational Experience." *Classical Bulletin* 76, no. 2 (2000): 169–80.

———. "William Sanders Scarborough and the Politics of Classical Education." In *Classical Antiquity and the Politics of America: From George Washington to George W. Bush,* edited by Michael Meckler, 55–68. Waco, Tex.: Baylor University Press, 2006.

———. "William Sanders Scarborough: The First African American Member of the Modern Language Association." *Publications of the Modern Language Association* 115 (2000): 1787–93.

Said, Edward W. *Culture and Imperialism.* New York: Vintage Books, 1994.

———. *Orientalism.* New York: Vintage, 1979.

Sandoval, Chela. *Methodology of the Oppressed.* Minneapolis: University of Minnesota Press, 2000.

Saunders, Tiasia. "[Howard's] Classics Department Cut Despite Outcry from Thousands." *Hilltop,* August 23, 3021.

Scarborough, William Sanders. *The Birds of Aristophanes.* Boston: Cushing, 1886.

———. "Chronological Order of Plato's Dialogues." *Transactions of the American Philological Association* 24 (1892): vi–viii.

———. "The Educated Negro and Menial Pursuits." 1898. In Scarborough, *Works of William Sanders Scarborough,* 201–6.

———. *First Lessons in Greek.* Classic Reprint Series. London: Forgotten Books, 2018. First published 1881 by Barnes (New York).

———. *The Works of William Sanders Scarborough, Black Classicist and Race Leader.* Edited by Michele Valerie Ronnick. Oxford: Oxford University Press, 2006.

Schueller, Malini Johar. Introduction to *A Colored Man Round the World* (1858). By David F. Dorr. Edited by Malini Johar Schueller. Ann Arbor: University of Michigan Press, 1999.

Schuyler, George S. "Our White Folks." 1927. In Roediger, *Black on White,* 71–84.

Sciarrino, Enrica. *Cato the Censor and the Beginnings of Latin Prose: From Poetic Translation to Elite Inscription.* Columbus: Ohio State University Press, 2011.

Simmons, Tracy Lee. *Climbing Parnassus: A New Apologia for Greek and Latin.* Wilmington, Del.: ISI Books, 2002.

Smith, Minnie Louise. *Elementary Latin.* Boston: Allyn & Bacon, 1920.

Smith, William. *A History of Greece, from the Earliest Times to the Roman Conquest.* New York: Harper, 1861.

Snowden, Frank, Jr. *Before Color Prejudice: The Ancient View of Blacks.* Cambridge, Mass.: Harvard University Press, 1983.

———. *Blacks in Antiquity: Ethiopians in the Greco-Roman Experience.* Cambridge, Mass.: Harvard University Press, 1970.

Span, Christopher M. *From Cotton Field to Schoolhouse: African American Education in Mississippi, 1862–1875.* Chapel Hill: University of North Carolina Press, 2009.

Spigner, Nicole. "Phillis Wheatley's Niobean Poetics." In *Brill's Companion to Classics in the Early Americas,* edited by Maya Feile Tomes, Adam J. Goldwyn, and Matthew Duquès, 320–42. Leiden: Brill, 2021.

Stallybrass, Peter, and Allon White. *Politics and Poetics of Transgression.* Ithaca, N.Y.: Cornell University Press, 1986.

Stauffer, John, Zoe Trodd, and Celeste-Marie Bernier. *Picturing Frederick Douglass: An Illustrated Biography of the Nineteenth Century's Most Photographed American.* New York: Liveright, 2015.

Sterling, Dorothy, ed. *The Trouble They Seen: Black People Tell the Story of Reconstruction*. New York: Doubleday, 1976.

Stowe, Harriet Beecher. "The Education of Freedmen." *North American Review* 129, no. 272 (1879): 81–94.

Strauss, Barry. "The Black Phalanx: African-Americans and the Classics after the Civil War." *Arion: A Journal of Humanities and the Classics,* 3rd ser., 12, no. 3 (2005): 39–63.

Tanner, Benjamin Tucker. *An Apology for African Methodism*. Baltimore, 1867.

"Teachers: Their Qualifications and Support." In *American Missionary*, 152. New Orleans: Amistad Research Center, 1866.

Terrell, Mary Church. *A Colored Woman in a White World*. Washington, D.C.: Ransdell, 1940.

Thomas, Kendall. "Strange Fruit." In *Race-ing Justice, En-gendering Power: Essays on Anita Hill, Clarence Thomas, and the Construction of Social Reality,* edited by Toni Morrison, 364–89. New York: Pantheon, 1992.

Tucker, David. *Black Pastors and Leaders: The Memphis Clergy, 1819–1972*. Memphis: State University Press, 1975.

Tunstall, Robert W. *Eleven Orations of Cicero, with Introduction, Notes, and Vocabulary*. Boston: Heath, 1910.

Tyler, William Seymour, ed. *The* Germania *and* Agricola *of Caius Cornelius Tacitus, with Notes for Colleges*. New York: Wiley & Putnam, 1847.

Van Steen, Gonda. *Liberating Hellenism from the Ottoman Empire: Comte de Marcellus and the Last of the Classics*. New York: Palgrave Macmillan, 2010.

Wadelington, Charles W., and Richard F. Knapp. *Charlotte Hawkins Brown and Palmer Memorial Institute*. Chapel Hill: University of North Carolina Press, 1999.

Waite, Cally L. "The Segregation of Black Students at Oberlin College after Reconstruction." *History of Education Quarterly* 41, no. 3 (2001): 344–64.

Walker, David. *Appeal to the Colored Citizens of the World*. Edited by Peter B. Hinks. 1829. Reprint, State College: Pennsylvania State University Press, 2000.

Watson, Veronica T. *The Souls of White Folk: African American Writers Theorize Whiteness*. Jackson: University Press of Mississippi, 2013.

Watson, Yolanda N., and Sheila T. Gregory. *Daring to Educate: The Legacy of the Early Spelman College Presidents*. Herndon, Va.: Stylus, 2005.

Watts, Jerry G. "Dilemmas of Black Intellectuals: What Role Should We Play?" *Dissent Magazine* (Fall 1989): 501–7.

Weisenburger, Francis P. "William Sanders Scarborough: Early Life and Years at Wilberforce." *Ohio History: The Scholarly Journal of the Ohio Historical Society* 71 (1961): 203–26, 287–89.

West, Cornel, and Jeremy Tate. "Howard University's Removal of Classics Is a Spiritual Catastrophe." *Washington Post*, April 19, 2021.

Wheatley, Phillis. *Complete Writings*. Edited by Vincent Carretta. New York: Penguin Books, 2001.

Whitaker, Graham. "*Alterthumswissenschaft* at Mid-Century." In *Classics in Practice: Studies in the History of Scholarship*, edited by Christopher Stray and Graham Whitaker, 129–69. London: Institute of Classical Studies, School of Advanced Study, University of London, 2015.

White, Dorrance S. "Humanizing the Teaching of Latin: A Study in Textbook Construction." *Classical Journal* 25 (1930): 507–20.

———. "Latin and the Reconstructionists." *Classical Journal* 32, no. 5 (1937): 267–80.

Williams, Heather Andrea. *Self-Taught: African American Education in Slavery and Freedom.* Chapel Hill: University of North Carolina Press, 2005.

Williamson, Margaret. "'Nero, the Mustard!' The Ironies of Classical Slave Names in the British Caribbean." In *Classicisms of the Black Atlantic*, edited by Ian Moyer, Adam Lecznar, and Heidi Morse, 57–78. Oxford: Oxford University Press, 2020.

Wilson, Francille. *The Segregated Scholars: Black Social Scientists and the Creation of Black Labor Studies.* Charlottesville: University of Virginia Press, 2006.

Wilson, Henry. "Edward Wilmot Blyden, 1832–1912." In *Abroad in America: Visitors to the New Nation, 1776–1914*, edited by Marc Pachter and Frances Wein, 157–66. Reading, Mass.: Addison-Wesley, 1976.

Winterer, Caroline. *The Culture of Classicism: Ancient Greece and Rome in American Intellectual Life, 1780–1910.* Baltimore: Johns Hopkins University Press, 2002.

Withun, David. "American Archias: Cicero and *The Souls of Black Folk.*" *Classical Receptions Journal* 13, no. 3 (2021): 384–98.

Wolters, Raymond. *The New Negro on Campus: Black College Rebellions of the 1920s.* Princeton, N.J.: Princeton University Press, 1975.

Woodson, Carter G. *The Mis-education of the Negro.* 1933. Reprint, Chicago: African American Images, 2000.

———. ed. *Negro Orators and Their Orations.* New York: Russell & Russell, 1969.

Wormser, Richard, Bill Jersey, and Sam Pollard, dirs. *The Rise and Fall of Jim Crow.* New York: Quest Productions/Videoline Productions and Thirteen/WNET, 2002.

Wright, Richard, Jr. *87 Years behind the Black Curtain: An Autobiography.* Philadelphia: Rare Book, 1965.

Young, Robert J. C. "The Afterlives of *Black Athena.*" In Orrells, Bhambra, and Roynon, *African Athena*, 174–90.

INDEX

accommodationism, 16, 98, 100
Adams, John Quincy, 27
Addams, Jane, 113
Adler, Eric, 132n33
Aeneid (Virgil), 29, 59, 62, 65, 67–68, 79–80, 86, 141n14
Aeschines, 87, 93
Aeschylus, 34, 71, 82
Africa, 7–8, 21, 30–33, 37, 41
African Americans: learned societies for, 33–35; as objects of history, *vs.* subjects, 5–6. *See also entries at Black*
African American Writers and Classical Tradition (Cook and Tatum), 94–95
African Athena: New Agendas (Roynon), 14
African Methodist Episcopal Church, 15, 47, 55, 69–76, 139nn93–94
agency, 2, 5–6, 9, 77, 126
Agricola (Tacitus), 81–85
"Ain't I a Woman?" (Truth), 89
Alabama A&M, 64, 67–68
Alcorn State University, 47, 60, 64–65, 82
Allen, William G., 143n36
Altertumswissenschaft, 10, 25, 28, 95, 97–98, 132n32, 146n11
American Missionary Association, 6, 42, 47–51, 99, 102, 135n28, 137n48
American Philological Association, 72–73, 78, 95
Anabasis (Xenophon), 27, 71, 80–81
Anderson, Eric, 6, 61–62
Anderson, James, 6, 70, 139n95
Anna T. Jeanes Foundation, 61
Antigone (Sophocles), 81
antiquities, plundering of, 22–23
Aphrodite of Melos, 22
Apology (Plato), 71
Apology for African Methodism, An (Tanner), 69
Appeal to the Colored Citizens of the World (Walker), 14–15, 35–39
Appiah, Kwame Anthony, 131n15
Aristotle, 133n38, 142n15
Armstrong, Samuel Chapman, 60, 62, 100,

138n69
Arnett, Benjamin William, 71
Arnold, Matthew, 89
Aryan master race, 132n33
Assing, Ossilie, 92
Atlanta Baptist College, 55
Atlanta University, 50–51, 54–58, 81, 91, 97, 103, 116
Augustine, 36
Augustus, 31
Auld, Sophia, 21
Avery Institute, 50, 53–54, 137n48
Ayer, Charles, 108–12

Babylon, 33
Baldwin, William, 61
Barnard, John Levi, 10, 14, 24, 30, 143n37
Barrett, Luther G., 109
Bartlett, Thomas, 136n39
Before Color Prejudice (Snowden), 14
Bell, Derrick, 130n6
Benedict College, 49–50
Bernal, Martin, 14, 26, 132n33
Betrayal of the Negro, The (Logan), 7
Bhambra, Gurminder K., 14
Biddle Memorial Institute, 80
Bingham, Caleb, 88, 90, 94
Black agency, 2, 5–6, 9, 77, 126
Black Athena (Bernal), 14, 26
Black bodies, 26, 132n34
Black colleges: African Methodist Episcopal Church and, 69–76; catalogs of, 11–13, 42–43, 47–48, 51, 71, 80–81; enrollment at, 135n26; founders of, 47–68; modern university system and, 4; number of, 13; obstacles faced by, 43; philanthropy and, 60–68; practical instruction and, 12–13, 53–54, 56–57, 65, 130n22, 137n44, 139n95; remedial instruction in, 43. *See also* specific institutions
blackface, 89
Black humanism, 14
Black humanity, 18–19, 30–31
Black inferiority, 19–21, 25, 74, 78, 85, 98, 100

165

Black insurgency, 7
Blackness, 24
Black pedagogy, 6
Black servants, 9
Blacks in Antiquity (Snowden), 14
Blok, Josine H., 132n33
Blyden, Edward Wilmot, 32–33, 72
bodies, African American, 26, 132–34
Boggs, William E., 102–3
Boise, James Robinson, 81
books, 79–81, 141n3, 142n16
Boston College, 134n8, 135n17
Boston Literary Society, 34
Bowman, Nelson, III, 6
Brazzell, Johnetta Cross, 99
Brown, Charlotte Hawkins, 109–11, 113, 125
Brown, William Wells, 85
Brownlee, Fred L., 137n43
Brownlee, Joe M., 54
Brown v. Board of Education, 16
Bumstead, Horace, 116–17, 145n3
Burrus, John Houston, 60
Burton, Richard, 21

Cabell, Paul, 139n86
Calhoun, John C., 27–28, 132n32, 143n45
Cardozo, Francis Lewis, 137n48
Carlson, Scott, 2
Carnegie Foundation, 61
Carretta, Vincent, 24
Casey, Hubert D., 109
catalogs, college, 11–13, 42–43, 47–48, 51, 71, 80–81, 83–84, 87, 100, 116, 118, 120, 121, 135n18, 136n34, 137n46, 141n6
Cato the Elder, 143n42
Catullus, 62, 86
Channing, Edward T., 89
Chapman, Samuel, 60
Chase, Thomas, 79, 81, 83, 86
Child, Lydia Maria, 32
choir, 59–60
Cicero, 15, 29, 45, 57, 62–63, 65–67, 71, 79, 80–83, 87, 90, 92–93, 94, 132n34, 138n67, 143n36
citizenship, 147n3
Civil War, 1, 30
Clark University, 55
Classica Americana (Reinhold), 78
"Classical Antiquity and the Proslavery Argument" (Harrington), 27

classical culture, 5, 8, 13, 18–19, 21–23
classical education, 1–6; Howard University statement on, 118–19; life-forming purpose of, 78; Oberlin and, 45–46; resistance and, 12; role and value, 14. *See also* liberal arts
classicism: racialist, 35–39; scientific, 25–28
classicists, 8
classics, 7–8; Black humanity and equality in defense of, 30–33; emancipation and, 39; historians, 83–85; leadership and, 43; moral power of, 94–95; philosophy, 82–83; poetry, 86–87; race and, 116–17; rhetoric, 87–92; subversive readings of, 44; texts, 79–80; in Yale Report of 1828, 41
Collar, William Coe, 65, 68
College-Bred Negro American (Du Bois and Dill), 120–21, 135n26
College of the Holy Cross, Worcester, 129n8
colleges. *See* Black colleges
colonialism, 21–23, 130–14, 137n43
Colored Man Round the World, A (Dorr), 31
Colored Woman in a White World, A (Terrell), 89
Columbian Orator (Bingham), 88, 90, 94
Complete Latin Grammar, A (Harkness), 80
Congregationalism, 45
Conspiracy of Catiline (Sallust), 84
Cook, Samuel DuBois, 20
Cook, William W., 94–95
Cooper, Anna Julia, 114, 125, 138n67
Cooper, Helene, 124
Coppin, Fanny Jackson, 7
Cornelius, Janet Duitsman, 19
Cornish, Samuel Eli, 30, 34
Correct Thing to Do, to Say, to Wear, The (Brown), 111
Cravath, Erastus Milo, 59
Crogman, William Henry, 55
Crowell, E. P., 86–87
Crummell, Alexander, 28
cultural capital, 5, 97
cultural imperialism, 10
culture: classical, 5, 8, 13, 16, 18–19, 21–23; 26, 124–25, 132nn32–33, Western, 2, 25, 131n15
Culture and Imperialism (Said), 22
Culture of Classicism, The (Winterer), 78
Cyropaedia (Xenophon), 29

Dabney, Charles, 136n32
Dangerous Donations (Anderson and Moss), 6
Daniell, Moses Grant, 65, 68
Daring to Educate (Watson and
  Gregory), 7
De amicitia (Cicero), 71, 81, 83
democracy, 121, 147n3
Demosthenes, 15, 30, 45, 81, 87, 90, 93, 143n36
De natura deorum (Cicero), 83
Dennis, Michael, 138n69
De officiis (Cicero), 45
De oratore (Cicero), 29, 92–93
Derbigny, Irving Anthony, 121–22
De senectute (Cicero), 67, 71, 81–83
De viris illustribus (Nepos), 84–85
Dill, Augustus Granville, 97, 120, 135n15,
  135n26, 146n14
Diogenes, 91
Dionysius of Halicarnassus, 93
dissemblance, 10–11, 105, 108–12, 144n3
Doermann, Humphrey, 6
Dorr, David, F., 31
Douglass, Frederick, 1, 21, 31, 89, 92–94,
  139n94, 142n35, 143n37
Dred Scott v. Sandford, 20
dress code, 50, 136nn37–38
Drewry, Henry N., 6
Du Bois, W. E. B., 11, 60, 71, 73, 94, 97–98,
  101, 108, 113, 118, 120–21, 124–26,
  130n14, 135n15, 135n26, 136n37, 139n107,
  140–107, 146n14
Durrill, Wayne, 29

Easton, Hosea, 32, 39
Ebony Column, The (Hairston), 14
Edgcomb, Gabrielle Simon, 6, 47
education: emancipation and, 41, 133n47;
  Freedmen's Bureau and, 41–42; missionaries and, 42; practical instruction in,
  12–13, 99–101, 105–8, 130n22, 136n32,
  137n44, 138n71, 139n95; Reconstruction and, 57–58, 101; religious need for,
  34–35; remedial, 43; slavery and, 20–21; as
  subversive, 98; White power structure and,
  98–100. *See also* classical education
Education of Blacks in the South, The,
  1860–1935 (Anderson), 6, 70
effeminacy, 22
Egypt, 7–8, 21, 25–26, 31–32, 132n33, 133n49
Elementary Latin (Smith), 81

Eleven Orations of Cicero (Tunstall), 81
Elgin marbles, 22–23
Eliot, Charles W., 115–16, 145n1
Elliott, Charles, 150n8
Empire of Ruin (Barnard), 10, 14
Epictetus, 37
Epicureanism, 83
Epistles (Horace), 71, 82, 86
Epodes (Horace), 65, 86
Ethiopia, 32–33, 132n32
Euripides, 81
Eurocentrism, 10, 120, 146n11
Euthyphro (Plato), 82

Fairchild, James H., 45–47
Fanon, Frantz, 18
Fayetteville State University, 68
Figures in Black (Gates), 12
First Lessons in Greek (Boise), 81
First Lessons in Greek (Scarborough), 7, 46,
  72, 80, 94
Fisk, Clinton B., 59
Fisk Jubilee Singers, 59–60
Fisk University, 7, 15, 16, 42, 43, 50, 53, 58–60,
  81, 86, 90–92, 101–2, 136n37, 136n40
Flemming, Cynthia Griggs, 49
Florida Agricultural and Mechanical College,
  47, 64–66, 105–8
Florida State Normal and Industrial School, 11
Forest Allen, Frederic de, 80
Forgotten Readers (McHenry), 33–34
founders, of Black colleges, 46–47, 60–68
Franklin, John Hope, 140n106
Franklin, Vincent P., 18
fraternities, 6
Frederick Douglass: The Orator (Gregory), 92
Freedmen's Bureau, 41–42, 59, 101
Freedom's Journal, 30, 34, 91
From Swastika to Jim Crow (Edgcomb), 6, 47
Fuller, T. O., 108, 111–12
"Future of American Colleges May Lie, Literal-
  ly, in Students' Hands, The" (Carlson), 2
Fyffe, Charles Alan, 81

Gage, Francis, 89
Gallic War (Riess and Janes), 81
Gannett, William Channing, 42
Garnet, Henry Highland, 31
Garrison, William Lloyd, 34, 91, 143n37
Gasman, Marybeth, 6

INDEX **167**

Gates, George Augustus, 102
Gates, Henry Louis, Jr., 12
Geiger, Roger, 135n26
General Education Board, 61, 108, 140n108
Georgia State Industrial College, 102–5
Germania (Tacitus), 81–84
Gibbs, Ida, 106
Gildersleeve, Basil Lanneau, 26–30, 80
Gilpin Faust, Drew, 3
Gleason, Clarence W., 81
Gobineau, Arthur de, 132n33
Goings, Kenneth W., 7
Gold, David, 91
Gorgias (Plato), 45, 71, 81–82
grammars, 94–95
Grandgent, C. H., 117
Grandison, Kendrick, 145n49
Grayson, William John, 133n38
Greek artifacts, 22
Greek language, 2–5, 7, 28, 43, 50–52, 58, 65, 79–81, 86, 89, 104
Greeks, as White, 10
Green, John P., 76
Greener, Richard T., 72, 95
Gregory, James M., 92
Gregory, Sheila T., 7
Guide to Fundraising at Historically Black Colleges and Universities (Gasman and Bowman), 6
Gundaker, Grey, 20

Hadley, James, 80–81
Hairston, Eric Ashley, 14, 16, 131n24
Hammon, Jupiter, 131n21
Hampton Institute, 54, 60–63, 101–2
Hampton-Tuskegee model, 14, 61, 74, 76–77
Hankins, Barry, 44
Hannibal, 31, 36–37
Hanson, Victor Davis, 125
Harkness, Albert, 79–81, 142n16
Herodotus, 26, 31–32, 71, 83, 132n32, 138n67
Heroes of Greek Mythology (Kingsley), 94
Hesiod, 45
Higher Education of the Negro: Its Practical Value (Bumstead), 116
Hine, Darlene Clark, 144n3
Hinks, Peter, 36
historians, 83–85
historically Black colleges and universities. *See* Black colleges

Histories (Tacitus), 29
History (Livy), 81
History of Greek Tribes and Cities: Orchomenos and the Minyans (Müller), 25–26
History of Rome (Livy), 84
History of Rome, A (Leighton), 94
History of Rome, A (Liddell), 82
Homer, 23, 34, 71, 81–82
Hopkins, Pauline, 31
Horace, 23, 56, 62, 65, 71, 81–82, 86, 135n18
Howard, Oliver O., 69, 103
Howard, William H., 106–7
Howard University, 43, 46, 53, 68–69, 84, 87, 90–92, 118–19, 123, 135n24, 137n48, 147nn22–23
Howe Institute, 111–12
humanism, 3, 14
Hume, David, 19–20, 131n20
Hunter, Jane Edna Harris, 114
hypokrisis, 11, 98, 108

Iliad (Homer), 81–82
imperialism, 10, 15, 21–23, 130n14
inclusiveness, 9–10
industrial education. *See* practical instruction
industrialization, 129n8
Iphigenia in Tauris (Euripides), 81
Isocrates, 87

Jackson College, 108–9
James, George, 133n49
Janes, Arthur L., 81
January 6, 2021, Capitol attack, 147n7
Jarratt, Susan C., 15, 34, 78, 91–92, 97, 129n15
Jeffers, Honorée Fanonne, 131n29
Jefferson, Thomas, 10, 15, 19, 23, 25, 35–39
Jesuit colleges, 129n8, 129n10
Jewell, Joseph O., 146n11
Jim Crow, 8, 16, 55, 73, 99, 139n108
John F. Slater Fund for the Education of Freedmen, 60–61, 99, 109
Johnson, Nan, 88
Johnson C. Smith University, 80
Johnston, Harry H., 115
Jones, Beverly W., 113
Jones, Elisha, 81
Jones, Maxine D., 99
Jones, Thomas Jesse, 121
Josephus, 31
Julius Rosenthal Fund, 61

July, Robert W., 33
Juvenal, 29, 82

Kaesser, Christian, 25
Kennicott, Philip, 124–25
Kent, William, 71
Kentucky Normal and Theological Institute, 43
Kharem, Haroon, 120, 137n43
King, Martin Luther, Jr., 13
Kingsley, Charles, 94

land-grant colleges, 3, 63–64
Latin language, 2–5, 7, 43, 50–53, 63, 65,
    67–68, 80, 104
Laura Spelman Rockefeller Memorial Fund, 61
Lee, Benjamin F., 71
Lee, John Robert Edward, 107
Lefkowitz, Mary, 132n33
Leighton, Robert Fowler, 94
LeMoyne College, 112
Lewis, David Levering, 71
Lewis, Robert Benjamin, 31–32
liberal arts, 1, 2–3, 4–5, 8–9, 11–16, 21, 41,
    45–46, 48–49, 52, 54, 55, 57–58, 59, 60–61,
    65, 66, 68, 74–75, 76, 82, 88, 91, 96, 98,
    99–106, 108–9, 112, 113–14, 123, 125,
    130n22, 136n32, 144n28, 145n3. *See also*
    classical education
Liberating Hellenism from the Ottoman Empire
    (Van Steen), 22
Liberator (periodical), 34
Liberia, 32–33
Liddell, Henry George, 82
Lies That Bind (Appiah), 131n15
Life of Terence, colore dusco (Suetonius), 24
Light and Truth (Lewis), 31–32
Lightfoot, George Morton, 87, 119
Lincoln, Abraham, 29
literacy, 1, 18–20, 27, 33, 36, 42–43, 49, 98,
    114, 133n47, 145n59
literary associations, 33–34
Livy, 62, 71, 81–84
Lloyd-Jones, Hugh, 147n2
Logan, Rayford W., 7
Longinus, Cassius, 29
Lucretius, 83
Lysias, 81, 87, 93

Macleane, Arthur J., 135n18
Mahan, Asa, 46–47

Mahoney, Kathleen, 129n10, 134n8, 135n17
Malamud, Margaret, 133n38, 143n36
Mammy: An Appeal to the Heart of the South
    (Brown), 110
marginalization, 23
Martin du Tirac, Marie-Louis-Jean-André-
    Charles, 22
masculinity, 90
masks, 11–12, 98, 108, 129n19
McGrath, Earl J., 122
McHenry, Elizabeth, 33–34
McMillan, Lewis K., 64
McPherson, James, 49
Meier, August, 62
Memorabilia (Xenophon), 71
Merrill, James Griswold, 102
Metamorphoses (Ovid), 81
Methodists, 69
Methodology of the Oppressed (Sandoval),
    129n19
Miller, Kelly, 43
Minerva Society of Philadelphia, 33
Minyans, 25–26
missionaries, 42, 49
Mitchell, Samuel T., 71–72
Modern Language Association, 72–73
moral power, of classics, 94–95
Morehouse College, 55, 58, 84, 91, 100, 136n39
Morrill Act of 1862, 3, 63, 103
Morrill Act of 1890, 103
Morris Brown University, 43, 55, 56, 80–81,
    94, 137n46
Moss, Alfred A., Jr., 6
Müller, Karl Otfried, 25

Napier, James Carroll, 118–19
Narrative of the Life of Frederick Douglass
    (Douglass), 1, 21
Nash, Margaret A., 64
National Association of Colored Women, 71
Negro in the New World, The (Johnston), 115
Nelson, Charmaine A., 23
Nepos, Cornelius, 65, 67, 84–85
Nineteenth-Century Rhetoric in North America
    (Johnson), 88
"Niobe" (Wheatley), 24
nonviolence, 102–5
North Carolina State Normal and Industrial
    School, 68
Notes on Virginia (Jefferson), 10, 15, 19, 25, 37

INDEX **169**

Obama, Barack, 3, 13, 124–25, 147n3
Oberlin College, 15, 44–47, 55, 70–71, 135n15, 135n18
"Ocean" (Wheatley), 24
Odes (Horace), 56, 62, 65, 71, 81–82, 86
"Of National Characters" (Hume), 19–20, 131n20
"Of the Quest of the Golden Fleece" (Du Bois), 94
Ogden, John, 59
Ogilby, John, 141n14
Olynthiacs (Demosthenes), 81, 87, 93
On the Crown (Demosthenes), 45, 81–82, 87, 93
On the Sublime (Longinus), 29
oppression, 8–9
orality, 89. *See also* rhetoric
"Orient, the," 21–22
Orientalism, 21–22
Orrells, Daniel, 14
Oson, Jacob, 31, 39
Ovid, 23, 81, 86

Page, Walter Hines, 26–27
Palmer, Alice Freeman, 110
Palmer, Fred, 103
Palmer Memorial Institute, 109–11
pants, sagging, 136n39
passing, 12
paternalism, 49, 136n32
Paul, Nathaniel, 34–35
Payne, Daniel A., 70–71
Payne Theological Seminary, 74
Peabody Educational Fund, 61
pedagogy, 6
personhood, 78
Phaedo (Plato), 81–82
Phaedrus, 37
Phelps-Stokes, Caroline, 74
Phelps-Stokes Fund, 61, 74
philanthropy, 60–68
Philippics (Demosthenes), 81, 93
philology: pure, 9; scientific, 10
philosophy, 82–83
Pindar, 34
"pit schools," 12
Plato, 45, 71, 81–83, 94–95, 138n67
Plautus, 71, 86
Plessy v. Ferguson, 104–5
Pliny, 39, 62, 80

plundering, of antiquities, 22–23
Poems on Various Subjects, Religious and Moral (Wheatley), 23
poetry, 23–24, 80, 86–87, 131n21
Politics (Aristotle), 133n38
Polt, Christopher, 149n1
practical instruction, 12–13, 53–54, 56–57, 62, 65, 69, 96, 99–101, 105–8, 130n22, 136n32, 137n44, 138n71, 139n95, 145n3
Predominantly Negro Colleges and Universities in Transition, The (McGrath), 122
Price, Gregory N., 130n22
Progressive era, 7
Prometheus Bound (Aeschylus), 71, 82
Protestantism, 34
Psalms, Book of, 33
"pure philology," 9

Quintilian, 15, 82, 87–88, 90, 93–94, 143n38, 143n42

Raboteau, Albert J., 30
racial imperialism, 10, 15
racial uplift, 5, 8, 11, 13, 33, 39, 44, 75, 77, 78, 91, 108, 113–14, 116–18, 119, 145–59
racism: land-grant colleges and, 63–64; in readings of classics in American South, 28–30; in scientific classicism, 25–28
Ray, Charles B., 134n62
reading rooms, 33–35, 133n62
Reconstruction, 2, 7, 57, 75, 101
Reinhold, Meyer, 78
remedial instruction, 43
Reminiscences of School Life, and Hints on Teaching (Coppin), 7
Renaissance, 3, 5
Republic, The (Plato), 82–83
resistance, 9–12, 33–34, 97–98, 102–5, 108–12
rhetoric, 87–92. *See also* speech
Richards, J. Havens, 115
Richardson, Joe M., 42, 58–59, 101
Riess, Ernst, 81
Romans, as White, 10
Rome, 84, 132n34
Ronnick, Michele Valerie, 6–7
Roynon, Tessa, 14
Russwurm, John Brown, 30

Said, Edward, 21–22
Sallust, 83–84

Sandoval, Chela, 129n19
Sappho, 34
Satires (Horace), 71, 81–82, 86
Satires (Juvenal), 29
Scarborough, Sarah Cordelia, 72
Scarborough, William Sanders, 5, 7, 46, 55, 71–73, 74–75, 76, 78–80, 86, 92–95, 97–98, 125, 126, 140n107, 142n15, 143n44
Scherer, Robert, 139n95
Schueller, Malini Johar, 31
Schuyler, George S., 132n35
scientific classicism, 25–28
"scientific philology," 10
Scipio Africanus, 31
secondary sources, 94–95
secrecy, 12
Self-Taught (Williams), 2
servants, Black, 9
sexism, 90
Shipherd, John Jay, 45–46
Shorter, Joseph P., 72
signifying, 12
Simmons University, 43, 50
Skinner, Thomas E., 111–12
Slater, John Fox, 61
slavery, 4, 7, 8–12, 24–25, 41, 42, 47, 50, 56, 57, 84, 86, 110, 116, 130n6, 133n38, 137n46; Black inferiority and, 30–31; civilization and, 27–28; education and, 20–21; in grammar textbooks, 142n16; literacy and, 18–20; "natural," 19–21, 27–28; in transcendentalism, 44; in Walker, 36–39
Smith, Edward Parmalee, 59
Smith, Johnson C., 86
Smith, Minnie L., 81
Snowden, Frank, Jr., 14
Snowden, Samuel, 35
societies, learned, 33–35
Socrates, 91
Sophocles, 81
sororities, 6
Souls of Black Folk, The (Du Bois), 124
Souls of White Folk, The (Du Bois), 130n14
South Carolina College, 29–30
speech, 89, 92–94
Speech on the Reception of Abolition Petitions (Calhoun), 27
Spelman College, 7, 12, 51, 55, 80, 90, 99
Spence, Adam Knight, 58–59
Stand and Prosper (Drewey and Doermann), 6

Stewart, Philo Penfield, 45
Stoicism, 83
Stolen Legacy (James), 133n49
Stowe, Harriet Beecher, 41, 89–90, 120
Stuart, George, 79, 86
Suetonius, 24
Suliot, Theodore, 71

Tacitus, 29, 56, 62, 67, 71, 81–85
"Talented Tenth, The" (Du Bois), 101, 113, 118
Talladega College, 50
Taney, Roger B., 20
Tanner, Benjamin T., 69
Tatum, James, 94–95
teachers, Oberlin and, 46
Terence, 24, 37, 62–63, 71, 86
Term of Ovid, A (Gleason), 81
Terrell, Mary Church, 5, 46, 71, 89, 98, 113–14, 125
Tertullian, 31
textbooks, 47, 79–81, 88, 141n3, 142n16
Theocritus, 45
Thirkield, Wilbur T., 118
Thucydides, 81, 83, 138n67
Tolson, Melvin B., 91, 98
"toolsism," 16
Tougaloo College, 12, 52–53
transcendentalism, 44
Treatise on the Intellectual Character and Civil and Political Condition of the Colored People (Easton), 32
Truth, Sojourner, 89–90
Tubman, Harriet, 139n94
Tucker, David, 112
Tucker, Thomas De Saille, 46, 105–6
Tunstall, Robert W., 81
Turner, Henry McNeal, 74, 98
Turner, Nat, 12, 36
Tusculan Disputations (Cicero), 71, 81–83
Tuskegee Institute, 11, 54, 60–63, 76–77, 101–2, 106, 111, 136n38, 144n28

Underground Railroad, 45
United Church of Christ, 102
universities. *See* Black colleges

Van Steen, Gonda, 22
Vastey, Pompée Valentin, 31, 39
Venus de Milo. *See* Aphrodite of Melos
Virgil, 23, 29, 57, 59, 62, 65, 67–69, 79–81, 86,

101, 110, 141n14

Virginia Normal and Collegiate Institute, 139n86

vocational training. *See* practical instruction

Walker, David, 14–15, 35–39

Washington, Booker T., 9, 55, 60–61, 75, 101, 106, 110, 116, 139n95, 144n28

Washington, George, 24, 131n24

Watkins, William, 133n47

Watkins Academy for Negro Youth, 133n47

Watson, Veronica T., 100

Watson, Yolanda N., 7

Weisenburger, Francis P., 72

Western culture, 2, 25, 131n15

Wheatley, Phillis, 14, 18, 23–25, 131n21, 131n24, 131n29

When I Can Read My Title Clear (Cornelius), 19

Whiteness, 10, 21–23, 120, 124–25; as property, 19, 130n6

White power structure, 98–100

White privilege, 23

White supremacy, 2, 8, 10, 24, 55, 100, 123, 130n6, 138n71

"whole man," 15

Wilberforce, William, 70

Wilberforce University, 6–7, 12, 46, 70–76, 84, 86, 90, 94, 103, 135n22, 139n96, 140n107, 142n15

Williams, Daniel B., 139n86

Williams, Francis, 131n20

Williams, Heather, 2

Wilson, Francille, 108

Wilson, Woodrow, 117

Winckelmann, Joachim, 23

Winterer, Caroline, 78

Wolf, Friedrich August, 25, 132n32

women, 3, 5, 7, 9, 12, 13, 15, 17, 33, 41, 43–46, 48, 49–51, 56, 62–65, 70–71, 90, 91, 98–99, 102, 107, 115, 117–19, 121–22, 125, 136nn37–38, 137n43, 140n106, 147n2

women's clubs, 98, 113–14

Woodson, Carter G., 120

Woodson, Sarah J., 71, 146n11

Wright, Richard, Jr., 103–4

Wright, Richard, Sr., 97

Wright, Richard, Sr. (college president), 103

Xenophon, 27, 29, 71, 80–81, 138n67

"Yale Report of 1828," 41

Young, Nathan B., 106–7, 144n28

Printed in the USA
CPSIA information can be obtained
at www.ICGtesting.com
CBHW031508250424
7541CB00002B/7